"*The Francis Effect* is a thorough look at speaking anxiety and how to control it. It provides a wealth of information that will help anyone who reads and applies it become a more competent, confident speaker."

—*Mark Sanborn, National Speakers Association Past President, President, Sanborn & Associates, author of* The Fred Factor

"A winner. Easy to read, understandable, and relevant. Whether you are new to speaking or not, have stage fright or not, this book will help you be a better speaker."

—*Jeff Schaeffer, Publisher, McFadden Communications Group*

"An honest, smart and thorough approach to public speaking in today's world. No tricks—just clear explanations and examples of what to do—and why."

—*Amber Baldwin D'Amico, Vice-President, The Inner Sanctuary*

"An excellent primer for both the experienced and the aspiring public speaker."

—*Milt Matthews, board member of Robert H. Smith School of Business, University of Maryland*

"I have had a lifelong fear of public speaking. The lessons helped me to relieve the problems that always appear immediately before I speak. I highly recommend this book."

—*Korry Stagnito, Vice President/Publishing Director, Stagnito Communications, Inc.*

"*The Francis Effect* is a masterful and well-thought-out guide to overcoming the anxieties and difficulties associated with effective and powerful public speaking. It is perfect for the on-the-go businessperson because the format allows for quick reading and easy reference."

—*J. Brian Lovely, Esq., General Counsel and Creative Director of Product Development, Sideout Footwear, Volatile Shoewear*

"Great content, very informative, and easy to read, with excellent real-life examples. *The Francis Effect* definitely does the best job of thoroughly conveying 'how to get over it.'"

—Jennie Jones, Vice President, Marketing, SND Coffee

"A very simple and complete guide to improving your performance at presentations and public speaking. Learning about the skills necessary to put together an effective presentation is extremely useful."

—Tom Joyce, Vice President, Customer and Industry Affairs,
The Hershey Company

"*The Francis Effect* is outstanding. It is readable and well-organized. This book will resonate with those who struggle with presentations."

—Catherine Morse, Labor and Employment Law Director,
Freescale Semiconductor

"In an age where image and personal brand are increasingly important, this book takes the fear out of public speaking. It helped me get beyond the 'speaking' part and focus on effective preparation and delivery. A must-read for anyone who speaks to an audience—be it two or two thousand."

—Jane Berzan, Senior Vice President, National Association of
Convenience Stores

THE FRANCIS EFFECT

THE FRANCIS EFFECT

THE REAL REASON
YOU HATE PUBLIC SPEAKING
AND HOW TO GET OVER IT

M. F. Fensholt

Oakmont Press

Oakmont Press
2890 Inland Empire Boulevard, Suite 102
Ontario, CA 91764
Tel: (866) 833-7377   Fax: (866) 833-7388   www.oakmontpress.com

Ordering Information
Quantity sales. Special discounts are available on quantity purchases by corporations, associations, and others. For details, contact the "Special Sales Department" at the address above.

Orders for college textbook/course adoption use. Please contact Oakmont Press.

Orders by U.S. trade bookstores and wholesalers. Please contact Biblio Distribution: Tel: (800) 462-6420; Fax: (800) 338-4550.

Printed in the United States of America

Cataloging-in-Publication Data
Fensholt, Mary F.
    The Francis effect : the real reason you hate public speaking
and how to get over it / Mary F. Fensholt.
    p. cm.
    Includes bibliographical references and index.
    ISBN-10: 0-9755578-7-4   ISBN-13: 978-0-97555-787-7
    1. Public speaking. 2. Oral communication. 3. Speech anxiety.
4. Business presentations. 5. Performance anxiety. I. Title.
HF5718.22 .F46 2006
808.51—dc22   2005904529
FIRST EDITION
10 09 08 07 06   10 9 8 7 6 5 4 3 2 1

Interior designer: Beverly Butterfield, Girl of the West Productions
Copyeditor: PeopleSpeak
Indexing: Rachel Rice

In loving memory of my father, Edward
And with love to my daughter, Emily

If a child is to keep alive his inborn sense of wonder,
he needs the companionship of at least one adult
who can share it, rediscovering with him the joy, excitement,
and mystery of the world we live in.
RACHEL CARSON

CONTENTS

PREFACE

After fifteen years of helping people learn to speak effectively to groups, I can promise this: there is no magic pill that can make you a completely comfortable speaker overnight.

This book is not a quick fix for the common anxiety associated with speaking to groups. If a quick fix existed, you, and the millions of others who share this anxiety, would have already heard about it. You would have already used it. At least, you would have if it was available, affordable, legal, and not harmful to your health! (And I've met some people who would have been willing to be flexible on the last two qualifications.)

What this book will do is take away the mystery and frustration associated with the anxiety. You will learn how normal and healthy this anxiety is. This is a critical first step. Without this understanding, it is very, very difficult for intelligent, self-aware, and ambitious people to feel they have really achieved deep-seated competency. Building on this critically important understanding, the book will give you the tools you need to minimize the anxiety, to manage what might remain so that it becomes more invigorating rather than distracting, and even to hide any nervousness that remains!

Knowing that knowledge is power and that solid preparation is vital to successful performance, this book answers all the critical questions about speaking to groups. You will find what you need to put together a great presentation, deliver it effectively, and answer even the toughest questions with grace under pressure. You will find very specific guidelines, suggestions, tips, and examples you can use in the real world. The information will go well beyond just the basics and will help you speak successfully in today's more complex and collaborative world. Although written primarily for the person who makes presentations in business, almost all the information, and all the basics, will apply just as well to speakers in the professions, education, public service, and nonprofit organizations. If you speak to a group, this book was written for you. If you know people who do, this book was written for them. If you know people who should, but don't, this book was written for them. To support the idea that this book is for everyone who speaks to groups, I usually alternated pronouns for unnamed persons by chapter. Odd-numbered chapters generally use masculine pronouns for unnamed individuals; even-numbered chapters generally use feminine pronouns.

Great speakers were not born that way. As with any other skill, real proficiency in speaking to groups (and the comfort that comes with it) will be the result of becoming familiar with the basics, practicing, evaluating your success, and exploring what might work better next time. Computer users know this. Singers know this. Golfers know this. Rock climbers know this. Anybody who has ever put together a bike on Christmas Eve knows this. You know this. The information you gather every time you speak to a group can be put to use to increase both your comfort and your effectiveness.

I wish I had had this book when I was in college. I wish I had had it when I started my first job. I wish I had had it when I made my first business presentation and when I first spoke at a charity fund-raiser. But mostly, I am so glad that I can finally offer it to all my clients who have said over the years, "You should write a book."

So here it is. And here's to you for being the kind of person who wants to grow.

PART ONE

THE REAL REASON
FOR ANXIETY

1

All of us are born with a set of instinctive fears—of falling, of the dark, of lobsters, of falling on lobsters in the dark or speaking before the Rotary Club and of the words "Some assembly required."

DAVE BARRY

You Are Not Alone

The Fear of Public Speaking

His turn came. The young man rose and walked to the front of the room. He turned to face us and shifted nervously. Eleven colleagues watched and waited in silence. He looked at me, standing in the back of the room with my video camera trained on him. I nodded, and he began to speak.

His introduction was similar to the four or five introductions we had already heard from his colleagues. He told us his name, his job title (a midlevel management position in a national financial services firm), his home (a suburb of San Francisco). And then he spoke of why he had chosen to attend this presentation skills training seminar.

"In my second job out of college I was a broker for another firm. Presentations made me so nervous that I couldn't think straight. I mean, my knees would shake and my voice would shake and I'd sweat." He smiled ruefully. "I mean really sweat!

"And it happened every time! It was so bad that my boss decided to help. He told me he'd come to my next presentation and give me some advice when I was done." He rolled his eyes. His colleagues groaned and chuckled.

"So he did. He sat in the back of the room. I looked at him a few times. The first time he just stared back at me. After that, he was shaking his head. Then he put his head down and covered his face with his hands. I mean, it was really awful.

"When I was done, he took me for a beer. Next thing I know we're sitting there in silence drinking our beer. Finally, he looks at me and says, 'Jeez, John. They're not going to eat you!'"

The group laughed, but squirmed in their seats.

"So I'm really here because . . . I know they won't eat me! But now I've been in this business for almost twelve years. I feel like I know what I'm talking about. I don't sweat, or at least not as much. But I still feel the same way every time I have to give a presentation. So I came because I'll take any advice I can get!"

He returned to his seat as his colleagues nodded and clapped. A woman in the back row leaned and whispered to her neighbor, "That's for sure!"

How Common Is Anxiety about Speaking to a Group?

The anxiety associated with speaking to groups is so common that most of us have come to expect it in ourselves and others. The fear of speaking to groups is by far the most common form of what researchers call "communication apprehension." Communication apprehension itself has been defined as an "individual level of fear or anxiety associated with either real or anticipated communication with another person or persons."[1] Most of the people I have worked with over the years report that speaking to groups is the *only* communication apprehension they have. They report they are much more comfortable in any other communication setting: one-on-one, small groups, the telephone, parties, and on and on. And many are convinced that the anxiety they experience about speaking to a group is worse than most others feel. They are puzzled and frustrated by the intensity of the anxiety. They are worried that their listeners will see it. And many people make life and career choices based on the need to avoid speaking to groups. I was one of those people.

Shy for as long as I can remember, I kept a low profile throughout school. I earned two degrees in communication studies without ever taking a class in public speaking. I gave only two brief presentations during my college and graduate school years, and while I got through them, I didn't enjoy the experiences.

Ironically, the area of communications I entered professionally was conducting seminars that helped people design and deliver effective business presentations. For ten years, I watched people struggle with the fear of public speaking. I heard horror stories about their experiences. And I became frustrated with the fact that no one seemed to have a convincing explanation for this common fear.

Much of the literature dismisses the fear of public speaking as being caused by "performance anxiety." In short, the experts will tell you that "you are anxious about performing because of performance anxiety." This clearly begs the question. You might as well say, "It's painful because it hurts."

The question remains: What is performance anxiety? Is the fear of public speaking really performance anxiety? Is it *only* performance anxiety? Why is it so universal, so debilitating? And why can it hit with a power so out of proportion to the importance of the event and the real risks involved?

My clients were frustrated because they were intelligent, high-functioning, rational people and yet they could not understand or explain their own fear and anxiety. I couldn't explain it. We certainly knew that no one could tell us how to prevent it. Without understanding the cause or causes, we had no way of knowing whether the steps we took to prepare for a presentation were at all effective in helping us minimize and manage the anxiety and fear.

Not finding satisfactory answers to the question in the traditional fields—psychology, sociology, and interpersonal communications—I began to look for clues in other fields, such as biology, anthropology, and physiology. The answers I found became the basis for this book. Helping my clients understand these answers has made a huge difference in their ability to accept, minimize, and manage the almost universal anxiety and fear associated with public speaking. Understanding these answers can help you do the same.

You just had to love her! From the moment she entered the training room on the first day of the seminar, Audrey had a wonderful effect on us all. She came in a bit tentatively but gave me a big warm smile as soon as I walked over to greet her. After putting on her nametag and getting a cup of coffee, she walked over to the group of three other early arrivals.

The seminar, offered by the corporate university of a large computer company, was attended by people from throughout the organization. Since they came from diverse business units, they had never met before. They stood in a circle, chatting a little awkwardly. Their conversation centered on why they had come to this presentations seminar.

Within two minutes Audrey had the group laughing. Each new arrival was quickly drawn into the conversation. Audrey made sure she introduced everyone, and her openness, genuine curiosity, and warmth made the conversation flow freely.

Soon it was time to start the seminar. As the ten participants took their seats, they jokingly argued about who should get to sit next to Audrey.

I briefly introduced the seminar. Then each participant introduced him- or herself from the front of the room. A few looked almost as uncomfortable as they claimed to feel. One man never looked up from the floor as he spoke. The listeners applauded politely as each speaker walked back to his or her seat.

Audrey was the ninth person to speak. She walked to the front of the room and gave us that big smile. Her introduction was wonderful. She spoke with satisfaction of how she had risen from administrative assistant to marketing director. She spoke with loving pride about her husband and two daughters. She told us she was really looking forward to the seminar. She finished speaking. The group applauded with genuine enthusiasm.

Audrey remained in the front of the room. She looked questioningly at me, standing in the back with my video camera. She seemed to be asking,

"Can I say one more thing before I sit down?" I nodded. When the applause died down, she looked again at the audience. Her shoulders collapsed. Hunching, she squinted apprehensively at the group and said, "Please tell me honestly. Can you see my hair standing up?"

Anxiety Can Be Invisible to Listeners

Most of the time listeners can't tell how a speaker feels. Listeners can't see the pounding heart, the tightness in the stomach, the dry mouth, the sweat trickling down the rib cage. Listeners can't see the hair standing on end. Even when a speaker is visibly nervous, when a very close look reveals the knees or the hands shaking, the listeners want the speaker to do well. Think how you felt the last time you listened to a nervous speaker. You were likely more supportive than judgmental.

When a speaker is visibly nervous—when he rocks back and forth, fidgets with his fingers or jams his hands deep in his pockets, when we hear his voice shake and crack, or see his eyes dart from side to side or floor to ceiling—we don't tend to judge that speaker harshly. We know how speakers feel! We feel for him. We may take on some of his tension. We hope he will relax as he continues talking. Yet even though we typically don't judge a nervous speaker harshly or with contempt, think about our response to a clearly confident speaker.

Think about how you felt the last time you listened to a speaker who was truly in command. It is impossible not to notice the contrast. What a pleasure it can be to listen. When a speaker is eager to share with us, and does so with obvious confidence and skill, listening feels a lot like being engaged in energetic conversation. We are absorbed and attentive. We focus on the content of the talk more easily. We feel more willing to ask questions.

If the nervous speaker and the confident speaker are equally competent at the technical parts of their jobs, which one do you think most listeners would want to work with? Buy from? Hire? Promote?

In a recent survey, a global research firm found that 94 percent of executives and managers rated communicating well as the most important skill for success in management.[2] The ability to speak effectively to a group is an important part of being able to communicate well. Speaking to a group increases your visibility. As you rise within your organization, speaking well rises in importance too. Whatever your position, the mastery of public speaking increases your ability to share your ideas, sell your products and services, influence others, and motivate them to greater achievements. Excellent presentations help you make a greater contribution to whatever organizations you belong to. And you, as well as your organization, will reap the rewards of those contributions.

But the promise of all the rewards in the world won't eliminate the anxiety, the fear, and the uncomfortable physical changes that so often come with public speaking. It is precisely because the anxiety and discomfort are so common that they shouldn't just be expected and accepted. They need to be understood, minimized, and managed. This book will help you do that.

Summary

The anxiety associated with public speaking is so common that it has come to be expected. It is usually accepted as unavoidable. But the severity of the symptoms of this anxiety often causes physical and emotional discomfort and stress. These symptoms—and the resulting discomfort and stress—cause frustration and embarrassment in otherwise confident and knowledgeable people. Too often, the result is the avoidance of public speaking. The person who avoids the opportunity to speak to groups loses the opportunity to share information, to inform, to persuade. His ability to be visible, productive, and successful is often diminished.

Don't let this happen to you. Rather than accept the anxiety as mysterious and inevitable, learn to understand why it happens. Then you can minimize, manage, and ultimately master it.

Dangers bring fears and fears more dangers bring.

RICHARD BAXTER

The Downward Spiral

How Anxiety Causes Anxiety

Before we look more closely at the fears and anxieties caused by public speaking, we should be clear about the difference between the two. Both fear and anxiety are real emotional and intellectual responses to a perceived threat. But there is an important difference.

Fear is a response to a well-defined threat, such as suddenly discovering your car's brakes don't work while on the freeway off-ramp or finding a strange, large, growling dog blocking your path. Anxiety is the result of a vague or ill-defined threat. Unprovoked worries about your child's safety or an unlikely turn for the worse in your financial affairs are possible examples of anxiety.[1]

If you are like most people living in the industrialized world, you experience few true physical threats. Most of us will never experience a sudden brake failure, for example. We know that our audience will not harm us physically. But in our fast-paced and competitive business world, we often experience psychological threats. Many business presentations and speeches are an opportunity to gain or lose credibility, status, prestige, and money. So how do we typically respond when that "opportunity" lands on our schedule? With anxiety. The anxiety is vague at first, but it can turn to dread as the date draws closer.

Feelings of anxiety drive speakers to look for an explanation, to analyze the cause. When they do, most speakers have no problem coming up with at least two or three specific fears. Here are some I often hear.

What if I don't have the right information? What if I bore them? What if I can't get them to understand? Or I confuse them? What if I can't answer all their questions? Or I don't get any questions at all? What if I just don't convince them?

What if my voice shakes? Or cracks? What if my mouth gets dry? What if I sweat so much everyone can see it? What if I talk too softly? Or too fast? What if I forget what to say? Or start to ramble and can't stop?

If you look again at the concerns in the last two paragraphs, you will find that each paragraph contains a different kind of concern. The concerns in the first paragraph are related to selecting and preparing content: the topic, the information covered, the support material used, who the audience will be, what they want and need. Let's call these "content concerns." The concerns in the second paragraph are related to personal performance, that is, how the speaker delivers the content. Let's call these "performance concerns."

Content concerns most often come into play when lack of knowledge or information is a factor. Perhaps you don't know how to get started organizing your presentation. Or you're not sure how to help the less technical audience members understand how your newest product works. Or you're wondering how much detail to include on your slides. Or the CEO is coming, and she's known for asking really tough questions. You can find advice and answers to these questions, and many more, in parts 2 and 3. But what about situations like the following?

- *You are standing in for someone else.* You have been "asked" to fill in for your boss at the last minute. You will speak for thirty minutes to a group of important customers at your company's executive briefing center. You and a small team of engineers have been immersed in a challenging project for the last four months. You have had minimal contact with your boss. You have general knowledge of her topic, but you don't feel like an expert.

- *You have been assigned a vague topic.* You have been asked to speak for ninety minutes at an industry conference. You agreed because you want to raise your own visibility, as you plan to become an independent consultant next year. Your topic and the title of your presentation were assigned by the organizers of the conference. The title is "Evaluating Operational Efficiencies."

- *You have limited information about your audience.* You just received a brand new set of forty-two product information slides from your marketing department. You've been instructed to use the slides in your sales presentations. You have an important presentation this afternoon. You know your products pretty well. You have seen the slides only once before, at a meeting last week. You suspect the client is close to making a purchasing decision. You are not sure who will attend.

The concerns you would have in each of these cases are content concerns. There is no substitute for thorough knowledge of your topic and enough information about your audience to enable you to tailor your talk just for them. With either of these missing, it is very difficult to speak with confidence. Here's why.

The Downward Spiral

Unresolved content concerns are the first level of a downward spiral of increasing anxiety. They quickly lead to emotional fears, the second level. At this level we ask ourselves more questions.

What if I appear uninformed, ignorant, or even stupid? What if I lose this opportunity, the income, the status, the prestige? What if I fail my company, my boss, my colleagues, myself? What if I damage my reputation, my career, my confidence?

The performance concerns of the second level, stemming from the content concerns, are experienced by most speakers. They create even more anxiety. This increased anxiety is the third level. At the third level we start getting anxious about the anxiety itself and become nervous about our nervousness. We ask ourselves, What if I get so nervous that my anxiety becomes obvious? What if they see it? What if they hear it?

What if I forget what to say? Say the wrong thing? What if my voice shakes or cracks? What if my legs shake? What if I talk too fast? Too soft? Too loud? What if I sweat profusely?

Anxiety about how visible and/or audible these performance issues will be to the audience can make them even worse. The downward spiral of anxiety and discomfort picks up speed. It becomes harder and harder to stop. Let's quickly review the steps in this downward spiral.

1. I'm not sure about my content.
   Therefore, I'm not sure I can succeed. I may fail.
   The consequences of failure would be painful.
   The thought of suffering painful consequences makes me afraid of failing.

2. Because I am afraid of failing, I am nervous.
   Because I am nervous, I will probably sweat and _____ .
      (Fill in the blank with your favorite performance concern.)
   The audience will see me sweat and _____ .
   They will know I am nervous.
   They will think less of me because they know I am nervous.

3. Knowing they will think less of me makes me more nervous.
   My increased nervousness means I will probably sweat and I will
      _____ even more.
   Knowing I will sweat and _____ makes it more likely
      the audience will notice and know I'm nervous.
   They will think less of me because they see I am nervous.
   And so on.

When we fear performing poorly, we continue a downward spiral that can cause our fears to become reality, a classic self-fulfilling prophecy. Experiencing this spiral of anxiety just once is enough to convince many people to avoid speaking to a group for the rest of their lives. So is this advice the answer to our fears? "Always know your content and your audience well before you speak to a group."

This is part of the answer. It's good advice. Follow it whenever you can. But it's not that simple. In the real world there are times when you won't be able to know your content or your audience as well as you would like. As you rise in an organization, you will probably be asked to speak more often and on a wider variety of topics. You will have less time to prepare. Your audiences will become more diverse. In many speaking situations you will be less likely to have detailed knowledge of your content and your audience.

> I was dreading winning. I didn't even plan a speech—I was worried that I would slip up or do something horrible. I was shaking in my seat, putting on a posed smile. Inside I was petrified.
>
> LEONARDO DiCAPRIO

As much as you might like to follow this advice, you can't always do so. Even if you could, there is another problem.

Sometimes you have no logical reason for content or performance concerns. You are the expert. You are the highest ranking person in the room. You are delivering good news. Your audience respects and may even love you—and yet the anxiety still hits.

Terry lives on the west side of Los Angeles. He is a gifted actor and playwright. He has appeared in television shows and commercials and has written a play that ran for years. He has a great sense of humor and keen insights into the absurdities of human behavior. He has coached others in presentation skills for fifteen years. He has given many well-received speeches.

Asked to give a speech at a business convention on the importance of good public speaking skills, Terry was happy to agree. The speech was scheduled for early on a Tuesday morning. The week before the speech, Terry prepared.

He drafted notes. He chose his slides. He booked a flight for the trip to San Francisco. He made hotel reservations near Moscone Center, the huge convention center that was to be the site of his speech. He was ready.

Monday afternoon Terry boarded the plane to San Francisco. As the plane climbed and circled out over the ocean, Terry put his seat back, closed his eyes, and thought about the next morning. He decided to mentally review his speech. He imagined himself walking out onto the stage. Anxiety hit hard.

His breaths got shorter as his chest tightened. He felt his hands and forehead begin to sweat. He felt his stomach churn. Then his mind got in the act.

Maybe the convention has been canceled, he thought hopefully. Or maybe today's speakers ran long and they'll have to finish in the morning. Maybe they won't have enough time for my talk.

His mind considered these possibilities. It decided these events were unlikely. It went back to work looking for other possibilities. Maybe this plane will crash! Terry thought hopefully.

As illogical as it may be, even experienced speakers and performers feel the anxiety. Many highly successful entertainers report they feel this anxiety before every performance.

The play has been running for months with great reviews and she has never forgotten a line. He has sung these songs hundreds of times. She has performed this monologue in clubs all over the country to enthusiastic applause and laughter. And each time these performers are anxious.

Many seasoned businesspeople experience that same anxiety. I hear the examples from puzzled and frustrated people often.

- "We went to sixteen cities on that road show. I must have done that presentation twenty-five times. It got easier after a while, but I still got nervous every time."

- "I wrote that presentation! I wrote my dissertation on it! I know as much about it as anyone in the country. And I left out one of the most important points!"

- "My voice always shakes so much I feel like I'm singing opera."

- "I've learned to stand with my feet far enough apart so my knees don't knock together."

- "I don't do presentations in good silk blouses any more. I had to throw my favorite one away after the last conference."

- "Every time I do a demo, my hands get so wet they practically drown my mouse!"

The evidence clearly shows that although a speaker knows her material well and is sure it is the right material for that audience, the anxiety can still hit. It can hit often. And hard. When it does, the body responds the only way it can.

Why Does the Human Body React So Strongly?

The human body reacts to content and performance concerns in exactly the same way it does to physical danger. It can't tell the difference!

In our ancient environments, when life was "nasty, brutish, and short," most of the dangers we faced were physical. Rough terrain, poisonous snakes and insects, dangerous wild animals, and many other physical dangers were part of our daily life. The design of the human body is much older than the relatively recent inventions of cities, complex commercial and legal systems, and sophisticated technology. It is much older than the need to deliver presentations. It still operates with the evolved ability to respond physically to perceived danger.

How big is the gap between the design of the body and the demands placed on it by modern life? The present design of the human body is approximately two hundred thousand years old. This design is based on designs that are much, much older.[2] Starting about 5000 BC, human society, economic systems, and technologies evolved at a rapid pace. The human body did not. We give presentations in a modern world. But we do it with Early Stone Age bodies. And these Stone Age bodies respond to psychological and emotional threats in the same way they do to physical threats—with physical changes.

Collectively, these changes are called the "fight-or-flight response." The physical changes of the fight-or-flight response include a sharpening of the senses to help us detect and avoid physical dangers. They also give us increased physical strength and speed to fight or flee if the danger can't be avoided.

No passion so effectually robs the mind of all its powers of acting and reasoning as fear.

EDMUND BURKE

The changes do not enhance our memory. They do not improve our analytical skills. They do not help us think more quickly or clearly. They do not give us easier access to our vocabulary. Just when we really need all our modern wits about us, when we need to think clearly and quickly, when we need to manage ourselves in a professional way, we get exactly the wrong kind of help from our bodies.

When we don't understand the nature of the fight-or-flight response, it can catch us by surprise. Even when it is not a surprise, when we have experienced it before and during other presentations, it is not welcome. Even less welcome is the anxiety that hits when we have no real content or performance concerns.

Some anxiety is understandable if we aren't as well prepared as we would like or when the stakes are high. But what about when we are thoroughly prepared? And when the stakes are low? What about unexplainable anxiety? What about anxiety, like Terry's, that hits for no apparent reason? What can the body possibly be responding to? When there seems to be no logical reason for the anxiety and it still hits, a logical person becomes understandably frustrated. When that logical person is accustomed to feeling competent, in control, even powerful, feeling helpless to prevent the anxiety can be even more frustrating.

Frustration is negative, but something positive can come from it. It can motivate you to take action and improve your situation. You can take action and improve your situation by reading the next two chapters. In these chapters you will discover a better explanation for the anxiety and fear.

Summary

Concerns about both content and performance contribute to the fear of public speaking. Content concerns are those concerns related to selecting and preparing the content of the presentation. They include the appropriateness of the topic, specifics of the information covered, the support material used, the nature of the audience, what members of the audience want and need, and how the audience is likely to respond.

Performance concerns are concerns about how the speaker will deliver the information and manage the event. Will she demonstrate knowledge and expertise? Look and sound confident and believable? Be able to successfully answer audience questions?

When a speaker has concerns about the adequacy or appropriateness of her content, she can easily feel anxiety and fear. When a speaker believes that the symptoms of this nervousness may become visible or audible to the audience, her nervousness increases. This increase in nervousness also increases the chances that her nervousness will be noticed. This downward spiral of fear and anxiety is difficult to control or break.

Experiencing this downward spiral can discourage a speaker from speaking in public. Excellent preparation is one key to minimizing and managing the anxiety and fear caused by content concerns.

But anxiety often exists even when there is no logical reason for content or performance concerns. When a speaker experiences anxiety—and the physical symptoms of anxiety known as the fight-or-flight response—the downward spiral can begin even without the existence of content concerns. Then frustration is often added to the emotions she experiences. This frustration can motivate the speaker to take action—to learn more about how to minimize and manage the anxiety.

In classical antiquity the wolf was thought of as a "ghost animal"
whose very gaze could strike people speechless.

HANS BIEDERMANN

Wolves and Other Phobias

Natural History and the Real Reason

Preparing as thoroughly as possible is an important part of minimizing and managing anxiety. Knowing you have done everything you can to prepare makes it easier to feel confident. It also helps to put the importance of the presentation into a larger and longer-term perspective. Asking, "What is the worst thing that can happen if this doesn't go well?" is an excellent way to remind yourself that your career and your life will go on long after the presentation is forgotten. Many people do this, and report that it helps.

What Else Is Going On Here?

But if the anxiety could be resolved that easily it would not be so common. Why does anxiety still hit when content and performance concerns should logically be nonexistent? Or when risks in the situation are so low that there is no real way to "fail"? Why do so many experienced speakers and performers, even those who repeatedly and consistently experience success, continue to feel the anxiety? Why does it affect even those of us who are not at all shy in other social settings?

There is another reason, one that may be even more deeply rooted and powerful than anything we have examined so far: the body knows something the mind may not.

What Is This Powerful Cause of Anxiety?

When we stand in front of a group, we become the "salient object"—the most noticeable person, the center of attention. Everyone is looking at us. Why is this not a pleasant experience?

When human beings become the salient object—center stage—the result is a heightened state of consciousness. Psychologists call this heightened state of consciousness "hypervigilance." In this state we are conscious of so many stimuli—both external and internal—that we can easily feel overwhelmed. Our physical surroundings, the audience, our own intellectual, emotional, and physical states all compete for our awareness—our consciousness. When we deliver a speech or presentation, our conscious minds are very active and alert. But the conscious mind is only a part of the total human being. Antonio Damasio, MD, PhD, is a neurologist and leading thinker and writer on consciousness and on the connection between brain, mind, and emotion. He writes,

> The unconscious, in the narrow meaning in which the word has been etched in our culture, is only a part of the vast amount of processes and contents that remain nonconscious, not known in core or extended consciousness. In fact, the list of the "not-known" is astounding. Consider what it includes:
>
> • All the fully formed images to which we do not attend;
>
> • All the neural patterns that never become images;

- All the dispositions that were acquired through experience, lie dormant, and may never become an explicit neural pattern;

- All the quiet remodeling of such dispositions and all their quiet renetworking—that may never become explicitly known;

- And all the hidden wisdom and know-how that nature embodied in innate, homeostatic dispositions.

Amazing, indeed, how little we ever know.[1]

All of these nonconscious factors affect our intellectual, emotional, and physical states when we address an audience. But it is the fifth item that I want to examine here: "All the hidden wisdom and know-how that nature embodied in innate, homeostatic dispositions." I believe this factor offers us the best explanation for the intense anxiety that often appears when we "step into the light" of a presentation.

An understanding of what is meant by "innate, homeostatic dispositions" is important here. "Homeostasis" is the maintenance of physiological stability in spite of changes in the environment. The first person to use the term homeostasis was Walter Cannon, an American physiologist. Cannon wrote an essay titled "The Wisdom of the Body." He explained that homeostasis allowed organisms to maintain, within a range allowing for survival, a consistent internal state.[2] For example, we sweat to cool down when the temperature rises, we tan when exposed to sunlight to protect our skin, and the irises of our eyes dilate and constrict as light levels change. Cannon explained that the mechanisms that contribute to homeostasis, this "wisdom of the body," have evolved over the eons to ensure survival. But are physical changes the only mechanisms that humans have for achieving homeostasis?

In his book *The Feeling of What Happens*, Damasio writes "for certain classes of clearly dangerous or clearly valuable stimuli in the internal or external environment, evolution has assembled a matching answer in the form of emotions . . . emotions are not a dispensable luxury. Emotions are curious adaptations that are part and parcel of the machinery with which organisms regulate survival."[3]

A great and growing body of evidence suggests strongly that Cannon's "wisdom of the body" and Damasio's "hidden wisdom and know-how that nature embodied" in us are basic parts of the anxiety that often surfaces at the very *idea* of public speaking.

Let's now look more closely at just who we are as humans. Let's explore part of what this hidden wisdom and know-how might include. And let's consider its impact.

Humans and Other Animals

René Descartes (1596–1650) is widely recognized as one of the most important Western philosophers of the past several centuries. Known during his lifetime as a mathematician, physicist, and physiologist, it is as a philosopher that he is most frequently remembered and read today. Two of the best known of Descartes' philosophical ideas are those of a method of extreme doubt and the argument that, though we may doubt, we cannot doubt that we exist: "I think, therefore I am."

Descartes held that this ability to think, and the ability to speak, proved that humans have minds—and souls. He argued that animals, although they may be capable of some feelings and emotions, do not have a mind. Without a mind they are very different from humans. For the last three and a half centuries, the belief that humans are distinctly different from (and superior to) animals has been the basis for much of Western thinking on this subject. Western culture reflects and reinforces the Cartesian idea that humans reason and decide while animals act instinctively or react to outside forces. This is why humans are not commonly believed to possess "instincts." It follows that, without instincts, we are born as "blank slates," waiting for experience and learning to "write" our abilities and character into place. So nurture, not nature, determines character and behavior.

But is the distinction really that clear?

No, say many eminent scientists. In the last three and a half centuries, we have learned a great deal that Descartes never knew.[4] Support is growing for the belief that nature plays a much larger role in determining our behaviors and feelings than previously thought. A growing body of evidence shows that

21

emotions and feelings affect our thoughts and reasoning processes. The ongoing debate about the importance of "nature versus nurture" is generating a great deal of thinking, theorizing, and research.[5] The findings of strong similarities in twins raised apart give us significant insight, and the ever-expanding research in human genetics provides more conclusive information about the roles of genetics and the environment in human development and human behavior.

The more we look at both animals and humans, the more closely related they turn out to be. Research shows surprisingly significant genetic similarities between humans and other primates. Genetic surveys are converging on the conclusion that about 98.7 percent of the DNA in humans and chimpanzees is identical.[6] Some geneticists now classify chimpanzees as more closely related to human beings than any other primate.[7] Zoologists and sociologists find strong similarities between the behavior of humans and other primates.[8]

Descartes assigned great significance to the ability of humans to speak, citing it as an indication of the superior intellectual capacities of the human mind. But there is a growing recognition that only humans have the physiology needed for the production of speech. In 2001, geneticists at the University of Oxford found that a single mutation of one gene robs humans of fine motor control of the mouth. This same mutation causes them to lose the ability to understand some aspects of grammar.[9]

Also interesting is that animal communications are proving to be more varied and more complex than Descartes ever imagined. Animals use a wide variety of vocalizations, facial expressions, body postures, and even chemical communications.[10] All these findings are combining to challenge the clear-cut Cartesian distinction between an instinct-based animal nature and a reason-based human nature.

Certainly humans (or most humans, anyway) have the ability to reason, to think logically, make decisions, and control our impulses. But one doesn't have to look too closely at humans to realize that we don't always operate by reason alone. Emotions, passions, unexplained intuitions, snap decisions that don't seem at all logical, and mysterious anxieties and unreasonable fears are also parts of the human experience and of human nature. One of the most common components of human nature that fall into the category of the unexplained and mysterious is the phobia.

What Exactly Is a Phobia?

A phobia is an irrational, abnormal, and persistent fear of a situation or object despite the awareness and reassurance that it is not dangerous. To qualify as a phobia, a fear must be so excessive and disproportionate that it compels the person to avoid the situation or object. The avoidance interferes with the person's life—with his thoughts, activities, or sleep.

Modern psychiatry recognizes three types of phobias: specific phobias, agoraphobia, and social phobias. Let's look briefly at each of these and then, more importantly, at the connection between the three.

Specific phobias include a fear of animals or insects; a fear of elements of the environment, such as heights or water; situational phobias, such as a fear of flying, entering tunnels, or crossing bridges; and medical or injury phobias, such as a fear of the sight of blood or needles.

Agoraphobia is the fear of being in a place or situation from which escape might be difficult or embarrassing, fear of losing control when in a public place, or fear of being in a place or situation in which help might not be available in the event of a panic attack. In a sense, agoraphobia is the fear of being afraid.

Social phobias are elicited by exposure to certain types of social or performance situations, especially situations that are perceived to involve scrutiny or judgment by others. (Does public speaking come to mind here?) Social phobias, unlike shyness, cause avoidance, and so they affect the person's ability to function in work and relationships.

But are these types of phobias really so clearly separate? Surely the fear of social situations can lead to agoraphobia. The downward spiral we discussed in chapter 2 might be classified as agoraphobia (the fear of finding oneself behind a lectern giving a speech) brought on by a social phobia (the fear of being scrutinized and judged by the audience). And what if someone with specific phobias of flying and crossing bridges had to do both on the way to delivering a speech?

But could a more specific phobia be an underlying cause as well? The eminent psychologist Martin Seligman was one of the first to propose that people may be prepared by nature to acquire certain phobias.[11] Further research has supplied strong evidence to support this idea.[12] For millions of years, people who quickly learned to avoid environmental dangers, such as poisonous snakes, insects, and heights (not to mention saber-toothed tigers) had a better chance of staying safe—both alive and healthy—than those who did not. And they had a better chance of passing their genes to the next generation. They are the ancestors of us all.

This brings us back to public speaking. Is it possible that the fear of public speaking, so common and often so much greater than the circumstances of a talk would seem to justify, has some basis not in the environment or the circumstances but in human nature itself?

As we consider the possibility, let's look at another eminent scientist's explanation for many of these human fears, these common phobias. Edward O. Wilson is a leader in the fields of evolutionary biology, sociobiology, and conservation. This insight is from his Pulitzer Prize–winning book *On Human Nature*:

> We can search among the unconscious, emotion-laden learning rules for the kind of behavior most influenced by genetic evolution. Consider the phobias. Like many examples of animal learning, they originate most frequently in childhood and are deeply irrational, emotionally colored, and difficult to eradicate. It seems significant that they are most often evoked by snakes, spiders, rats, heights, close spaces, and other elements that were potentially dangerous in our ancient environment, but only rarely by modern artifacts such as knives, guns, and electrical outlets. In early human history phobias might have provided the extra margin needed to insure survival: better to crawl away from a cliff, nauseated by fear than to walk its edge absentmindedly.[13]

Many discussions of the fear of public speaking include the "Ten Worst Human Fears" (in the United States) found in the *Book of Lists*. According to this ranking, the ten worst fears, in order of frequency of occurrence, are

1. Speaking before a group
2. Heights
3. Insects
4. Financial problems
5. Deep water
6. Sickness
7. Death
8. Flying
9. Loneliness
10. Dogs[14]

Looking at this list again in light of Wilson's suggestion that these common phobias are "most often evoked by . . . things that were potentially dangerous in our ancient environment" gives support to his theory. His case becomes even more compelling if we substitute "wolves and hyenas" for dogs and "the loss of my environment (the lifestyle I live)" for financial problems.

Let's think about this list a bit more. The fear of heights is really more a fear of falling from the height than of the height itself. We don't turn and run when we see a tall tree or a mountain—we just may not rush to climb either one. And, while flying was not a part of everyday life in our ancient environment, the fear of flying is less a fear of flying than it is the fear of falling, of having the wrong type of "landing"—like Icarus. So the fear of flying is really just a modern incarnation of the fear of heights. Now let's consider the number one fear: the fear of speaking to groups.

The fear and anxiety that accompany being the salient object seem to be rooted too deeply to be explained just by concern about what to say. Many people report that noticeable anxiety begins with the *thought* of doing a presentation.

Let me share the results of an experiment with you. I've done this experiment literally hundreds of times in seminars and workshops. Often the first presentation I have workshop participants do is a self-introduction. Logically, this is one of the simplest kinds of presentations of all. The subject matter is very familiar. Each speaker is the world's expert on his subject. The small group of eight or ten other people gathered for a workshop are most often peers, often people the speaker will never see again after the workshop. Logically, this task should be easy. Yet I have seen and heard firsthand, with thousands of people, that this request almost inevitably causes anxiety. But, when I give workshop participants this choice, "For the next one or two minutes you can either stand in front of the group and introduce yourself or simply stand in silence," the results are thoroughly predictable. First they laugh uncomfortably, even groan. Then, inevitably, they choose to speak.

The conclusion? It is not just the speaking that causes the fear. The stronger fear is the fear of just standing in front of the group, alone. The very *thought* of doing this causes anxiety. It *feels* dangerous. Our bodies feel the danger. And the body responds.

How does the human body respond when faced with sudden and immediate danger? With the fight-or-flight response. The body prepares to stand and fight or to flee as fast as it can. The senses become more acute, heart rate increases, adrenaline floods the bloodstream. In our ancient environments the fight-or-flight response gave us the ability to respond quickly to physical dangers with the strength and stamina we needed to increase our chances of surviving unharmed—or just surviving.

But why is the fight-or-flight response so intense even when the risks of public speaking are low—when the speaker is well prepared, experienced, and in a low-risk, or no-risk, situation?

The fear and anxiety that trigger the physical changes of the fight-or-flight response are not rooted in content and performance concerns alone. The fear we feel so strongly is the fear of being the salient object, the center of attention—scrutinized, alone, outnumbered, and vulnerable.

After years of helping intelligent, well-educated, competent, and generally confident adults deal with this fear, I have come to believe that the common fear of public speaking is at least as much a "hard-wired" biological response, a built-in phobia, as it is the result of content and performance concerns.

And although other species don't have the highly developed language skills of humans—or complain about the fear of public speaking—the fear that for us comes with public speaking is not unique to humans. Nor is it truly, or only, a fear of speaking or of some other type of performing. It is the manifestation, in humans, of a fear we share with many other species. This fear is part of our biological makeup—our animal and, therefore, human nature. It is a fear that has contributed to the survival of the unbroken chain of ancestors whose genes we carry. It is a part of what makes us human.

Safety in Numbers, Danger in Solitude

This fear comes naturally when we violate one of the most basic survival rules of animal nature. Schools of fish, flocks of birds, herds of antelope, prides of lions, packs of wolves—many, many species of animals know instinctively that there is safety in numbers and great danger in solitude.

Primates, our closest relations in the animal world, depend on membership in a group for survival. The following passage describes the group-centered social style of primates. The author and insightful observer of human beings Desmond Morris explains: "Because of the static nature and abundance of the food, there is no need for the primate group to split up in search for it. They can move, flee, rest, and sleep together in a close-knit community, with every member keeping an eye on the movements and actions of every other . . . Even in those species that do split up from time to time, the smaller unit is never composed of a single individual. It lacks the powerful natural weapons of the carnivore and in isolation falls easy prey to the stalking killers."[15]

More insight into our discomfort at being separated from a group and the center of attention—the salient object—comes from Robin Dunbar in his book *Grooming, Gossip, and the Evolution of Language.* Dunbar lists three ways that groups provide protection for the members in the world of animals. All of them apply to primates, to early man, and to us.

First, he explains, groups provide multiple pairs of eyes to watch for predators. Some members can focus on the necessities of daily life, such as searching for food and caring for young, while others keep watch. Second, larger groups are a deterrent to predators. All else being equal, the larger army will probably win the battle. The likelihood of passengers and air marshals coming to the aid of a flight attendant may deter a potential hijacker. Third, a large group creates confusion. When distracted and unable to concentrate on singling out a specific victim, an attacker is less likely to be successful. And the confusion can create the time potential victims need to escape the danger. Dunbar writes, "So primates live in groups as a mutual defence against predation. Indeed, sociality is at the very core of primate existence; it is their principal evolutionary strategy."[16]

Public Speaking Violates the Law of "Safety in Numbers"

We don't have the means of fight or flight that give other animals a margin of safety. We lack fangs, claws, a tough hide, or great physical size or strength. We cannot run like a cheetah or spring like a gazelle. We can't fly away. Certainly, being caught out in the open, alone, in clear view of predators, could have dire consequences.

But weren't even the earliest humans intelligent enough to outsmart animal predators? Sometimes they were, sometimes not. Anthropologists have found ample evidence that for hundreds of thousands of years, early humans were not just hunters and gatherers. They—we—were also prey.

In an article in *Natural History* magazine, authors Noel T. Boaz and Russell L. Ciochon describe one such find. In "The Scavenging of 'Peking Man,'" they describe their work analyzing fossil remains of *Homo erectus pekinesis,* historically known as Peking man. This human relative lived from about six hundred thousand to three hundred thousand years ago. The authors examined the partial remains of about forty-five individuals found in a cave about thirty miles from Beijing. In addition to the Peking man remains, the cave originally held thousands of animal bones. The most common and complete animal skeletons found in the cave were those of a now extinct giant hyena, suggesting that the hyenas were the occupants of the cave. How, the authors ask, did the *H. erectus* bones get to the cave?

In the author's words, "Had *H. erectus,* instead of being the mighty hunters of anthropological lore, simply met the same fate as the deer and other prey species in the cave?"[17] The fact that all of the *H. erectus* skeletons were incomplete, often lacking the extremities—forearms, hands, lower leg bones, and feet—suggests strongly that the individuals died in other places and that only their partial remains were brought to the cave.

Two-thirds of the *H. erectus* bones showed some sign of damage inflicted by an animal such as the giant hyena. The damage visible included puncture marks from a carnivore's fangs; long, scraping bite marks; and the marks of stomach acid, suggesting that one of the bones had been swallowed. Without going into all the gruesome details, it seems pretty clear that the hyenas were the cave's home team, and that the home team was winning. The answer to the author's question looks like yes.[18] This, and a wealth of other evidence, shows that humans were prey.[19]

As humans evolved, as our intellect and language skills developed, we relied on safety in numbers. Humans who lived by this rule survived. Those who straggled or strayed did not. For most of our history, finding ourselves apart from the safety of our own group and in full view of another group was an enormous danger. For millions of years, being alone greatly increased our chances of becoming a meal for other animals.[20]

> Drive Nature from your door with a pitchfork, and she will return again and again.
>
> HORACE

We are all the descendants of survivors. We are all the descendants of humans who understood this well enough and long enough to pass on their genes. These survivors bequeathed to us our deeply rooted abhorrence of placing ourselves in the position of salient object. Like the fear of snakes, insects, heights, or the dark, we live with this part of our nature in the modern world.

In *The Songlines,* author Bruce Chatwin provides more support for the theory that humans retain an innate warning system as a defense against the predators that threatened our survival for so many eons. In this passage he explains the thinking of John Bowlby, renowned expert in child development,

> in his speculation about the underlying cause of many childhood fears. Chatwin writes,

The greatest source of terror in childhood is solitude.

WILLIAM JAMES

"Penetrating . . . into the causes of anxiety and anger in the very young, Dr. Bowlby concluded that . . . the child's fear of the dark, and of strangers; its terror of rapidly approaching objects; its invention of nightmarish monsters where none exist; in short, all those 'puzzling phobias' which Freud sought to explain but failed, could, in fact, be explained by the constant presence of predators in the primaeval home of man." [21]

Bowlby explains that a child left alone in his bed in the dark "is yelling—if you transpose the cot to the African thornscrub—because, unless the mother comes back in a couple of minutes, a hyena will have got it . . . Visitors to a baby ward in hospital are often surprised by the silence . . . Yet if the mother really has abandoned her child, its only chance of survival is to shut its mouth." [22]

The work of Bowlby and many others strongly supports the idea that humans do retain certain defensive behaviors, and that these behaviors are triggered by situations we face today. These are situations that our body believes to be inherently risky—situations like public speaking.

The Real Risks of Public Speaking

In our modern environments the physical challenges and dangers threatening our survival are greatly reduced. Now we typically face more intellectual and emotional challenges than immediate physical dangers. The risks we face in the modern world are more often risks to our personal and professional reputations, our ability to prosper, and, perhaps most importantly, to our self-image.

Speeches, and especially business presentations, are a chance to communicate our messages and influence others. But they are more than that. They are a way to gain credibility, status, prestige, and often, financial rewards. So we take the opportunity, walk to the front of the room, climb the stairs to the stage, and step into the light as the center of attention, the salient object.

How does the body respond? With anxiety. The human body can't tell the difference between facing an audience and facing a pack of giant hyenas. It's all the same to the body. And the body reacts the way it is designed to react. It prepares us to protect and defend ourselves in the same way it always has.

> **Whenever man forgets that man is an animal, the result is always to make him less humane.**
>
> JOSEPH WOOD KRUTCH

Humans have the powers of imagination and visualization. More than any other animal, we have the ability to live in the past as well as the future. We have the ability to anticipate and imagine possible events in great detail. We do this based on our past experiences, the stories of others, and our own imaginations.

Imagination and the power to visualize the future will evoke and intensify emotion. As our emotions intensify so will our physical responses. This may make us even more likely to experience the fight-or-flight response than other animals. The very thought of placing ourselves in a risky situation is often enough to trigger the heart pounding, breathing changes, muscle tension, and other symptoms that indicate the beginning of the fight-or-flight response. So it is the human body's hidden wisdom, our innate disposition, even more than content or performance concerns, that triggers the fight-or-flight response. The response is primarily an evolutionary reaction to the physical visibility and vulnerability inherent to public speaking. This, more than any other factor, is a cause of the powerful flight or fight response.

Anxiety Is a Normal and Healthy Human Response

This last cause is the most important to understand because it is the most difficult to prevent or control. As natural as breathing, this response is part of being human. Start with the dry fuel of content concerns, add the oxygen of performance concerns, and then toss in the spark: the innate phobia of being in front of a group, the salient object, and vulnerable. The resulting fire is the common human fear of speaking to groups—the intense and seemingly irrational anxiety lit by the inborn defenses of our nature. Too often this fear erupts into a bonfire, a raging case of the fight-or-flight response. Designed over the time it took to design modern man and perpetuated by the survival of those who experienced it and heeded its warning, it is a part of what and who we are.

Throughout history some people have had a special ability to "communicate" with animals. Those who are gifted in working with animals have an ability to see, understand, and work with the animal's nature. They notice the animal behaviors that signify fear, reluctance, contentment, boldness. They consider, Is this animal one that is highly territorial? Hierarchical? Cooperative? Does it hunt prey? See well in the dark? Live alone or in groups? Does it mate for life or mate at any opportunity? What is the natural range of differences in any one characteristic of a species?

These gifted people have keen observation skills, awareness of the traits that are similar in different species, and sensitivity to the traits that make each unique. With keen observation and understanding comes the knowledge that enables them to work with the nature of the animal, not against it. As humans we need to do the same with ourselves, our colleagues, our employees, our students, our children. In seeing, understanding, and working within our human nature, we find the key to minimizing and managing the fear. Happily, more than any other animal, humans have the ability to do this.

The Good News: You're in Charge!

Your human intelligence gives you the ability to understand your nature. It also gives you the ability to work within that nature without yielding to it completely. You can consider and experiment with new behaviors. You can learn new skills. You can deliberately expand your range of options. This is true for most of life. It is also true for speaking to groups.

But the most important point to know now is this: The experience of intense anxiety is normal, natural, and healthy. It is part of your human design.

It is a biological response that has simply outlasted much of its usefulness in the modern world. It will be experienced more intensely by some and less intensely by others. It will probably never disappear entirely. But it is not simply a sign of emotional insecurity or lack of preparation. When you acknowledge this and have a basic understanding of the physiological changes our bodies experience—both what and why—you can accept the anxiety and begin to move beyond it. You can minimize and manage the remaining anxiety. It can be done. And you can do it.

The Six-Pack Solution to Anxiety

The solution in this section is a different kind of six-pack than the one you're probably thinking of. The anxiety related to public speaking can be minimized and managed six ways. It is almost always accomplished by combining several of these ways:

1. Understanding the nature of the fear of public speaking

2. Getting training in the design and delivery of presentations

3. Practicing good presentation skills

4. Making stress-reducing lifestyle changes

5. Performing relaxation exercises before speaking

6. Taking medication

Of all of these, an understanding of the reasons why public speaking triggers the fight-or-flight response is most important. I have seen the tremendous difference it has made for thousands of people. When you understand the evolutionary basis of the fear, you can work from a solid base of knowledge. This knowledge base removes the frustration and puzzlement you would otherwise have when anxiety occurs. It eliminates the need to explain the anxiety with

> **Knowledge—that is, education in its true sense—is our best protection against unreasoning prejudice and panic-making fear.**
>
> FRANKLIN D. ROOSEVELT

negative self-talk. It makes it possible to move on, to focus your energy on learning and practicing the skills you need to become a fabulous speaker.[23]

Attempting to explain the fear and anxiety associated with public speaking without understanding the evolutionary reason for the fear is a mistake. These attempts continue to cause unnecessary puzzlement and frustration. They perpetuate self-doubt and misplaced energy for many thousands of people. They have done so for the last several thousand years.

Francis and the Wolf

There are many versions of the following story. The version I like best is told by John Shea in his book *Starlight*.[24] He credits it to the storyteller Bob Wilhelm. I have condensed it here, adding a few final details from the version found in *St. Francis of Assisi: A Biography* by Omer Englebert.[25]

In thirteenth-century Italy the small city of Gubbio was nestled in the foothills of a great mountain. It was a beautiful city full of fountains, churches, and sculptures. The people of Gubbio were justifiably proud.

One night, out of the deep and dark woods surrounding Gubbio, a shadow emerged. It prowled the streets of the city until it came on someone walking alone. Then it pounced.

In the morning the people of Gubbio discovered a mangled and gnawed body. In anger and shock they asked, "How could this happen in Gubbio?" The people agreed: it must have been the work of a stranger passing through. That night the people locked their doors and stayed inside. All except one woman.

In the morning her body was found, mangled and gnawed. The people of Gubbio again agreed it could only be the work of a stranger. But then one old woman spoke.

"I could not sleep. From my window I saw a wolf. A large grey wolf with blood dripping from his mouth!"

Two men, eager to be admired, decided to rid the town of the wolf. That night, heavily armed, they took to the streets to wait for the wolf. In the morning what remained of their bodies was found. Now terrified, the people of Gubbio gathered and shouted demands that the wolf be found and dealt with. But how?

Finally a small girl spoke of a holy man in a neighboring city. This man could speak to animals. An old man said he, too, had heard of the holy man. Could it hurt to try? The delegation formed to fetch Francis received many suggestions from the people of Gubbio.

"Tell him to tell the wolf to honor the commandment 'Thou shalt not kill.'"

"No, appeal to the good in him. Tell him to love his neighbor!"

"A wolf is a wolf! He cannot change! Tell him to go to Perugia. They deserve a wolf! Or to Spoletta! In Spoletta they wouldn't even know he was there!"

When the delegation reached Francis, the members told him of the horror in Gubbio and begged him to come. They asked him to tell the wolf to obey the Commandments or go to another town. St. Francis listened, told them he would see what he could do, and asked them to go home.

The next morning the people of Gubbio woke to find Francis standing near the fountain at the center of town. As a crowd gathered, the people demanded to know what St. Francis had told the wolf to do. He waited, and when they became quiet he said, "My good people of Gubbio, the answer is very simple. You must feed your wolf." Then he walked away and returned to his own city.

The people shouted, "What does he mean? This is not our wolf! We did not ask the wolf to come! How can he say, 'You must feed your wolf?'"

But that night, a platter of food was offered to the wolf. The food was taken, and the killing stopped. The wolf was fed the next night and the next until every man, woman, and child had fed the wolf. The town continued to care for the wolf, and the wolf came and went freely, bothering no one. When it died of old age, the townspeople grieved, for they had become attached to it.

Our fear is our "wolf." Like the wolf of Gubbio, it can appear suddenly and refuse to leave. Denying the fear, or hoping it will disappear, is as ineffective as hoping the wolf is just passing through, ordering the wolf to obey the Commandments, or demanding that it move to Perugia. Like the people of Gubbio, we must learn to live with our wolf. When we do, we have taken the first, most important step to reducing anxiety and increasing our confidence.

The Francis Effect is the reduction of anxiety and the increased confidence that come with truly understanding the body's natural response to public speaking. And the Francis Effect starts with understanding and accepting our human nature.

Just as the townspeople of Gubbio were unwilling to accept that the wolf was "their" wolf, many people find it hard to accept that the anxiety they feel is a normal, natural response to the challenge of making a presentation. Even more difficult to accept is that most of us will never be able to convince our wolf to move to another town. But like the people of Gubbio, we can learn to understand the nature of our wolf, learn what to do to keep it from "biting" us, and learn to peacefully coexist with it. We may even grow fond of it. It could happen. Think of the way participants in extreme sports thrill in the risks they take. And even if you aren't the kind of person with a high tolerance for risk, you can come to recognize that the energy that comes with anxiety can be harnessed to help you deliver more successful presentations!

What does reason demand of a man? A very easy thing— to live in accord with his own nature.

SENECA

Summary

The fear of speaking in public, like other common phobias, is part of human nature. It is a normal and natural part of what we are as humans.

It is present in differing degrees in different people. Like phobias such as the fear of snakes, heights, and the dark, it helped protect us in our ancient environments. The fear we feel when finding ourselves separated from the safety of our group—alone, exposed, vulnerable, and the object of scrutiny—evokes a natural and deeply rooted fear: the fear of becoming prey. The public speaker finds himself in exactly this position.

The human body, the product of millions of years of evolution in physically dangerous environments, is designed to respond defensively to the perception of danger. Although the logical human brain may realize that public speaking presents no real physical danger, the human body retains an innate warning system. This system triggers the fight-or-flight response. The body doesn't distinguish between intellectual challenges, emotional challenges, or physical challenges. Instead, it responds in the only way it knows how—with a flood of hormones that increase our body's ability to deal with physical dangers.

To ignore or deny the reality of this response is not productive. The Francis Effect begins to operate when we understand, accept, and learn to work with the natural responses of our bodies, not against them. The Francis Effect leads to reduced anxiety and increased confidence. To experience the benefits of the Francis Effect, we must first accept that the fear and anxiety associated with public speaking are normal and healthy. Then, rather than use our energy in frustration or denial, we can invest it in mastering new skills. These skills will further increase our confidence and comfort. They may even lead to a real enjoyment of public speaking.

Fear is that little darkroom where negatives are developed.

MICHAEL PRITCHARD

Recognize Your Wolf

Why You Need to Know

Eddie, age four, played outside as the sun sank on a hot summer night. His mother walked out onto the screened porch and flipped the switch to turn on the backyard light. Eddie looked up and watched as moths gathered around the light, batting against the glass globe. He swatted vaguely at a mosquito buzzing around his head and looked down. A large spider was crawling across the driveway, stopping and starting, changing direction from time to time. Eddie moved toward the spider, crouched down, and put his flattened hand directly in the spider's path. It stopped briefly, then started on its way again, and climbed onto Eddie's palm.

Delighted, he raised his hand to eye level and examined the spider closely. For a moment the spider seemed to examine him back, but then again began walking, heading toward the tips of Eddie's fingers. He quickly closed his palm and then peered in the small hole created by his thumb and pointer finger. Yes! The spider was safely inside. He ran to the porch door, threw it open, and rushed across the porch into the kitchen.

"Mom! Look what I got!"

"Just a minute, Eddie. I'm on the phone with Mrs. Price."

As he waited for his mother to finish, Eddie could feel the spider move. The legs tickled his hand. He smiled and again raised his fist to look inside. As his mother hung up the phone, he raised his fist above his head and opened his palm. His mother screamed and jumped back. Eddie screamed and jumped back. The spider fell to the floor between them and scurried away to safety under the dishwasher just before his mother's foot stamped the floor nearby.

"Eddie!" she said. "That's a spider! Don't pick up spiders! And never bring one into the house!"

Eddie exhaled with a wail. Sobbing, he ran to his mother and put his arms around her waist.

"Will the spider come back?" he sobbed, peering fearfully out from under his arm at the floor near the dishwasher.

Eddie is my brother. The story of the spider was retold from time to time while we were growing up. Most people who heard the story were amused by the unspoken points: How funny that Eddie had no fear of spiders until our mother screamed. How funny that he would be so proud of the spider that he would present it to our unsuspecting mother. How funny that our mother's fear was so instantly contagious. Less funny was the point that children need adults to teach them how to interact with all the dangers lurking in the big world.

But the story has another point to make. Eddie's story is an example of "prepared learning." The theory of prepared learning holds that some learning, although triggered by a stimulus (either the learner has direct experience or the learner observes someone else having the actual experience), attaches to a very narrow set of stimuli. It also holds that without one of those stimuli (experience or exposure), learning will not take place. Interesting for our purposes is that the stimulus, whether a snake, a spider, or a speech to a group, does not have to be experienced directly. Research has shown that just hearing about the bad experience of another person can trigger the emergence of a phobia.[1] Would Eddie have learned to fear spiders if our mother had responded with delight and interest (assuming the spider didn't bite him)?

A series of interesting experiments, designed and conducted in the early 1980s by a graduate student at the University of Wisconsin, Susan Mineka, explored the question. Mineka knew that scientists had believed for years that laboratory-bred baby monkeys showed an inherited fear of snakes. She showed that when exposed to snakes while separated from their mothers, baby monkeys showed no fear of snakes.[2] When mother monkeys born in the wild showed a fear of snakes in front of their baby monkeys, the babies quickly became terrified of snakes.[3]

Mineka found clear evidence that the fear was a result of prepared learning. She showed lab-bred monkeys a video of adult monkeys reacting in terror to the sight of a snake and responding calmly to the sight of a flower.

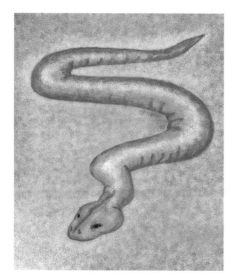

The baby monkeys reacted as predicted, becoming terrified of snakes but showing no fear of flowers.

But then she went on to prove that the baby monkeys' terror was not triggered by the terror of the adults alone. Mineka spliced the video to construct a tape that showed adult monkeys reacting with terror to the sight of a flower but reacting calmly to the sight of a snake. She showed baby monkeys this tape. Did any of the baby monkeys become afraid of flowers? No, not at all.

Would Eddie have been terrified of his first ice cream cone if his mother had showed fear of it? How about his first toy truck? Probably not.

And here's another question. Did Eddie learn to fear the spider because it was our mother who screamed? That is, would he have been less likely to react with fear if a stranger had shown fear of the spider? Again, probably not. Here's why.

In other experiments, Mineka showed that monkeys learned to fear snakes as easily from strange monkeys as they did from a parent. She also showed that monkeys could learn to fear snakes just as easily from another monkey who had also learned it secondhand. These experiments ruled out the likelihood of prepared learning being eradicated in only a few lab-bred generations (the equivalent of a modern snake-free environment). In short, Mineka's work shows clearly that instinct does play a role in learning.[4]

In the last chapter we looked at Edward O. Wilson's explanation of common human phobias. As you'll recall, Wilson explained phobias as innate survival mechanisms. Phobias still protect humans from elements that presented danger in our ancient environment. He noted that phobias of modern artifacts, even dangerous ones, are very rare.

In other interesting studies, humans were conditioned to fear snakes, spiders, electrical outlets, and geometric shapes. In one study, loud bangs were used to condition subjects to fear either snakes or guns. The results of these experiments showed that the fears of snakes and spiders lasted much longer than the fears of the modern objects.[5]

Which leads us to ask two obvious questions: Is the common anxiety in response to public speaking—of standing alone, unprotected, scrutinized by a group—an innate fear that will inevitably surface? Or is it a fear that must be learned?

I don't know the answers to those questions, but after working with thousands of adults, I do know that for most people anxiety is a normal part of public speaking. The challenges we explored in the last chapter and years of experience watching thousands of people of all ages struggle through those challenges leads me to firmly believe that most people will inevitably feel some anxiety.

Biology Is Not Destiny

But what is inevitable does not have to be enduring—or unendurable. We can learn to minimize it greatly, in some cases completely. We can learn to manage any remaining anxiety so that it doesn't interfere with our ability to speak effectively, so that it doesn't show, and so that it doesn't prevent us from taking advantage of the opportunities that public speaking offers.

Just because a fear is easily learned doesn't mean it can't be prevented, eliminated, minimized, or managed. All of us have at some time—through education, determination, and practice—mastered a skill that at first seemed daunting. We learn to sleep in the dark, to swim in deep water, to get on airplanes and look out the window at the scenery far, far below. We explore new cities and strange countries. We are fascinated by snakes and spiders (although most of us learn to manage these fears by keeping our distance or looking through plate glass). We even learn to delight in the shock or the shivers that a really gruesome mask or movie gives. And we help our children learn to do the same.

How is this done? Two very important factors in reversing or minimizing anxiety, fear, and phobias are these: education and control.

Education

How and when we are introduced to something that has the potential to blossom into a phobia makes a difference. Children raised with friendly family dogs are unlikely to show fear when they meet a strange dog. And have you ever watched a group of three-year-olds zipping down a hill on skis? Gradual and increasing exposure to the feared thing or activity is the basis of many therapies.

Researchers have pointed out that positive or neutral experiences with an object or situation can outweigh its negative aspects. For example, we know that cars can be dangerous, but we have so many positive experiences with them that any tendency to fear them might be "overruled." We usually don't fear knives because they have many daily uses that improve our lives. Using guns for target practice (and playing video games) can be challenging and fun.[6]

Control

Further research led Mineka and others to suggest that people are more likely to develop phobias for objects that they cannot control and situations that they cannot predict or control.[7] Knives and guns, for example, are not likely to attack under their own power, to drop from overhead, or to slither across the floor. Electrical outlets are even more predictable. (But people in an audience can be unpredictable, and speakers commonly fear being asked a question that they are unprepared for.)

Finally, many psychologists believe that people with a panic disorder develop social phobias or agoraphobia because they are afraid of having a panic attack in public. They fear the resulting helplessness and embarrassment. Again, it is the fear of lack of control that is the culprit.[8] Here again the answer can be gradual exposure and step-by-step mastery of the elements that make up the experience they fear. Learning, determination, and practice reduce the fear and make positive change possible.

Education, determination, and practice—all three are important. Determination drives us to learn new skills and find opportunities to practice them. But education is critical. Without knowledge we have very little power. So, to become even more knowledgeable, let's look at the answer to another common question.

Why Shouldn't People Just Accept That Their Anxiety Exists?

Is there any danger in not understanding the nature of this anxiety? Isn't it just as good to simply accept that we will get nervous when speaking to a group? Why can't we just stiffen our spines and soldier on? Does understanding the biological underpinnings really serve any useful purpose?

It does. It is a vital part of minimizing and managing the fear and increasing our confidence and comfort. Let's take a look at the problem that a lack of understanding can cause.

We Need Consistency of Action and Belief

When we humans experience something new, especially something unexpected or unpleasant, we feel the need for an explanation. When we behave in a manner inconsistent with our beliefs or our logic, we look for some way to explain that behavior. This explanation often comes by changing our attitude or belief so that it is more consistent with our behavior.

This explanation, known in social psychology as the theory of cognitive consistency, grew out of the work of Kurt Lewin, and was developed more fully by Leon Festinger in *A Theory of Cognitive Dissonance*. The *theory of cognitive consistency* states that behavior that is at odds with an established attitude creates a state of discomfort. Festinger called this discomfort *cognitive dissonance*. To reduce or eliminate the dissonance, a change is needed to achieve consistency between the behavior and the attitude. This change usually takes the form of changing the original attitude to conform more closely to the actual behavior. So the theory of cognitive consistency predicts that when a person behaves differently than her attitude would predict, she will also change her attitude. To put it more simply, when we think or say one thing and do something very different, it makes us uncomfortable. So we do something to reduce the discomfort. If changing our behavior is not easy or simple, we change what we think.[9]

This brings us right back to the same question that opened this book: I'm intelligent, knowledgeable, and mature. Why am I still so uncomfortable speaking to groups?

This very question is an example of cognitive dissonance. When we believe that we have no logical reason to experience the discomfort caused by public speaking and yet we still suffer the physical changes—the accelerated heart rate, the shaking, the forgetfulness, the sweaty hands, the dry mouth—we look for a way to reduce the dissonance. Without understanding these responses, it is very difficult to reduce or eliminate them. And that's the problem.

When we can't understand or eliminate the physical symptoms of anxiety, we resort to adjusting our attitude or belief. We tell ourselves

- "I must not be as prepared as I thought."

- "Maybe I don't know this stuff as well as I thought I did."

- "I must be afraid they are going to ask questions I can't answer."

- "I'm okay talking to people one-on-one, but not to groups."

- "I must not be as confident a person as I thought."

- "Am I really this fearful? I guess I'm just not a very brave person."

- "I never got over forgetting my lines in the junior high play."

- "I can't believe I got myself into this!"

- "Maybe I don't belong in sales/marketing/management/politics."

- "Public speaking just isn't for me."

- "I'm never going to do this again!"

- "I hate public speaking."

The tragedy occurs when we start to believe these explanations. When we believe that the fight-or-flight response is the result of a weakness of character or personality, we sabotage ourselves.

Fundamental Attribution Error

Another factor is at work here. Humans have a strong tendency to attribute behavior, especially the behavior of others, to fundamental character traits rather than to specific factors in the environment, the situation, or the context. Psychologists call this tendency *fundamental attribution error.* They believe this tendency to attribute behavior to character rather than to situation and context may be an attempt to simplify and understand a very complex world. Again, we are more likely to make this mistake when interpreting the behavior of others than of ourselves.[10] This is one of the reasons why first impressions are important. If someone says or does something unexpected, unconventional, seemingly irrational, quirky, or goofy the first time we meet her, we are very likely to conclude that she is irrational, unconventional, quirky or goofy. We often don't look for an explanation other than her character or personality.

We also, on some level, are aware that others may make this mistake when judging *us*. Have you ever tried to explain to someone why you made a decision that later (with more information available) turned out to be a mistake? Have you found yourself struggling to explain all the reasons why you did what you did? And why it seemed like a good idea at the time? Have you been frustrated at your inability to make the listener understand, consider all the factors involved, and conclude that your action wasn't really as irrational as it seems in hindsight? Have you watched her look at you with a combination of skepticism and impatience as you talk? Have you come to the conclusion that you will probably never be able to convince her that you aren't really a thoughtless, careless, or stupid person? You are frustrated because (even though you probably couldn't name it) you are watching her make a fundamental attribution error—*about you*. And you don't know how to prevent it!

When you are anxious about looking anxious or sounding anxious or making some kind of a mistake while delivering a presentation, you are probably also aware that others may be drawing conclusions about your character, your knowledge, your ability. These conclusions may be wrong. They are based on an incomplete picture of you. But without the ability to deliver a presentation with confidence, *you don't know how to prevent them.*

Now let's look at another important possibility. Without an understanding of the evolutionary reasons for our anxiety, we may be making a fundamental attribution error about ourselves. When we experience physical and emotional anxiety that is out of proportion to a situation, we look for an explanation. We attempt to make sense of our own anxiety. We try to eliminate our cognitive dissonance. But in the absence of another explanation, we may make a fundamental attribution error in our attempt to eliminate our cognitive dissonance. We explain our own physical responses to public speaking by blaming them on our character, our personality, or our innate ability— or disability! The self-defeating messages listed earlier may provide the comfort of an explanation. But the explanation is not accurate, satisfying, or productive. The body's evolved response to becoming the salient object is so powerful that it can cause physical anxiety without the help of these other factors. Adding these self-defeating messages to the mix only intensifies the effect and makes things worse. The result is another downward spiral.

This downward spiral begins with not understanding the evolutionary reasons for the anxiety and the body's physical response. Attempts to explain the power of the response with mistaken attitudes and beliefs about our own abilities continue the negative spiral. We only increase our anxiety by believing the explanations in the list above, and that can hurt our performance. The spiral continues on and on.

My real estate agent recently told me a story that vividly illustrates how this spiral works. She is bright, personable, attractive, and makes a good living by communicating successfully with people in high-stress situations. Yet she told me she had an experience in college—now more than twenty-five years ago—that made her give up public speaking for good. It was a classic experience. When anxiety hit, she couldn't remember what to say; she couldn't even relax enough to use the notes she had prepared. She told me that her friends were "shocked" by what happened, that she still doesn't understand why she got so nervous, and that she will never speak in front of a group again because she is still afraid the same thing might happen. How many times each day is this same story told?

Mastery of the anxiety about speaking to groups must start with both acceptance and understanding. Acceptance and understanding come when we know that our anxiety has a variety of causes, all legitimate, all normal, and all natural to our human nature. This inconvenient part of our nature is our "wolf." Just as the townspeople of Gubbio were unwilling to accept that the wolf was "their" wolf, many people find it hard to accept that their anxiety is a normal, natural response to the challenge of making a presentation.

Even more difficult to accept is that most of us will never conquer this fear completely. We will never be able to convince our wolf to move to another town. We need to learn to feed him—to give him what he needs in order to remain as placid as his nature will allow.

Before we look more closely at the nature of nervousness, and at how to "feed our wolf," we need to consider just one more reason why presentations can feel so uncomfortable. This reason will be explained in chapter 5.

Summary

The common fear of public speaking is, like many other phobias, an example of prepared learning. According to the theory of prepared learning, some learning is triggered by one of a very narrow set of observations or experiences. Without one of those observations or experiences, exposure to the anxiety associated with public speaking, for example, learning (to fear public speaking) will not take place. Experiencing illogical and unexplainable anxiety can stimulate this fear. Even observing others experience the fear is enough to trigger the fear in humans.

The situation gets worse when we don't understand the evolutionary reasons for the anxiety. Without an understanding of the evolutionary reasons for our own often strong reaction, we are likely to explain it in other ways. Common reactions to first feeling this anxiety include thoughts like these:

- I don't know why that happened!

- I tried to pull myself together but everything was just *gone!*

- My friends couldn't believe it because I'm so comfortable in a small group!

Our own surprise and puzzlement at the intensity of our anxiety leads us to explain it to ourselves with statements like these:

- I must not be totally prepared.

- I must not be good at public speaking.

- I hate public speaking.

In the absence of a better explanation, these statements become beliefs. These beliefs can then change our self-image in ways that can be self-defeating. Believing we lack confidence, skill, or a good memory, we become reluctant to speak in public. We avoid opportunities to speak in public, and we lose the ability to reap the benefits, including the benefit of practice. Knowing that experiencing this response when speaking in public is natural and normal is an important part of meeting the challenges of the fight-or-flight response. Instead of making the problem worse by adopting false beliefs, we can begin to identify and practice the habits that will help us minimize and manage the anxiety.

Learning is not compulsory . . . neither is survival.

W. EDWARDS DEMING

Doing What Comes Unnaturally

Flexing to the Challenge

It was Wednesday evening and Emily was preparing for the most important presentation of her life. She was six years old and nearing the successful completion of first grade. Her presentation was scheduled for tomorrow. She would share something with the class. Mrs. Hizon, her teacher, had said it should be "something important to you."

She would share Caroline, the American Girl doll Grandma Dorothy had given her for Christmas.

Her mother asked, "What will you tell the class about Caroline?"

"Well, first I'll tell them that her name used to be Samantha. But I changed it to Caroline because Caroline is my middle name and she looks just like me. She has the same color hair as me and the exact same color eyes! And that Grandma Dorothy gave her to me for Christmas."

"Will you tell them anything else?"

"I'll tell them that Caroline has her own bed that fits her and three outfits and that Grandma might get us matching outfits next Christmas. Oh, and

I'll tell them . . . " This went on for another minute or so. Emily seemed well prepared.

Caroline went to school with Emily on Thursday morning. Thursday afternoon Emily's mom asked, "How did sharing go this morning?"

"Okay."

"What did you tell the class?"

"Nothing."

"Nothing?"

"Well, Mom, when I looked at them they were all staring at me. And I started to tell them but then I couldn't."

"Then what happened?"

"They got to ask me questions."

"What kind of questions did they ask?"

"Oh, like where did I get her and what was her name and why do I like her and stuff like that."

"Did you answer the questions?"

"Yes . . . and then I did tell them about the matching outfits and her bed."

Delivering a presentation or speech is an unnatural way of communicating. When we deliver a monologue, we are violating the normal rules of speech communication.

Dialogue is our natural mode of speech. For our purposes, we will define dialogue simply as a conversation between two or more people. And dialogue has different rules than monologue.

Humans the world over learn to speak their first words by exchanging sounds with their parents and other caregivers. At first this is just one word, then two, then simple phrases and sentences. We know this. But we may not be aware of the "dialogue" that goes on far before a baby's first words.

Renowned child development expert John Bowlby looked closely at language acquisition. He found that at three weeks of age an infant will already engage in a kind of dialogue, taking turns "speaking" with the mother or caregiver. After close observation of how these dialogues develop, he concluded,

"The speed and efficiency with which these dialogues develop and the mutual enjoyment they give point clearly to each participant being preadapted to engage in them." In another study with children from twelve to twenty-four months of age he again observed the turn-taking of dialogue. He concluded, "The ability of the pair to take turns and avoid overlapping was not only strikingly efficient but as characteristic of the younger as of the older infants. Thus, long before the appearance of words, the pattern of turn-taking so characteristic of human conversation is already present."[1]

Humans are designed and built for dialogue. A mother is intuitively ready to bring out the natural turn-taking of dialogue even in her tiny infant. And the infant responds with "dialogue" when his brain is only half the size it will be when he first uses words.[2]

Dialogue is natural for humans. We are hard-wired for it. As we acquire language, we quickly develop this natural use of dialogue. We observe our environment and comment on it. We interpret it and share our thoughts with others. We gossip. We access information from our memory banks and deliver it in the form of brief comments, responses, or questions. We listen to the responses and contributions of our dialogue partner. And the process is repeated, over and over again. Soon we become dialogue experts.

Monologue is not natural. Delivering a monologue with comfort and confidence demands a flexibility that must be developed.

We are not built for monologue. We don't learn how to do it in the course of our normal early development. We don't practice it. It is not en-

couraged. We have very little opportunity or incentive to become skillful and practiced at organizing and delivering monologues. It is unrealistic to expect to be able to deliver a monologue with comfort and confidence unless this skill has been both taught and practiced.

As we acquire social skills, the importance of listening, sharing, and responding to the thoughts and input of others is continually emphasized. Imagine a typical cocktail party with groups of three or four people chatting. Now imagine one person in a group speaking for twenty minutes without engaging another person in dialogue.[3]

Years may go by before we ever have to "deliver" more than a short paragraph of information without frequent intermittent input and responses from at least one other person. Our memory banks seem predisposed to deliver information in response to brief comments and questions rather than to help us memorize scripts. We generally do not decide exactly what to say next until our dialogue partner or partners have responded to us. Emily was easily able to answer the questions of her classmates—to engage in dialogue—even when her planned monologue evaporated.

> The trouble with her is that she lacks the power of conversation, but not the power of speech.
>
> GEORGE BERNARD SHAW

Dialogue makes it possible for us to "connect" with other people. The dialogue between a mother and her infant strengthens their connection. It was the dialogue of Emily's question-and-answer session that helped her move beyond her own self-consciousness and anxiety. It was dialogue that made it possible for her to connect with her classmates. When she did, she also remembered what she had *planned* to say.

How Can I Connect with My Audience?

I often have clients ask me to teach them how to "connect with the audience." What they are really looking for is the sense of connection that comes from dialogue. They want to know that their messages are understood. They want to get a sense of how members of the audience are responding. They want to know if the audience agrees or has reservations. They want to know what the audience members think and feel. And they want to communicate their own conviction and enthusiasm, their own gravity and concern, to the audience.

Why is this feeling of connection so difficult to achieve in a monologue? Monologue lacks two important components of dialogue. The absence of these components is the major reason monologue feels so different from dialogue.

The lack of one of them is enough to create a loss of understanding and a feeling of detachment during a dialogue. The lack of both of them is what makes it so difficult to connect with the audience.

Grounding

The first component is *grounding.* Grounding is the process by which we let our dialogue partner know how we have understood his messages, that is, what we think the messages mean. We also seek evidence from him that our messages have been understood the way we meant them. Grounding enables us to coordinate actions and to discover and fix misunderstandings.[4]

We ground our communications in many ways, some verbal, many nonverbal. For example, a listener's raised eyebrow can show skepticism, which the speaker can investigate. Intermittent nodding shows that the listener believes he understands the messages being given. A pertinent question shows the speaker his argument has been followed. Paraphrasing a speaker's message shows that the listener wants to check that he really understands.

Grounding happens most quickly and effectively in face-to-face dialogue when the participants can observe each other closely. The need for grounding is a major reason for the sale of airline tickets; people want to observe each other closely when they conduct important business. It is why so many sales calls are done in person. It is why high-stakes negotiations are done face to face. It is why, at some point, even Internet friends need to meet in person if their relationship is to develop further.

Lack of effective grounding causes miscommunication. When you hear "it was just a communication problem" or "our wires must have gotten crossed," you can be sure there was inadequate grounding between the people involved.

The need for grounding can make telephone conversations more difficult than face-to-face communications. On the telephone, we can't use or observe many of the subtle nonverbal cues that greatly contribute to grounding. Even videoconferencing presents barriers to grounding because subtle nonverbal behavior can easily be missed.

Giving a presentation in monologue mode makes it even more difficult to ground our messages than when we are on the phone. In many ways we are "working in the dark." We can't possibly observe the body language and the subtle reactions of everyone in the audience. And even more importantly, we can't take turns. We hear nothing from them—not their comments, not their questions, not their vocal tones. When we deliver a monologue, they are silenced. And the more formal the presentation, the more likely that much or all of it will be communicated as a monologue.

Entrainment

The second component of dialogue missing in monologue is called *entrainment*. A simple example of entrainment is the person who begins tapping his toe or bobbing his head to the rhythm of a piece of music.

Every living human body is a physically oscillating system. We vibrate. The rhythms of our breathing, of our heartbeat, of our brain waves are just a few of the vibrations we generate. We really do give off "vibes."[5]

When one physically oscillating system entrains another, the timing of repetitive motions of one system influences the motions of the other. Given time, they fall into a kind of rhythm with each other.

When we have a dialogue with another person, we begin to influence, and are influenced by, his vibrations. Our vibrations and those of the other person will begin to shift frequency as we move to synchronize.

Two Talking Humans Will Entrain

When we engage in dialogue with others, we will begin to entrain. We might slow our rate of speech a bit to match that of another person. Subtle changes may occur in the expansiveness and the speed of gestures we use. This subtle "dance" of entrainment is well documented.[6] We begin to synchronize vibrations, to influence and be influenced by the vibrations of others. In a very real sense, we begin to "tune in" to each other. We "resonate." We begin to move in time to the same unheard music.[7]

But just how basic and elemental is the synchronization of entrainment? In his classic book *Beyond Culture,* anthropologist Edward T. Hall tells us that this synchronization, observable even in the timing of movements between an infant and a speaker, is a universal human trait. In infants it is consistently observable the day after birth, possibly even as early as the first hour of life.[8]

So a connection is achieved when human bodies entrain with other human bodies during dialogue.

Can You Entrain with a Group?

It is virtually impossible to "tune in" to your audience in this way when delivering a monologue. If one person is a mass of vibrations, the vibrations from ten people are a cacophony. The vibrations of fifty people or five hundred people, now farther from us, will likely have trouble reaching us at all. If they do, we won't be able to entrain with this mass of vibrations. The feeling will never be the same as talking to an individual.

Our earlier definition of dialogue was just "a conversation between two or more people." Yet if dialogue is to lead to learning, to solving problems, to reaching agreement, dialogue must become much more. Peter Senge, author of *The Fifth Discipline,* believes the purpose of dialogue is to "go beyond any one person's understanding. In dialogue, individuals gain insights that simply could not be achieved individually . . . they are participating in a pool of common meaning, which is capable of constant development and change."[9] This "participation" is what communication is meant to be—and what monologue never is.

Monologue Is Uncomfortable Because It Is Unnatural

To sum up, monologue is not natural. We are not hard-wired for it. We don't learn it or practice it. Our memory banks are not designed to support it. By definition, monologue makes grounding and entrainment, two vital components of dialogue, impossible. For all these reasons, the use of monologue makes it very difficult to connect with your audience.

Understanding Makes It Easier

If you don't understand and expect this difference in the feeling of a monologue, it can be very disconcerting. It can add to any anxiety you already feel. If, in the past, you have experienced the discomfort that comes with this difference, the remembered sense of discomfort can add to your concern about speaking the next time. When you deliver information as a monologue, the nature of monologue itself presents a communication challenge.

Help Is on the Way

Parts 2 and 3 of this book will give you many suggestions for leveraging the power of dialogue. You will learn to use the physical behaviors characteristic of dialogue to make your presentations more genuine, natural, and comfortable. You will learn many ways to incorporate the natural rhythms of dialogue into the delivery of your content. You will learn how to enter into genuine dialogue with members of your audience without losing control of your presentation.

But first, the next chapter will give you a greater understanding of the physical and intellectual effects of the fight-or-flight response. Understanding why we react as we do will make the reactions less frustrating, annoying, or frightening. Some of them may even amuse you! But even if you are not amused, understanding the nature of your responses is the foundation of the Francis Effect—the understanding you need to work with your human nature to become an excellent presenter.

The last chapter in this part will give you specific activities, exercises, and tips for minimizing and managing the anxiety you feel. Recognizing how the anxiety is most likely to affect you, choosing the strategies that address the reactions you may experience, and following the suggestions given can make a huge difference in your ability to minimize and manage the anxiety.

Summary

Monologues—speeches and the majority of presentations—are an unnatural form of human communication. Humans are predisposed to dialogue. We have a strong preference for dialogue.

Humans begin to babble in the vocal rhythm of dialogue in the first few weeks of life. We learn to speak using dialogue and continue to use dialogue for the vast majority of spoken communications during our lifetime.

Lack of practice is one reason delivering a monologue is difficult. The reduced ability to connect with our listeners makes it more difficult. Both grounding, ongoing checking and confirming understanding, and entrainment, synchronizing to the rhythm of speech and motion of your partner in dialogue, are close to impossible when delivering a monologue.

Understanding that these normal parts of human communication are absent during a monologue helps us understand the "disconnect" from our listeners that we often feel during a presentation. This understanding can also motivate us to learn and practice techniques (explained in parts 2 and 3) that help us make a stronger connection with our listeners.

Let us face ourselves bravely as we are. For only a philosophy
that recognizes reality can lead us into true happiness,
and only that kind of philosophy is sound and healthy.

LIN YUTANG

Getting to Know Your Wolf

Smile at the Symptoms of Anxiety

You know that your body responds to the intellectual and emotional stress of content concerns and performance concerns in much the same way it responds to physical danger. You know that delivering a substantial amount of information in monologue mode is an additional challenge. You know that when you become the salient object, the center of attention, your body responds with the fight-or-flight response to the "danger" of being exposed, vulnerable, and outnumbered. As a result, your wolf of anxiety wakes and growls.

What happens to the normal and healthy human body when anxiety hits? Let's look at the list of symptoms speakers typically report experiencing in the minutes before, during, and after their presentations to the group. These are frequent comments:

• My heart was pounding.

• I couldn't get my breath.

- I felt myself blushing.

- My palms were sweating.

- I heard my voice shaking.

- I forgot what to say.

- My mouth was dry.

- I felt tightness in my throat/chest/whole body.

- I felt my hands/knees/legs/whole body shaking.

- My voice kept cracking.

A closer look at the biology and physiology of what occurs will help you understand, and better manage, your reactions. (If you don't particularly enjoy reading about hormones and the nervous system, skip the next few paragraphs and go to the list of common symptoms.) The very brief explanations of these symptoms—of what the body is trying to do for you—will give you something to smile about before your next presentation.

The human nervous system has two main components. The voluntary nervous system controls those actions requiring thought, such as picking up a book. The autonomic nervous system controls all activities that do not require thought, such as breathing.

The autonomic nervous system is itself divided into two components: the sympathetic division, which controls the fight-or-flight response and is our main concern, and the parasympathetic division, which controls normal breathing, digestion, growth, and so on.[1]

The challenges of preparing and delivering a presentation are usually enough to stimulate the sympathetic nervous system to respond. This response, an evolutionary response to danger, activates in two distinct phases. The first phase, known as the SAM (sympathetic-adreno-medullary axis) is the all-too-familiar fight-or-flight response.

The Fight-or-Flight Response

When the fight-or-flight response is triggered, the body goes through many powerful changes in a matter of seconds. The brain shoots a message down the spinal cord to the medulla, the core of the adrenal glands. The adrenal medulla begins to synthesize and secrete adrenaline and related hormones, such as cortisol and aldosterone, into the bloodstream. The body will experience the effects of adrenaline in a matter of seconds.[2] To prepare for the perceived emergency, blood pressure and heart rate increase dramatically. The liver pours out glucose and accesses fat reserves to be processed for energy. The circulatory system diverts blood from the surface of the body and nonessential physical processes, like digestion, to the brain and muscles. The effects of these changes explain many of the symptoms experienced by speakers, especially just before the start and during the first few minutes of a presentation.

Here are some of the common symptoms of anxiety followed by an explanation of what the body is doing to "help" us.

- *Pounding heart.* The fight-or-flight chemicals increase the rate and force of contraction of the heart muscle. This pumps more blood to the muscles to deliver more oxygen for the coming fighting or fleeing.

- *Dry mouth.* A dry mouth is the result of the suspension of nonessential physical processes so the body can use energy where it really matters. The body is in effect saying, "Digestion can wait until later. We have bigger problems right now!" When digestion stops, the flow of saliva also stops.[3] A temporary stop to digestion allows an increase in the blood—and oxygen—supply to the muscles needed for fight or flight.

- *Deeper and more rapid breathing.* Dilation of the bronchioles (the tiny branches of air tubes in the lungs) and acceleration in the rate of breathing increase the supply of oxygen to the lungs and heart.

- *Increase in blood pressure.* Restriction of surface blood vessels raises arterial blood pressure. This may help equalize the drop in blood pressure above the shoulders caused by standing up. It also may decrease the blood near the skin surface, lessening the loss of blood if a flesh wound is suffered.

- *Shaking, shivering, "goose bumps."* Shaking and shivering warm the body. They reduce the susceptibility to cold caused by the lessening of blood flow to the surface of the body. The raising of hairs on the body makes an animal with fur appear larger, stronger, and more threatening to an enemy.

- *Increased muscle tension.* Muscle tension increases to prepare the muscles for possible strenuous activity, like running or fighting.

- *Shaking voice.* Increased muscle tension and shaking for warmth can both cause your voice to shake.

- *Sweaty palms.* Sweating palms is another phenomenon that has outlived its usefulness. Human sweat glands most probably evolved from the fluid-producing eccrine glands found in many mammals. These glands produce a clear fluid, very close in composition to plain salt water. A thin layer of fluid on the skin adds traction. It is why we might lick a finger before turning the page in a book. In animals, it helps prevent slipping. Primates that live in trees have eccrine glands on their hands and feet, and some tail-swinging monkeys even have them on their tails. Nonprimates, including domestic cats and dogs, have them only on the pads of their feet.

In *The Scars of Evolution,* author Elaine Morgan writes:

A monkeys' palms sweat, not in response to a rise in temperature, but in response to a consciousness of danger. When the monkey makes a decision to launch itself into space to leap from one branch to another, the brain sends out a signal which quickens its heartbeat, sharpens its perceptions, and at the same time dampens the palms to ensure a good grip on the branch it is aiming for. Our own palms sweat in exactly the same way. They do not respond to changes in temperature. Instead, the wetness breaks out when we are tense or apprehensive—standing in the wings with stage fright, being introduced to someone we are in awe of, or contemplating a crucial shot in a snooker final so that the hands have to be dried on a cloth before cueing.[4]

All of these "symptoms" are part of a normal, healthy human response to a perceived threat. The response may be outdated because the pace of change in society has outpaced changes in the human body, but it still has a predictable and powerful effect on most speakers. Knowing this allows us to experience these symptoms without becoming overly concerned. When we greet the arrival of these symptoms with understanding, acceptance, and even amusement, we help break the downward spiral of anxiety that might otherwise occur.

But Why Does My Mind Go Blank?

Most people who have given presentations or performed have experienced the frightening feeling of "going blank." This is one of the problems my clients fear the most. Their responses to this phenomenon include a wide variety of emotions ranging from exasperation to embarrassment to sheer terror. Always they feel a sense of frustration and puzzlement at this loss of intellectual control. I often hear comments such as these:

- "Sometimes I can't even remember to check my notes!"

- "I designed the slide, and I couldn't think why!"

- "I can't believe I couldn't remember that word!"

- "I forgot the client's name!"

- "I left out two main points!"

As part of the fight-or-flight response, the body produces a hormone called *cortisol*. The stress-induced production of cortisol may play an important part in the temporary loss of memory.[5] Studies suggest that stress-induced cortisol may reduce the ability to recall information during and immediately after a stressful event. Recent studies show that both the ability to retrieve memories and the ability to form new memories are temporarily impaired when cortisol levels peak in the brain. This happens about thirty minutes after the onset of a stressful event. An example is the speed with which a new mother often forgets the pain of labor as soon as she has successfully given birth.[6] This stress-induced elevation in the level of cortisol in the brain may explain the common experience of forgetting information while delivering a speech or presentation. It may also explain why a speaker will easily remember what she had planned to say once she has finished, sat down, and begun to relax.

Memorizing Is Not the Answer

So even if you have successfully memorized your content, it may not be available to you when you really need it. Perhaps your wolf is just trying to help! Perhaps the wolf believes that your best chance of survival in a really threatening situation is not to stand and compute your odds or to formulate and deliver an articulate argument. Your wolf is convinced that your best chance of survival is to fight or flee. So your senses sharpen, your muscles grow stronger, but your more sophisticated intellectual processes abandon you in your modern-day moments of need!

Knowledge Is Power

You know the causes of the symptoms of anxiety. Understanding what your body is trying to do for you is the next step to minimizing and managing it. You certainly don't have to remember everything you have read about the symptoms. But do remember that they are normal and natural even if they are thousands of years out of date. The next time your wolf growls, you can smile at him. He's not unexpected or mysterious. He's just a normal wolf, a rather old wolf. You know why he's there.

The next chapter will take you through a number of ways you can minimize and manage the symptoms of anxiety when they do occur. You'll find exercises and tips to use before and during your presentation. These, combined with your new understanding of anxiety, will go a long way toward taming that wolf for good.

The early morning sun gleamed off the round silver towers of the software company's headquarters. Scheduled to work with a new client for four precious hours, I wanted to be ready by 8:30 a.m. A gracious, well-dressed woman was waiting to greet me, and I was quickly ushered to a large conference room, given coffee, and told my client had called and would arrive by 8:30. As I set up my camera and arranged training materials on the conference table, I regretted that I hadn't been able to speak with the client in advance. I only knew that he was a vice president of the company, thirty-four years old, and wanted "general skill improvement."

He walked into the room at 8:30 sharp. He looked very young. But as we introduced ourselves and chatted, it quickly became apparent that he was friendly and warm, very articulate, very ambitious, and very interested in the success of both his latest project and his team. I asked him to sit with me at the table. I told him I'd like to spend a few minutes learning about his position, the types of presentations he did, and any specific goals he had for our session.

He immediately became very serious. He looked me right in the eye and said, "I want to know why the water is in all the wrong places."

I paused. "What water is that?"

He said gravely. "My water."

I looked at him and raised my eyebrows.

He spoke more emphatically now. "I want to know why every time I get up in front of a group, my mouth gets dry and my hands get wet. Every time! Even in front of my own team. I know what I'm doing, and they like me! It doesn't make any sense!"

So I told him about the natural history of the fear of public speaking. He learned why his mouth got dry and his hands got wet.

When I finished, he said, "That makes sense. That makes a lot of sense." He smiled and said, "Let's get started!"

Summary

The fight-or-flight response evolved to help animals (including humans) cope with perceived danger. Many of the symptoms of anxiety so often associated with public speaking are part of the fight-or-flight response. Accelerated heart rate, breathing changes, muscle tension, shaking, sweating, and dry mouth all help the body prepare to fight or flee.

Other symptoms may include heightened sensitivity to sights and sounds and the temporary inability to remember some information or to form new memories. The result of these changes is an increased awareness of one's immediate environment combined with a temporary reduction in higher intellectual functioning. These changes are a response designed by evolution. They allow us to temporarily devote all our available energy to handling immediate physical danger. Intellectual processes that have longer term value, such as memory functions, may be temporarily sacrificed for the benefit of physical survival when faced with a clear and present danger, for example, a saber-toothed tiger, a giant hyena, or a band of hostile strangers.

Understanding that these changes are normal and healthy parts of the human experience is the key to acceptance. With acceptance comes reduced frustration and a new ability to focus our energy on minimizing and managing the effects of the fight-or-flight response.

> To use fear as the friend it is, we must retrain and reprogram
> ourselves . . . We must persistently and convincingly tell ourselves
> that the fear is here—with its gifts of energy and heightened awareness—
> so we can do our best and learn the most in the new situation.
>
> PETER MCWILLIAMS

Feeding Your Wolf

Minimizing and Managing Anxiety

There are many different ways to help minimize and manage the body's natural responses to the challenge of delivering a presentation. But before we go through them, let's take a look at the bright side of anxiety.

First, the Good News

In *The Anxiety and Phobia Workbook,* author Edmund J. Bourne identifies a number of personality traits often shared by people who have anxiety disorders. Many of these traits are positive and can be extremely helpful in preparing and delivering a successful presentation.

Creativity and emotional sensitivity are two positive traits often shared by people who experience anxiety.[1] Exercising creativity while conceptualizing, planning, and organizing a presentation is essential if one is to capture the minds and hearts of members of the audience. Emotional sensitivity and related gifts such as intuitive ability and empathy are tremendously valuable when communicating with others. The ability to engage in dialogue, build rapport, successfully exchange ideas and information, and reach true understanding is greatly enhanced when these abilities are used.

One aspect that may make presentations more of a challenge for intuitive, sensitive, and empathic people is the one-way nature of monologue. Without frequent responses and contributions from the listeners, a natural part of dialogue, the sensitive communicator may find himself more uncomfortable than someone who is typically less "tuned in."

And the Not-So-Good News

Other traits, which tend to increase and perpetuate anxiety, are likely to be present in people prone to anxiety. These traits are

- Perfectionism

- Excessive need for control

- Excessive need for approval

- Tendency to ignore physical and psychological signs of stress[2]

The intellectual, emotional, and physical demands of doing a presentation, especially a high-stakes presentation, can bring out some form of these tendencies in most of us. Of course, we will want to do a perfect presentation. Of course, we will want to feel in control. Of course, we will want the approval of our audience. And we will have to show up, and speak up, even if our bodies and minds are telling us they would rather not. We have to ignore the signs of stress and focus on the presentation at hand. How can we deal with this dilemma?

If you suffer from severe anxiety and recognize that you have issues related to one or more of these traits, there is help. Many books and organizations exist to help with anxiety. As a start, see the information on anxiety in the resources section at the back of this book. Ask your doctor if you would like more information on what to do.

It is very likely that even if you usually have none of the above traits, some signs of them will appear about the time you agree to do a presentation. Then excellent preparation and practice are important because they will give you the best chance of being as close to perfect as is reasonably possible, staying as much in control as possible, being most likely to earn the approval you need, and reducing your physical and psychological stress.

> Remember that fear always lurks behind perfectionism. Confronting your fears and allowing yourself the right to be human can, paradoxically, make you a far happier and more productive person.
>
> DR. DAVID M. BURNS

It is also important to remember that absolute perfection does not exist. Different members of your audience will appreciate different parts of what you say and how you say it. And humans relate better to human qualities, not god-like ones.

How Can I Minimize and Manage the Anxiety?

You now know that the anxiety related to public speaking is normal, even healthy. But that doesn't mean you have to like it. The first step to minimizing the anxiety is to identify the causes. Once you have identified your areas of concern, you will know where to begin.

The rest of this chapter will give you suggestions for dealing effectively with the anxiety. You will find a number of time-tested intellectual and emotional strategies. You will also find physical strategies that can help keep both anxiety and its symptoms to a minimum. You will learn to reduce and manage it when it appears. You will find exercises and tips you can apply in advance, just before you speak, and while you speak. Knowledge is power, but practice makes perfect. The more you practice these techniques, the easier and more effective they become. Choose the ones that work best for you.

Identify Your Concerns

We have seen that the symptoms of anxiety are the result of several factors. Below you will find a list of the four major factors we have discussed. Grab a piece of paper, and for each factor, list specific worries you have. (Do this with a particular presentation or speech in mind as your worries may change with different events.) For the last factor, physical concerns, list the physical changes and behaviors you noticed during previous presentations, for example, sweaty palms and rapid speech.

1. Content concerns

2. Performance concerns

3. Monologue concerns

4. Physical concerns

Once you have compiled your list, let's get to work. The rest of this chapter offers tips for managing the fourth major factor—the physical symptoms of anxiety. For help with the other three factors, here's where to look.

For Content and Performance Concerns

We know that many of the intellectual fears can be alleviated with solid preparation, and this can greatly minimize the emotional fears. Parts 2 and 3 of this book will give you the information you need to prepare excellent content and deliver it with skill and confidence. The chapters on analyzing your audience, organizing your content, and enhancing your content are extremely helpful if you have content concerns. The chapters on verbal and nonverbal delivery skills, using notes effectively, and moving from monologue to dialogue will be especially valuable to you.

Nature, Mr. Allnut, is what we are put in this world to rise above.

KATHARINE HEPBURN

as Rose Sayer in *The African Queen*

For Monologue Concerns

The chapters on organizing your content, using notes, nonverbal delivery skills, and moving from monologue to dialogue give excellent suggestions for helping make your content and your delivery as much like dialogue as possible. Practicing out loud, even talking through your topic in the car or shower, will help you become accustomed to communicating effectively in monologue mode. And giving presentations often is the best way to become accustomed to the different "feel" of monologue.

For Minimizing and Managing the Physical Symptoms of Anxiety

As we know, the wolf of anxiety may be sleeping, but he hasn't moved away. We need to know what to do when he wakes up hungry. The following practices, exercises, and tips can be used before and during your presentation. You'll learn intellectual and physical strategies for keeping your wolf at bay. Choose those that make sense to you, and begin practicing them well before an important presentation. They will help you feel more relaxed and confident and encourage you to make presentations more often. Feed your wolf well!

In the Days before Your Presentation

Remember, preparation is key. Try these tips well before your presentation.

Get Enough Rest

Over the several days (and nights) before your presentation, get plenty of sleep. For at least three hours before bed avoid any stimulants—nicotine, coffee, tea, and soft drinks with caffeine. Avoid after-dinner drinks. Alcohol can help you fall asleep, but the sleep you get will be light and fragmented, not restorative.[3] Sleep allows your body to reset your thermostat, recharge your battery, and top off your fluids. Lack of sleep makes it more difficult

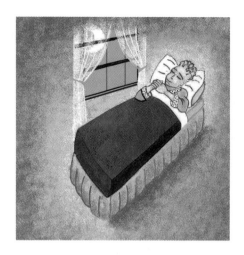

for your body to handle the normal stress of a presentation, slows your thought processes, and decreases your ability to remember.

Eat Smart

Reduce your intake of refined sugar. Too much can cause low energy, dizziness, or light-headedness.[4] Soft drinks, candy, ice cream, pastries, and desserts are high in refined sugars. Even "natural" sweets like honey, corn syrup, molasses, dried fruits, and fruit juices can have extremely high sugar content. Simple starches such as pasta, potato chips, and white bread break down into sugars when consumed. Substitute fresh fruit for sweets and replace simple starches with complex carbohydrates such as whole grain breads, vegetables, and brown rice.[5] By eating smart you can avoid the mood swings that are caused or aggravated by rapid changes in the level of blood sugar. These include light-headedness, anxiety, weakness, trembling, and palpitations. All of these exacerbate the normal stresses of presenting.

Exercise

Get plenty of exercise. Two days before your presentation is not the time to become a "weekend warrior." You don't want to become stiff and sore, exhausted, or injured. But gentle exercise, especially a combination of aerobic, strength, and flexibility training will help you minimize your feelings of anxiety. Exercise reduces your skeletal muscle tension and increases the rate of metabolism of excess adrenaline in your body. This helps minimize the negative effect of the fight-or-flight response. Exercise increases the flow of oxygen to the brain, increasing alertness and concentration. Exercise also stimulates the production of endorphins, natural substances that increase your sense of well-being and confidence.[6] Tests show that after thirty minutes on a treadmill young men show a 25 percent reduction in measurable stress and an increase in activity in the prefrontal cortex, linked to a sense of self-possession.[7] Exercise helps you relax and feel more confident.

Get a Massage—or Two

Massage has been shown to improve lung function in asthma sufferers, improve immune function, and even improve performance on math tests![8] Premature infants who receive regular massages have been shown to gain weight much more rapidly and leave the hospital sooner.

At Your Presentation

Try these tips on the day of your presentation.

Arrive Early

Plan to arrive early. The speaker's checklist (chapter 20) gives you many great suggestions for arriving on time, being under control, and checking that everything and everybody is ready for you. You can avoid increasing your natural anxiety with worries about being late or having to deal with unexpected problems if you arrive in plenty of time.

Mingle

Mingle with the audience before your presentation. If appropriate, greet and introduce yourself to members of the audience as they arrive. Chat with them. Learn about them: their reasons for coming, their challenges and concerns. Confirm what you assumed, discover what you didn't know. Learn their names. If you mingle with the audience beforehand, you can present to acquaintances, even friends, rather than strangers. You can tailor your presentation based on what you learned and use examples or references most meaningful to the audience. You can much more easily create the look and feel of dialogue.

Intellectual and Emotional Strategies

Understanding and practicing techniques that reduce intellectual and emotional anxiety will allow you to start with confidence, think more quickly, and focus more effectively on your listeners. Try the suggestions below as you wait to begin.

- *Concentrate on a simple mental task.* Mentally drive a familiar route, naming each street and visualizing the buildings you pass. Try to remember all the words to a song or poem. Add up all the costs of a project.

- *Recall and celebrate a positive experience.* Remember a success. Visualize it happening. Recall the feeling. Feel the satisfaction, joy, pride.

- *Use coping self-statements.* Tell yourself things that are both positive and true:

  - "My body is reacting as it is designed to."
  - "Anxiety is normal. I will do well even if I am uncomfortable."
  - "I am well prepared."
  - "My goal is to share this information with people who need it."
  - "Breathing deeply helps me relax."

- *Use simple externalization.* Consciously and deliberately use your senses to focus on something external. Observe and silently describe the people around you. Note their physical appearance, items of clothing, colors, fabrics, in as much detail as you can. Do the same for their physical behavior. Do they move slowly or quickly? How would you describe various facial expressions? Their tones of voice? Listen closely. Note as many sounds as you can: the hum of the ventilation system, the ticking of a clock, footsteps, the rustle of clothing, conversations going on around you, sounds from an adjoining room or hallway. Feel the temperature and texture of your clothing. Notice the temperature of your chair, table, or desk. Feel the texture of papers you hold.

Physical Strategies

Addressing the physical changes brought about by the fight-or-flight response can be done in several ways. Breathing, moving, and consciously using physical activity in ways that help you relax are all effective ways to minimize and manage anxiety.

Breathing well is one of the most powerful relaxation techniques you can use. It will relax your muscles, energize your entire body, and oxygenate your brain for peak performance. Use the technique below frequently in your daily life. Remember to use it just before you begin your presentation.

Diaphragmatic Breathing

Diaphragmatic breathing—breathing more slowly and deeply than we tend to do when anxious—can reduce many of the physical symptoms of anxiety in two ways. First, slower, deeper breathing can help reverse two reactions to the fight-or-flight response: increased rate of respiration and tightness in the muscles of the upper body, especially the chest and throat. Second, deeper breathing can reduce the tendency to hyperventilate. Hyperventilation can cause symptoms very similar to the fight-or-flight response. This breathing exercise can help you to relax. You will probably notice the effect quickly, but try to allow enough time to continue the exercise for at least several minutes.

Step 1. Place one hand lightly on your abdomen. Inhale slowly through your nose. This warms and moistens the air fully before it enters your lungs. Inhale until you feel your hand rise slightly as the abdomen slowly expands. Count to four or five. You may feel your chest move slightly, but your shoulders and neck should remain relaxed. Inhale until you feel comfortably "full."

Step 2. Remaining quiet and still, hold your breath for several seconds. You may want to visualize the oxygen flowing to all parts of your body or visualize any pleasant and relaxing scene. Hold your breath only as long as you are comfortable doing so.

Step 3. Exhale slowly and gently through your mouth or nose until your lungs feel comfortably empty. Do not force or blow the air out. Let your muscles relax as you exhale.

Step 4. Take two or three "regular" breaths. Allow your body to determine the speed, depth, and rhythm of these breaths. As you continue with this exercise, let your body decide what is comfortable.

Step 5. Continue this cycle of one slow, counted diaphragmatic breath and two or three regular breaths for several minutes.

This diaphragmatic breathing exercise is most effective when you become familiar and comfortable with it. Practicing it daily can give you this comfort. The benefits of deep breathing will help you manage daily stress.

Movement/Physical Activity

Look for ways to engage in mild exercise before, and even during, your presentation. The information on "spark" skills in chapter 14 will give you specifics on using your body effectively during your presentation. These specific instructions will help you both look and feel more relaxed and confident.

Try the following suggestions for anxiety-reducing physical activity in the time just before your presentation.

- *Go for a brisk walk.* Even a five-minute walk will help you relax, loosen your muscles to relieve tension, and give you a circulation boost that will increase the flow of oxygen and help you think clearly. The rhythm of brisk walking, so soothing to infants that the rocking chair was invented to mimic it, may do a great deal to relax and soothe you when you need it.[9]

- *Exercise in place.* Stretching, bending, arm circles or other simple exercises will give you many of the same benefits even when you can't go for a walk.

- *Flex your muscles.* When even stretching and bending are not possible (for example, if you are seated on the stage for some time before your turn to speak) tighten and then release your muscles repetitively while you breathe slowly and deeply. You will get many of the benefits of more vigorous movement.

- *Stand up early.* I often hear people say, "The first couple of minutes of a presentation are always the worst!" Standing up several minutes before you begin speaking can be a big help. When we first rise to a standing position, blood drains from the upper body, including the heart and the brain. It takes the body several minutes to readjust the blood volume. During this time the brain has less oxygen than it needs for peak performance. Just when you need to think most clearly—to step on the gas and be firing on all cylinders—you will be operating with too little fuel! Standing up several minutes before you begin speaking will allow your body to readjust before you begin your presentation.

- *Engage in repetitive activity.* Count ceiling or floor tiles. Count the number of chairs you see. Tap your fingers or your foot rhythmically. Fold and unfold a piece of paper in a complex pattern. Both focusing on something other than your anxiety and the rhythm you establish can be soothing.

Medication

I don't recommend beta blockers or any other drugs, including alcohol, to minimize the symptoms of anxiety. Understanding the reason for symptoms, accepting them, and being thoroughly prepared so you can create an atmosphere of dialogue with your audience are the best ways to reduce and manage anxiety.

Some people, however, choose to use a beta blocker to reduce the physical symptoms of anxiety. A small dose before a speech can reduce the flow of adrenaline that occurs with anxiety.[10]

The effects of beta blockers are not always positive. Some users report a loss of energy. Other possible side effects include dizziness, light-headedness, and allergic reactions.[11] Beta blockers can be dangerous for people with asthma, diabetes, and certain other allergies. If you do decide to use a beta blocker, discuss it with your doctor. Also ask your doctor about the possibility of trying a test dose before the day of your presentation to make sure you have no negative side effects.

The Benefits of Stress

Finally, know that moderate stress can actually help you grow, change, improve your skills, and cope more effectively with life's challenges. Stress causes the release of norepinephrine. This neurotransmitter, which improves mood, helps you perceive problems as challenges and encourages creative thinking.[12] Eustress, the type of stress caused by anticipating and experiencing positive events—completing an important project or falling madly in love—can produce positive responses in the body. And small amounts of stress serve as a dress rehearsal for the body, helping us stay strong and ready to change, grow, and survive. Professor Paola S. Timiras of the University of California at Berkeley credits mild stress with more efficient DNA repair, strengthening the immune system, decreasing mortality due to cancer and infections, and thus increasing life span.[13] Professor Bernard Griego, also of UC Berkeley, reinforces the idea that some stress is beneficial. He believes stress makes people more "psychologically hardy" and makes them better able to deal with different stress levels.[14]

That which does not kill us makes us stronger.

FRIEDRICH NIETZSCHE

Just think what a marvelous opportunity you have if you are nervous about public speaking! Not only do you have the chance to learn new skills, increase your ability to persuade and motivate others, increase your visibility and opportunities for reward, but you can also become more psychologically hardy and physically healthy. How much better can it get?

Summary

The natural anxiety response that so often comes with public speaking takes on several forms. Intellectual anxieties are centered on content. Physical anxieties include all the symptoms of the fight-or-flight response. They can stem from intellectual anxieties, from the evolutionary response to being the center of attention—the salient object—or from both. Emotional anxieties often follow both intellectual and physical anxieties. They center on what our listeners will think of us.

Some personality traits tend to increase and perpetuate anxiety. These traits are perfectionism, excessive need for control, excessive need for approval, and the tendency to ignore physical and psychological signs of stress.

Understanding the nature of anxiety, the positive results stress can bring, and the ways you can minimize and manage negative stress are your first steps to becoming a comfortable and confident speaker.

PART TWO

PREPARING YOUR
PRESENTATION

8

There are two types of people. Those who come into a room and say, "Well, here I am!" and those who come in and say, "Ah, there you are."

FREDERICK L. COLLINS

It's All about Them

Reach Your Audience, Then Your Goals

Your presentation is scheduled. You are committed. You know how important it is to be prepared, so don't procrastinate. Getting started early is a wonderful way to prevent the buildup of anxiety. Nothing will increase your comfort level more than getting started early.

But the questions you have are these: Where do I begin? How do I begin? What do I do first?

What do you want to do?

What do you want to accomplish by giving your presentation? So much has been written about the importance of goals that I won't lecture you here. I'll just remind you of the old saying "If you don't know where you're going, you're likely to end up there."

You will probably have a number of goals for your presentation. Some may be personal, some professional. This contributes to your challenge. But awareness of all your goals is one key to designing and delivering a great presentation. And we have ways to help you meet your goals. Let's get started.

Take a look at the list below. How many of these goals do you share?

- Build rapport and trust
- Inform the audience
- Educate the audience
- Persuade the audience
- Entertain the audience
- Create new relationships
- Expand a relationship
- Improve a relationship
- Preserve a relationship
- Control a crisis
- Contain damage
- Demonstrate knowledge
- Learn from the audience
- Change the listeners' minds
- Help the listeners agree
- Increase my visibility
- Sell a product or service
- Practice my speaking skills
- Enjoy myself
- Survive

Most likely you have multiple goals. Most likely your goals are interdependent. For example, could you expand a relationship or change your listeners' minds without also building trust? Could you persuade them or change their minds without also educating them? To achieve your goals you must know enough about your listeners to tailor your content and delivery to them.

Who Is Your Audience?

Three very basic elements to consider in assessing your audience are credibility, psychographics, and demographics.

- *Credibility.* How much credibility do you have with the audience? How well do they know you? How do they perceive your competence, your character, your confidence, and your intentions? How do they perceive each other?

- *Psychographics.* How do you relate to the audience in terms of attitudes, values, belief systems, and ideologies? How do they relate to each other? What do they value? Do you share those values? Where might you differ from the audience? How fundamental are these differences? Should you attempt to overcome them or work within them? Can you do either?

- *Demographics.* How do you relate to the audience in age, sex, religion, family status, educational level, and socioeconomic class? What cultural differences or language differences do you need to consider? To what extent do members of the audience differ on these factors?

Consider the following more specific questions about your listeners. Answering these questions will help you identify and describe your listeners in detail. With this knowledge and understanding you can tailor your information to them. This will help alleviate content concerns, increase rapport, enhance your credibility, and help you be most persuasive! Knowledge is power, and power builds confidence.

- Who will attend? What are their names? Job titles? Job responsibilities?

- What are their ages? Genders? Levels of education? Cultural backgrounds?

- What do they believe they need? What challenges do they have?

- What problems do they need to solve? What limitations do they have?

- What are their attitudes about your subject? Your organization? You?

- What do they know? How familiar are they with the issues? How much technical understanding do they have? What concepts will you need to explain? What terms should be used, defined, or avoided?

- How important is the topic to your audience? How much do they care? What emotions do they have around this topic or issue? Why do they feel this way?

- What are the costs to them in terms of money, time, effort, risk? Are they able to pay the costs? Are they willing to pay?

- What special considerations exist? Does your audience have any unusual needs? Do you need to take their history into account? Are some topics taboo?

- Who makes the decisions? What decision-making power do they have?

- Who influences the decisions? What power of influence do they have?

Make Educated Guesses

Once you have identified the "need to know" information, jot down the answers you have. Sometimes you will have specific information. Sometimes

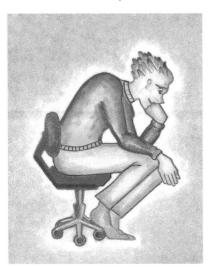

you can make an educated guess. Your answers are likely to come from a wide variety of sources. These may include previous contact with audience members, research you have done, your previous experience, and your knowledge of the industry. You may be surprised by how much you do know. After all, you were asked to speak for a reason!

Fill in the Blanks

You can learn more about your intended audience in many ways. If you will be speaking at an industry conference or user conference, find out what kind of information is gathered as part of the attendance reservation process. Often you can discover organizations, job titles, geographic information, and much more this way. If you will be speaking as a technical expert as part of a sales effort, learn as much as you can about the situation and the client

> People will sit up and take notice if you will sit up and take notice of what makes them sit up and take notice.
>
> FRANK ROMER

from the account manager or event host. Depending on the nature of your talk and your audience, one or more of the following options can help you learn what you need to be most effective:

- Ask people who plan to attend: in person, by phone, by e-mail.

- Visit the Web site of the organization you will address.

- Read the corporate report of the company you will speak to.

- Read industry publications.

- Search on-line for press coverage.

- Send an e-mail survey to those who will attend.

- Include a survey as part of registration to attend.

- Chat with audience members as they arrive for your presentation.

- Take a "show of hands" survey at the beginning of or during your presentation.

The Basic Types of Business Listeners

When you have answered the above questions, added your educated guesses, and done any needed research, you will often be able to identify your listeners as belonging to one of the following groups: executives, experts, technicians, customers, suppliers, or end users. Understanding the responsibilities, interests, and needs of these different types is another great way to make sure that your content, level of detail, and delivery methods will be on target.

Can you identify your listeners as belonging to one or more of the following groups?

Executives

Executives make business, financial, legal, administrative, governmental, and political decisions. They are concerned with shareholder value and market share. They decide whether to approve, fund, build, and market new products and programs. They decide whether to continue, expand, or shrink ongoing efforts. They must consider overall strategy and long-term goals and consequences.

Experts

Experts know their company's and/or industry's products and services extremely well. They designed them (or similar products or services), they tested them, and they understand their history, strengths, weaknesses, and opportunities for improvement. They understand the theories and issues related to these products and services. They often have advanced degrees and operate in research and development or academic areas of business or government. They are especially appreciative of elegance of design. Experts generally present information to other experts, to technicians, and to executives.

Technicians

Technicians build, operate, administrate, maintain, and repair the products that the experts theorize about, design, modify, and improve. They have detailed knowledge and extensive experience. Their knowledge is usually more practical and immediate than that of experts.

Customers

Customers purchase or recommend the purchase of your products and/or services. They may be executives, experts, technicians, or end users, and, occasionally, suppliers. In large organizations your customers are most often executives and experts in other organizations.

Suppliers

Suppliers provide products or services that contribute to other organizations' ability to satisfy their own customers and employees. They may be executives, specialists, or technicians, or in marketing and sales positions.

End Users

End users of your product, service, or idea are typically nonspecialists. Their interests are usually highly practical—they want to use the product, service, or idea to accomplish their tasks. They often have immediate needs and think shorter term. They may have very little technical knowledge. Nonspecialists are least likely to understand what experts and technicians are saying. Demonstrations and hands-on time are often highly effective with nonspecialists.

If all the members of your audience have similar needs and expectations, you will be able to eliminate content fears that come from not knowing what your audience wants. But often, when you think about these questions, it will become clear that different audience members have different wants, needs, knowledge levels, and opinions. What do you do if members don't all have the same wants and needs?

Planning for a Diverse Audience

The opportunity to speak to an audience with members who have identical backgrounds and interests is a rare luxury in today's world. Most audiences have members with a variety of educational backgrounds, training, experience, specialties, and expertise. Their interests in attending may be very different, and their ability to understand specialized information may vary widely. This is more the norm than the exception today.

There is no one way to please all of the people all of the time. It is unlikely you will be able to deliver the precise content, level of detail, and tone that will completely satisfy everyone. But happily, most listeners understand and expect this diversity. Your audience members will understand your challenge—and will appreciate your awareness of it—if you follow these recommendations.

I don't know the secret of success, but the key to failure is trying to please everyone.

BILL COSBY

Acknowledge the Situation

In your opening, tell the audience that you are aware of the differences in background and interest. You might say something like this: "I know that some of you have been using this software since the first release and will be especially interested in the new features. I understand that some of you will soon be implementing this system for the first time and will want a general understanding of the functions and benefits we offer."

When you acknowledge the diversity you accomplish two objectives. First, you demonstrate that you understand the audience, are aware of their goals, and care enough to want to give them all something of value. Second, you increase each member's awareness that others' goals may be different from his or her own. This goes a long way in establishing your credibility. It helps everyone understand and accept your next step.

Share Your Presentation Strategy

Present your strategy for dealing with this situation. Often, the best approach is to target the level of detail to the less technical or least specialized portion of your audience. Another option is to vary the amount of specialized or detailed information at different times. But no matter what your strategy is, share it with your audience.

Much unhappiness has come into the world because of bewilderment and things left unsaid.

DOSTOEVSKY

Let's look more closely at your options for working with a diverse audience.

Simplify or Reduce the Level of Detail

If you plan to simplify the information, tell the audience you have made this choice. Then let them know how you will provide more in-depth or technical information if they want it. Times and methods you can use to provide details and specialized information include

- During the question-and-answer session
- After the presentation
- In handouts or supplementary material
- By phone or e-mail
- On your Web site
- From customer service representatives
- From technical support representatives

Vary the Amount of Specialized Information

Another option is to acknowledge that you will vary the amount of specialized information during your presentation. Ask the audience to understand and bear with you when you do so. Just before you shift from less to more specialized information, let your audience know you are doing so, and give them an estimate of how long it will take. The less specialized audience members will be extremely grateful for any information about how long a section of your presentation will take. You might say something like this: "Now let's cover the specifics of the research design and the statistical tools used. This will take about three minutes. Then we will move right into our findings and recommendations."

Use Language the General Audience Will Understand

Specialized language has several uses. It allows for precision in meaning, but it is also a powerful tool that will unite or divide your audience. This is especially true when the audience has diverse backgrounds.

When specialized language is understood by the entire group, it can create a feeling of group cohesiveness. This comes from the unspoken awareness that "we are all enough alike to understand what she means." But it can also mystify and exclude. Lawyers are legendary for using unnecessarily complex language to mystify their activities. This creates a separation between themselves and their clients. It helps establish and preserve an aura of indispensable expertise. Having established themselves as experts, they increase their ability to operate with less interference from clients. And this expertise commands high fees.

The key to using specialized language effectively is to understand that it can unite or divide your audience. Meaning is easily lost if members of the audience aren't familiar with the specialized language, the acronyms, or the buzzwords used by a speaker. And the listeners who don't understand are immediately separated, intellectually and emotionally, from the listeners who do.

Just as important (and possibly more so), the inability to understand specialized language separates the listeners from the speaker. For a speaker trying to connect with both the minds and hearts of her listeners, the overuse of specialized language can create a wall that can't be scaled. So use acronyms and specialized language consciously and sparingly. Instead of saying, "The primary care practitioner apprised the interested party that the subject of her ministrations had experienced the ultimate irreversible and permanent negative healthcare outcome," say, "The doctor told her the patient died."

When you use specialized language, make it as understandable as possible to the general audience. If you must use acronyms, tell the audience what they mean. Plan to remind them of the meaning at least once.

Use Examples, Analogies, Anecdotes, and Stories

Use examples, analogies, anecdotes, and stories to increase understanding. But choose wisely. Simple examples may not be useful to experts, and highly technical ones will go over the heads of nonspecialist users and listeners. An analogy helps present new or complex information by comparing it to information that is already known and understood. A good anecdote or story will help listeners both remember your information and share it with others later. (Read the lessons on developing and using analogies and stories in chapter 11 for more information on how to use these tools well.) This will make a tremendous difference in how the less specialized members of your audience respond to your presentation!

Encourage Questions during Your Presentation

Another good way to handle mixed audiences is to have frequent, brief question-and-answer sessions. If time and protocol allow, invite your audience to ask questions at any time. Let them know how to get your attention (e.g., raising their hands), or after each major topic, stop and ask, "What questions do you have so far?"

The questions you get will give you information about the ability of the audience to understand your information and also about their interests and concerns. The answers will often give the less technical people a better understanding of the issues and help prepare them for the next topic. Also, answering questions is a great way to escape from monologue mode. Many speakers report that having a brief question-and-answer session early in the presentation creates a cooperative atmosphere and relaxes them tremendously.

Thoroughly researching and analyzing your audience is an important first step in preparing your presentation. If it seems to go slowly, remember this: presentations should be like painting your living room. Most—90 percent—of the time and effort is spent in advance. Really thinking about who your audience will be is like washing and priming the surfaces, applying painter's tape, and putting down drop cloths. Preparing thoroughly before you apply paint takes time, but it clearly defines the surfaces to be painted, helps make sure the paint will stick, and prevents messes and the need for cleanup afterward. Preparing thoroughly before you speak helps you be clear about both the scope and content of your information, helps you present information in a way that is likely to be understood and remembered, and prevents misunderstandings. Especially if presentations are new for you, you should plan to follow this guideline because it helps tremendously with the next steps. Remember to start slow to move fast.

Once the prep work is done you will be ready to create and organize the information that will become your notes. The ability to organize your content well and create useful notes is absolutely vital. The next chapter will help you learn to do this.

The methods you will learn will work in the real world. In an ideal world you would have lots of time to prepare, but this is not an ideal world. In this world the best laid schemes of mice and men often go askew. Sometimes you need to prepare really, really fast! So read on to learn to quickly and easily prepare great notes. The wolf of anxiety becomes very placid when he sees a speaker who has great notes!

Winning can be defined as the science of being totally prepared.

GEORGE ALLEN

Summary

When you can clearly state your presentation goals, you have taken the first important step toward achieving them. The next critical step is to gain an understanding of the needs and goals of your audience. Understanding the audience is vital so you can gather the right information, organize it appropriately, and deliver it in the most effective way. Three important considerations are the credibility you have with your audience, their psychographics, and their demographics.

To explore the needs and goals of your audience you can survey individuals who will attend. This can be done in the days before your presentation in person, by phone, or with a prepared survey. You can also visit related Web sites and review literature such as corporate reports, product or service brochures, and industry publications.

Special thought and care must be given to tailor the information for a highly diverse audience. Develop a plan for presenting information to a diverse audience, and share your plan with them. Consider the language choices you make, the examples you use or stories you tell, your use of humor, and how you plan to encourage and answer questions from the audience.

9

Improvisation is the essence of good talk. Heaven defend us
from the talker who doles out things prepared for us.

MAX BEERBOHM

Too much improvisation leaves the mind stupidly void.

VICTOR HUGO

Getting It Together

Preparing the Content

How much preparation should you do?
It depends! It depends on the breadth and depth of your knowledge of your subject matter. It depends on the formality of the occasion. It depends on the type of audience. It depends on how long the presentation will be. It depends on whether you are most capable and comfortable with highly structured and detailed notes or you prefer to talk more spontaneously. Understanding and working within your personal preferences for structure and detail is critical.

Levels of Preparation

The three basic levels of preparation of content are none, some, and all. The delivery of a presentation or speech given with no notice—"off the cuff"—and with no notes is called *impromptu*. Delivery from notes or an outline but not memorized is called *extemporaneous*. The third option is to deliver with every word chosen in advance. This message can be *memorized* or *scripted*.

While some situations may call for impromptu, memorized, or scripted presentations, most presentations today are extemporaneous. An extemporaneous presentation allows you to combine the benefits of preparation with those of a more natural, conversational, and flexible delivery. To use words borrowed from both Beerbohm and Hugo above, it gives us the benefits of improvisation without the fear of falling into a void. Preparing and using speaker notes is an important part of delivering information extemporaneously. Here are a few good reasons for choosing to speak extemporaneously and using notes that are separate from your slides.

First, if you know you will (or might) be called on to present a speech, some preparation is usually your best choice. Off-the-cuff presentations don't give you the opportunity to be as clear, as well organized, or as thorough as you can be with some preparation. Knowing you are prepared is an important part of minimizing any anxiety you may feel.

Second, putting all (or even most) of the things you want to say into slides almost always results in awful slides. They will take too much time to create, and they will be too complex for listeners to easily read, understand, or remember.

Third, reading word for word is very likely to sound stilted. It will be impossible to have good eye contact with your audience, so you will probably not look as confident or honest. You will be unable to see the changes in facial expression or body language that allow you to "read" your listeners' reactions. It will be much more difficult to develop rapport. You will not be able to make on-the-spot changes, such as give an example in response to puzzled expressions or dive more deeply into something that catches the listeners' attention. (Although the good news is you won't know you missed an opportunity! Ignorance may be bliss, but usually only in the short term.)

Fourth, memorizing a script and reciting it from memory will cause many of the same problems as reading the script. And since memory is unreliable under stress, the speaker becomes extremely vulnerable to memory loss. Finally, unless memorizing is absolutely your only option, it is a terrible use of your time.

When you have prepared and organized your notes, you will have thought through your information thoroughly. This makes you feel more confident.

With the flexibility to make changes as you speak, you will know you can do what it takes to best meet the needs of your audience. Knowing you don't have the added pressure of remembering memorized content is a great pressure reliever. In short, if you feel confident in your preparation it will be easier to relax and focus on your audience, your content, and your goals.

As you prepare your content, keep these important points in mind:

- *"Sell" to the audience.* Even if you don't think you are in sales, even if you are not selling products or services, you are "selling" ideas or choices. You must persuade your listeners to listen attentively. You must persuade them that you and your ideas are credible. The belief that your idea, choice, product, or service has value must be sold before anything else can be. The demise of most of the first wave of dot-com companies proved once again that catalogs alone—even on-line catalogs—are not the best way to sell. Catalogs of products, services, or ideas do not make good presentations.

- *Tell a story.* The best presentations tell compelling stories, stories tailored to that particular audience. They show how a listener's life can be enriched by the idea, belief, product, or service being offered.

- *Identify your goals.* As we saw at the beginning of chapter 8, you will most often have several goals for your presentation. Most of these goals can be achieved only when you accomplish others as well. For example, you can't inform or educate your audience without also demonstrating knowledge. You can't preserve a relationship or control a crisis without building rapport and trust. Think of all you must accomplish if you are to succeed in selling a product or service! This is why developing your notes methodically is important—and a good investment of time.

- *Remember the needs of your audience.* In the last chapter we looked at how you can develop a better understanding of your audience. Remember how important it is to keep the needs of the audience in mind. Now you can combine your knowledge about the needs of your audience with your

> It isn't working that's so hard;
> it's getting ready to work.
> *Andy Rooney*

97

knowledge of your own goals. You will be successful when you develop and organize your content so that it will meet your needs and those of your audience.

Getting Started

The classic rule for a presentation is to do three things:

- Tell them what you're going to tell them.

- Tell them.

- Tell them what you told them.

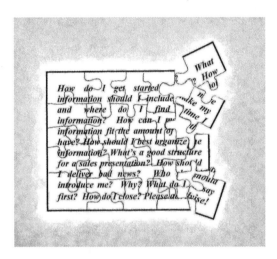

While there's nothing wrong with that advice, it isn't specific enough to be very helpful. It does clearly recommend that you use a three-part presentation structure: an opening, a body, and a close. But how to actually develop and organize these three parts can still be a puzzle. To learn the specifics of how to develop each of these three parts of your presentation, read on. The approaches you will learn here will follow that classic rule but will also give you the specific instructions you need to do a great job with all three parts! Now let's focus on developing well-organized and useful notes.

Developing Your Notes

The step-by-step process that follows is a simple one. You will learn two variations of the process and then choose the one that works best for you. When you use this process, you will be able to organize your content quickly. Next you can "tweak" your basic content to meet the need for more or less detail. You will end up with notes that will allow you to abandon any fear of forgetting something important. You will have a strong opening and closing. You will have a clear structure, one that you have consciously chosen to help the audience follow your argument. Finally, you will have the flexibility of changing the order of points you cover as you speak and still be able to get back on track.

Begin with the Middle in Mind

Let's start with the body of the presentation. Here's why. Once you have completed developing and organizing the body you will be able to look at the "big picture" very clearly. Then you can make a fully informed decision about what to say in the opening and closing. The content of the opening and closing—both what to say and how to say it—should enhance the more fully developed information in the body. Like a hat and shoes, the opening and closing should complement the suit you have already chosen.

The Step-by-Step Process

Follow these four steps as you develop the body of your presentation:

- Gather information.

- Group it.

- Structure it.

- Edit it ruthlessly.

The first two steps—gather information and group it—can be interchanged if the situation calls for it, creating two variations on the process. The variation you choose will depend on how completely you have mastered the content before you begin to organize it. The two variations of the step-by-step process are the *group and gather* approach and the *gather and group* approach.

The Group and Gather Approach

Use the group and gather approach when you have a very clear idea of the points you want to make and what you want to say.

Group First

Start with the main points you want to cover. A good way to do this is to jot each of these main points down on a separate sheet of paper. For example, if you are doing a project update presentation, your main points—and your page headings—may be

- Briefly review project goals, plan, and timeline

- Review progress to date

- Explain reasons for changes from timeline

- Summarize how changes are being handled

- Review revised timeline to completion

- Handle questions

Then Gather

Once you have identified and written down your main points you are ready to gather and add the information that will support each one. Now, revisit each page. Develop supporting information for one main point at a time. An easy way to do this is to jot down each supporting fact, point, or idea on a small adhesive note.[1] Keep it with the main point—on the same page, literally. Allow yourself some flexibility. It is normal for your mind to flood with ideas and information once you get going. Don't edit now. The important point is to capture information as it occurs to you, even if it is tangential to your main point or more strongly related to a different one. Your goal here is to capture as much information as possible in writing.[2]

When you have developed supporting information for each of your main points, stop. Check each piece of supporting information for any tangential information you have created. Does it really belong under one of your main points? Is it on the right page? If not, move it. If it seems truly tangential, put the note off to the side until later.

Your next step will be to organize your main points into a logical and effective order. The best and most logical structure may be obvious. In the project update presentation outlined above, the logical structure is quite obvious. At times, the best structure may be less obvious. It may help to consider the structures suggested in the next section of this chapter.

The Gather and Group Approach

If you are less sure of your main points, for example, if your presentation requires research or input from others or is more creative or interpretive, a slightly different approach may be more useful.

Gather First

It is never too early to begin to gather the information you will need. As soon as your presentation is scheduled, designate a folder—paper or electronic—that you can use to keep notes. All your information about the upcoming presentation now has a home. As you learn more, think of more you want to say, or remember questions you will need answered, make a quick note and put it in the folder. If your preparation requires further research, keep the results of the research in the same folder. When the time comes to organize and finalize your content, you will already have a good start.

But before you begin to organize your content you will need to add the information in your head to the information in your folder. You can do this in many ways, but here is one that works especially well.

Start jotting down your ideas and thoughts *before* you decide what the main points will be. On note cards or adhesive notes, capture as many ideas or thoughts as you can. Put each idea or point on a separate card or adhesive note. Add them to the information already in your folder. Although this process can be completed in one sitting, it is often more fruitful if you do it in two or three sittings. Walking away and returning later will often give you a fresh perspective and generate more and different information. (Keep your notes in your folder between work sessions for safekeeping.)

Then Group

When you feel you have captured all the information you need, group your information cards or adhesive notes by common or related ideas. Don't worry about deciding what to put with what. Just scan your notes and get started. The human brain is hard-wired to categorize and group information. You will quickly see how your notes practically rearrange themselves into groups. Now give each group a name. The names of each group become your main points or topics.

Legend has it that Abraham Lincoln used this method. According to the story, when engaged in the famous series of seven debates with Stephen A. Douglas in the summer and fall of 1858, Lincoln took notes as Douglas spoke, "filed" them in his stovepipe hat, and then spread them out on the floor at night to organize his responses and counterarguments. True or not, the story does make the point that this can be an effective approach.

Choose a Structure

Now that you have the main points and supporting content you need for the body of your presentation, it is time to choose a structure. The best and most logical structure may be obvious based on your knowledge of your content, your audience, and your goals.

Content Structures

The structures below are all choices you may wish to use. Different structures or combinations of structures may be needed at different times.

General to Specific

The general-to-specific structure starts with a general overview or the establishment of a general concept. Once this is done, the speaker covers specifics pertinent to the particular audience. For example, you say that your state is experiencing a budget crisis. Public school funding will be reduced next year throughout the state. In your district, state funding will be cut by 12 percent. You then present ideas for raising money locally to help cover the cost of special education programs within your district.

Specific to General

The specific-to-general structure takes you from the components or details to the overall picture or result. For example, you report the major initiatives, successes, and earnings of each division of your corporation for the last year. Then you report overall corporate earnings.

Order of Importance

The order-of-importance structure can be used in two ways: starting with the most important information or building to it at the end. Presenting the most important information first satisfies those listeners who want you to "cut to the chase." However, it may sacrifice the building of suspense that will help keep the listeners' attention later. Building to the most important information may create a sense of anticipation and excitement. But it may frustrate those who want you to "cut to the chase." Will they still be listening when you get to the critical information? Use your knowledge of your audience and your purpose to make your choice.

Order of Urgency

The order-of-urgency structure, like the order of importance, can be used in two ways. The first is to start with the most urgent information, usually an action to be taken, and move to the least urgent. The second is to start with the least urgent and move to the most urgent. This structure has the advantages and disadvantages of the order of importance. Also consider the implications of stating the most important action first. Will your audience remember it at the end? To make sure they do, restate it in your close.

Temporal

The temporal structure follows a timeline but most often does not include strong judgments about importance or urgency. It outlines a sequence of events. It is useful for giving historical overviews and outlining the steps to follow in a schedule of events. For example, if you discuss the history of United States naval uniforms in the early twentieth century, you might start with uniforms worn during the Philippine-American War (1899–1902), then move on to those of the Boxer Rebellion (1901–1902), the Latin American Campaigns (1906–1933), World War I (1917–1918), and the Yangtze Service (1926–1927 and 1930–1932). The temporal structure is often a component of the next two structures.

Geographic

The geographic structure follows the geography covered. A presentation on opportunities to market your products in the Pacific Rim might include a brief tour of the area. Moving clockwise, it might start with the North Pacific regions of Asia and eastern Russia; move to the Pacific regions of North America, Central America, and South America then the Pacific Islands, New Zealand, Australia, and southern Asia; and end with Southeast Asia.

Cause and Effect

The cause-and-effect structure lists or explains the cause or causes of something, then presents the effect. For example, some of the heat insulating tiles broke off the space shuttle Columbia during its launch. Reentry into the earth's atmosphere created intense heat. The missing tiles left the shuttle vulnerable to the heat. The vulnerability to heat resulted in structural failure. The shuttle broke up shortly before landing.

Procedure or Process

The procedure or process structure lists and explains a logical sequence of steps. Often, it explains the need for completing the steps in that order. For example, if you want an aquarium in your den, start by researching aquariums to determine the best kind for you. Salt water or fresh? How large? How much maintenance are you willing to do? How much do you want to spend? Next, purchase the aquarium and accessories. Set up the aquarium. Fill it with water. Add the necessary chemicals to balance the aquatic environment.

Wait the recommended amount of time. Do the tests needed to make sure the water is ready for fish. Add the chosen fish.

Compare and Contrast

The compare-and-contrast structure compares two or more concepts or objects in one or more ways. For example, several products might be compared on the factors of quality, durability, ease of use, and price to help determine the lowest total cost of ownership. Wines could be compared on the basis of sweetness versus dryness, sugar-to-acid balance, color, and the potential for aging well.

Pros and Cons

The pros-and-cons structure is similar to compare and contrast but also may examine just one concept or object or compare a proposed change to the status quo. It includes the making of value judgments. For example, a company may consider whether to move its factory to another state. Lower taxes and the local availability of raw materials may be pros but the anticipated turnover and relocation costs of the move may be cons.

Three Special Step-by-Step-Structures

Now let's look at three special structures. Each includes specific steps. These three structures are sale of a product or service, reporting of bad news, and problem to solution.

Sale of a Product or Service

These five steps are good ones to follow for a sales presentation.

1. *Show the need.* Discuss why and how the listeners need what you have to offer. Show that you understand the needs of your listeners. Acknowledge their situations, challenges, and goals. What problems occur that could be solved or prevented? What opportunities are lost because of the lack of what you offer? You may be able to give the listeners a bigger picture or a deeper understanding of their own needs. For example, will their current needs be intensified or changed by developing trends or anticipated changes in their environment?

2. *Increase interest and emotion.* Discuss the implications of the problems or lost opportunities. What if the problems become more serious? If the need is real and urgent, meeting it will be interesting to the listeners. If the need is irritating, painful, or frightening, the solution will be met with enthusiasm, relief, gratitude, and probably other emotions as well. Remember that evoking emotion is a key to creating a long-term memory. Don't be too concerned with remaining logical and professional at this point. A little drama is a vital ingredient here.

3. *Show how the product or service satisfies the need.* Explain why having your product or service is the best way to satisfy the need. How is the product or service better—more functional, more reliable, more powerful, more effective, a better value—than any other solution? What will the result be when the listeners' need is satisfied? Testimonials, examples, demonstrations, and visual aids will all help you accomplish this step.

4. *Help the audience members visualize themselves using and benefiting from the product or service.* The psychology of persuasion teaches us that belief follows action. If an individual takes action, he will most likely find a way to believe that action is a good one, a logical one, the best choice. By helping your listeners imagine themselves using and benefiting from what you offer, you are helping them persuade themselves. So paint a picture. Help them imagine themselves working more easily, more efficiently, more reliably, and less expensively. How will they use the time, energy, or money they will save? Will your listeners get credit for solving the problem? Will they be rewarded? How will they feel?

5. *Request action or approval.* Remember to close. Don't be shy. Define the next step you want your listeners to take. Ask directly for what you want. Then pause and wait for an answer.

Reporting of Bad News

These five steps will help you deliver bad news as effectively as possible. A good approach to take here is to sandwich the bad news between two positives.

1. *Buffer the bad news with a positive or neutral statement.* Start with a positive or neutral statement to help prepare the audience for the bad news. Be honest and realistic. Use a positive tone and demeanor, but don't be overly optimistic or saccharine.

2. *Connect to the bad news with a clear transition.* Avoid making negative value judgments here. The listeners will come to their own conclusions when they hear the news.

3. *Deliver the bad news.* State the news clearly. Do not hedge or try to soften it with obscure language. Report the facts you know. Explain why they happened or why they will happen. If more facts will come out later, state this.

4. *Suggest alternatives.* Alternatives soften the blow. Giving your listeners a choice of alternatives helps restore a sense of control. If these alternatives may change as new information comes in, tell your listeners this.

5. *Rebuild goodwill.* You may reinforce the positive, answer questions, listen to other suggestions, and so on.

Problem to Solution

These six steps are good basics to follow when discussing a problem and solution.

1. *Define and limit the problem.* A clear definition of the problem includes a statement of where the problem begins and ends.

2. *List all of the criteria the solution must meet.* Listing the criteria helps you avoid wasting time and effort on solutions that aren't possible or practical to implement.

3. *Identify the possible solutions.* Briefly state each possible solution. Consider the order in which you introduce the possible solutions. It may make sense to order them from best to worst or worst to best.

4. *Evaluate each solution against the criteria.* When you evaluate the solutions, here you might put to use one of the previous structures. For example, the pros-and-cons structure might be useful here.

5. *Choose the best solution.* Because you have lain the groundwork to choose the solution that is most effective and practical, your choice is likely to be accepted and supported by your listeners.

6. *Explain how the solution will be implemented.* Include whatever specifics you can about implementing the solution. For example, list the steps that must be taken. If possible, include individual responsibilities and the anticipated date of completion of each step.

Variations on this structure may be best for different problem situations. Consider the following questions as you decide whether a variation of the problem-solving structure is needed.

- *How much do the listeners already know about the problem?* If they know little or nothing about the problem, more information about the problem itself may be needed. Consider using the cause-and-effect structure to explain the problem.

  If they are already very familiar with the problem, spend more time on the recommended solutions. The six-step problem-solving structure may be a good one to use, with emphasis on steps 3, 4, and 5.

- *Are you reporting on a solution already implemented, or do you want to persuade your listeners to support the solution you recommend?* If you have implemented a solution that has solved the problem, less information about why it was chosen is necessary. If you must persuade the listeners to support a recommended solution, the six-step problem-solving structure may serve you well. This structure is a good one for outlining and explaining how you chose the solution you recommend. You may or may not choose to include step 6, discussing how the solution will be (or was) implemented.

Always Use Your Own Good Judgment to Choose a Structure

Your knowledge of your audience, your purpose, and your content will help you choose the best structure. It is possible that your presentation will not use one of the structures already discussed. You might find it appropriate to combine more than one of the suggested structures. You may choose to modify one to better meet your needs. But before you finish your preparations you should have a recognizable structure. Without it your presentation will not be as coherent or as effective as it could be.

Presenting Information within a Structure

Once you have organized your main and supporting points into a clear and logical structure, you can develop each of the points and ideas. How much detail does the audience need? How much do they want? How much can they handle?

At this point you may want to review the list below. You'll find a number of ways you can present information within the main structure of your presentation. Raising your awareness of these different ways of presenting information may give you additional ideas. It can also help you to deliver what you promise the audience. That is, don't tell them you are going to outline if you plan to expound. Don't tell them that you will prove a point if you are really going to interpret.

When you present information within a structure, you can

- Analyze: Separate into essential parts and examine or interpret each part.

- Compare: Examine two or more things in order to identify similarities and differences.

- Conclude: End or close, including a summary, result, inference, or decision.

- Contrast: Set in opposition in order to show differences.

- Criticize: Make judgments about merits and faults. Criticism often accompanies analysis.

- Define: State the meaning of, explain the essential qualities or nature of, determine the precise limits of.

- Describe: Convey an image or impression with words that reveals the appearance or nature of; give an account of; list parts, qualities, and characteristics of.

- Discuss: Examine by argument, consider and debate the pros and cons of an issue, explain conflicts. Discussion often includes analysis, criticism, and comparison.

- Enumerate: List several things: ideas, aspects, events, qualities, reasons, and so on; mention separately.

- Evaluate: Appraise carefully, determine the value or amount of. Include evidence to support the evaluation.

- Explain: Make clear and understandable. Make clear the cause or reason. Assign a meaning or interpret.

- Expound: Give a methodical, detailed, scholarly explanation.

- Illustrate: Explain by giving examples or making comparisons.

- Interpret: Explain, construe, or understand in a certain way. Give the meaning of something by paraphrase.

- Outline: Give a general account or report including only the main points or features.

- Prove: Establish the truth or genuineness of by evidence or argument.

- Rate: Estimate quality or value, assign to a classification, or assign comparative worth.

- Summarize: Briefly and concisely state or restate main points. Avoid unnecessary details. Include conclusions.

- Trace: Follow the course, development, or history of. Show the order of events or progress of a subject or event.

When you have completed the body of your presentation you are ready to develop an opening and closing that will do it, you, and your audience justice.

Opening Your Presentation

Your opening should increase interest and emotion. Your goal is to earn the attention you are given—quickly.

The Check-You-Out Response

When you begin speaking, you will almost always have the attention of the audience. I call this initial attention the "check-you-out response." As you take your place and begin to speak, natural human curiosity will make people look at and listen to you. You are, for a brief period of time, "where the action is." As we discussed in part 1, you are, for better or for worse, the salient object—the center of attention. The members of your audience are curious, eager for the action to begin, hungry for information. Because of this natural curiosity, I don't believe that speakers need to take extraordinary measures to grab attention.

But don't assume that you will keep the audience's attention simply by continuing to speak. People need a reason to continue to pay attention. Sitting quietly is not the same as listening attentively. You need to quickly convince them that paying close attention is a good use of their time. You need to convince them that listening has value. You need to increase their interest and tap into their emotions if you want to hold their attention beyond the "check-you-out response."

To Speak Is to Compete for Attention

As you speak you are in competition for the audience's attention. Not only are you competing with outside distractions or any physical needs or discomforts individual members of the audience may experience, but you are constantly competing with what is going on inside their own heads! The most reliable way to earn their attention and keep it is to give them what they want (within reason).

What do listeners want? They want you to answer four questions. When you answer the following four questions, you will have satisfied much of what the audience wants in an opening.

- *What is this about?* In most cases your listeners will have a good idea of the subject of your presentation. Most of us don't have the time or inclination to show up for a presentation without some knowledge of the topic and the purpose. In answering this first question, you will more often be defining and limiting the topic than truly introducing it. You can certainly confirm the subject of the presentation—the issue, the situation, the need, the problem, the opportunity. Then define the scope of your talk. What level of detail will you address?

- *Why should the listeners care?* What do you believe about the subject? Why does this matter? What is at stake? How important is it? How urgent? What implications could it have? How could these affect the listeners?

- *What should the listeners do?* What do you want the listeners to do during your presentation? What do you want them to believe and do after listening? What action should they take? What specific types of approval and support do you need? How much? When do you need it?

- *Why should they do this?* How will this action benefit the listeners? What needs of theirs will it satisfy? What will their return on investment be?

These questions should be answered as early, as clearly, and as succinctly as possible. The answers will compose the core message in your opening remarks. Here is an example.

"Good afternoon. Reducing the time it takes you to get a new product to market is critical to your continued success. I believe that using the CX-FAB will help you reduce the time it takes to develop and test a new product by an average of 40 percent. Please watch and listen as I explain the way you can achieve this speed by using the CX-FAB. Feel free to stop me at any point to ask me any questions you may have. As you listen, imagine how your customers will respond. Imagine what this could mean to your bottom line. I believe you will see that the CX-FAB will simplify the design and test processes for you. It will reduce your time to market and give you the advantages of more market share, more profit, and continued leadership in the industry."

> **Would you persuade, speak of interest, not of reason.**
>
> BENJAMIN FRANKLIN

Let's look at how the four basic questions were answered to compose the core message.

1. *What is this about?* The listeners need to reduce the time it takes to get a new product to market. Their success depends upon this.

2. *Why should the listeners care?* They will be able to reduce the time to market by 40 percent.

3. *What should the listeners do?* They should listen and imagine how their customers would respond. They should think about what it could do for their bottom line. They should use the CX-FAB.

4. *Why should they do this?* It will simplify the design and test processes, reduce the time to market, increase their market share, increase profit, and help them hold on to their leadership position in the industry.

Your Opening Is (Almost) Done!

Once you have answered these fundamental questions and can communicate the answers clearly and succinctly, you have almost completed the content for your opening. Consider the following suggestions for other elements you may or may not want to include in your opening. When you decide to include any of these elements, be brief. Remember that "less is more" as you put together your opening—the best way you can keep the attention of the audience is to get to the important information quickly.

Introductions

I find it surprising how many clients don't know whether they will be introduced or will be expected to introduce themselves. Leaving this discovery or decision until the last moment is at best a lost opportunity. Worse, it can cause confusion and awkwardness. Decide or discover who will introduce you. Then prepare accordingly.

Here are some reasons why having someone else introduce you is often a good choice. It can be difficult to introduce ourselves. We may be unsure of what to say or how much to include. Here's why. We are socialized not to talk too freely about our accomplishments. We know that people who publicize their own achievements can easily be seen as full of themselves. Listing your accomplishments may help establish your credibility with the audience, but it can make you so uncomfortable that you minimize them or come across as nervous. On the other hand, it is easy for someone else to praise you and your accomplishments. He can do so with respect, warmth, and a sense of pride in what you can offer the audience.

If you will introduce yourself, plan what you will say. Be brief, but be sure to mention information that will establish your credibility. Include something that will help you connect emotionally with the audience—a bit about a personal experience or shared interest will often do the trick. A very brief introduction may be appropriate if you were first introduced some time ago, for example, if you are one of a series of speakers introduced at the beginning of the event. But avoid being too repetitious. This doesn't work well: "As it says on this first slide and on the program, and as Dr. Livingston just said when she introduced me, my name is Endless Lee Repeated." Instead, start with an important point.

If you will be introduced, give the information you want covered to the person who will introduce you. This can help get you off to a strong start. If you will introduce and/or thank hosts, dignitaries, or colleagues, be prepared. Have the correct names, titles, and so on. Make sure you know correct pronunciations. Ask about any protocol issues, such as the proper rank order for the introductions.

"Thank You for Coming"

If you choose to thank the audience for coming, make it sincere and meaningful. A thank-you should sound genuinely felt. Don't make the mistake of sounding insincere just when you need to establish your credibility. Use vocal tones that sound like you mean it. Avoid tired phases like "I want to thank you for taking time out of your busy schedules" (to listen to you thank them for taking time out of their busy schedules?). Instead, use a more original or personalized way to thank them. For example, you could mention what is making them so busy that their attendance shows real interest or commitment. Or start with an important point. After all, if you really want to show gratitude for the time and attention you are given, give your listeners as much valuable information as possible in the time you have. If you finish a bit early, they will likely be grateful for the gift of time!

Other Considerations for Your Opening

Consider these points when planning your opening. Doing so will help you be succinct and set an appropriate tone for your presentation.

- *Avoid stating the obvious.* "I am here today to talk to you about" is obvious: you are obviously there, it is obviously today, and you are obviously talking. Instead, find a fresher way of introducing your topic. If the listeners already know what the topic is (and they almost always do) tell them why you will speak on it. Explain why it matters to them. Another good option is to limit the scope of your talk. You may want to state which parts of a larger issue or topic you will cover. If you are giving a talk on a specialized subject, you may want to state what level of knowledge you assume the listeners have when they come in. (This is especially helpful and appreciated if you have a very mixed audience; then you might also mention how you will handle the differences, for example, you will use nontechnical analogies to help less technical listeners understand the more technical information.)

- *Welcome listeners only if you are the first speaker.* If the listeners have been welcomed by all five of the previous speakers, they will probably be grateful if you get right down to business. If there is some compelling protocol that calls for you to welcome them again, make sure you sound like you mean it. Don't use a redundant or perfunctory welcome to begin your presentation. This makes a weak opening. It begins to lull listeners into a stupor before you have a chance to say anything important.

- *Don't apologize for your presence, your level of knowledge, or your state of readiness.* Apologizing can create the impression of a lack of confidence and detracts from your credibility. "I know you were expecting Dr. Gold. I'm sure you're disappointed. She had to handle a personal emergency, so I'm filling in. I just found out a couple of hours ago, so bear with me. I know many of you know more about this topic than me."

- *Don't express surprise at how many (or few) people came.* Expressing surprise sounds as if you were unprepared or out of touch. Expressing satisfaction or pleasure at the attendance is fine. Then give any information or instructions for resulting changes in timing, seating, and so on in a matter-of-fact tone.

- *Try not to be the one to cover logistical details, such as locations of phones and bathrooms.* Starting an important presentation with these details can reduce your ability to deliver a powerful opening. Have someone else do it before you start. If that is not possible, keep it brief. Then pause for at least several seconds before beginning your actual presentation.

- *Consider doing a destination check.* Starting your presentation before those who are in the audience by mistake are out of the room only creates a distraction. If you are at a venue with multiple speakers in multiple rooms, do a brief and clear "destination check." Wait until anyone who gets up to leave is out of the room (or at least out of the main body of the audience and into an aisle). A destination check might sound like this: "This is the presentation on ecologically sustainable perennial crops. The presentation on cloning mice with short telomeres is in the Cypress Ballroom." (Pause)

There are times when any or all of these elements should be included in your opening remarks. When you use them appropriately they can help build rapport and set people at ease. Just remember: the audience wants real value for attending, and the initial attention you receive is quickly lost when you spend too long "warming up." Before you include the elements just covered, think about whether you really need them. Covering the whole list could take a great deal of time. At any one presentation some of these elements may be unnecessary, may be done by others, or could be done one-on-one outside the context of the presentation. If you have questions about whether or not you will need to include any of these elements, find out ahead of time and plan accordingly.

Opening a Presentation to a Reluctant Audience

While most audiences are predisposed to give you their attention as you begin, you may occasionally (only occasionally, I hope!) face a situation when this is not entirely true. When listeners are "drafted" to attend, when you are one of a long series of speakers, when the room is very warm or dark, when some in the audience are feeling the effects of jet lag or a long cocktail party last night, you may find that you face more of a challenge.

If you feel that it is necessary to grab the attention of the audience, use a technique that isn't shopworn. Many of the often-used ways of opening a presentation have long lost their ability to engage the audience. They no longer contain any elements of surprise or novelty. I would be happy if I never again heard a speaker struggle through a not-so-successful joke or begin by reading the dictionary definition of the topic!

Some of the best ways of quickly earning the attention of the audience are the same techniques that will work for creating a feeling of dialogue with the audience. These are covered in more depth in chapter 16, but here are some that work well for opening a presentation.

- Ask a rhetorical question. Then pause to let the audience members think.

- Ask a question and request a show-of-hands response.

- Deliver late-breaking news.

- Share a startling fact or statistic.

- Tell a brief story or relate an anecdote.

- Use a powerful visual aid.

- Share a thought-provoking quotation.

Opening a Presentation to a Hostile Audience

Three steps can help you get off to a successful start when you are faced with the challenge of presenting to a hostile audience.

1. *Thank the audience sincerely.* A simple but sincere thank-you for being given the opportunity to speak will often establish a cooperative and respectful tone. Avoid the temptation to preach: "I'm sure we all appreciate the importance of free speech. Be open-minded. I know none of you would interrupt me."

2. *Establish common ground.* Briefly stress what you can agree on, for example, "We all have very strong feelings about this issue" or "We all want as much information as we can get. We need to learn everything we can to make sure nothing like this ever happens again."

3. *Use the appropriate nonverbal delivery skills.* Stay very conscious of the nonverbal signals you give. Now is not the time to risk looking or sounding arrogant, condescending, or aloof. Review the information on nonverbal communication in chapter 14. Avoid any behavior that could seem defensive or aggressive.

Once you have answered the four questions and included the elements you need for reasons of protocol, rapport building, and logistics, you should have an excellent opening.

Closing your Presentation

For better or for worse, almost nothing perks up an audience like the words "So, in conclusion." Use the attention you now have to your advantage! Closing your presentation is a great opportunity to pull concepts together, reinforce important information, motivate the listeners to action, and leave your listeners thinking about how much they could benefit from what you recommend. Do not be afraid to repeat important information. Repetition creates familiarity, and familiarity is one of the keys to long-term memory (learn more about this in chapter 11), so plan to repeat the critical points. You want to make sure the listeners leave with them in mind. The two elements you must always include in your closing are the call to action and the statement of benefits.

Call the Listeners to Action

The call to action can be the most important part of your entire presentation. What do you want the listeners to do next? Here are some examples of a call to action.

- "Starting immediately, use these criteria every time you make a decision on a commercial loan."

- "Have your selections on my desk by the first of December."

- "Stop by our booth this afternoon to see a demonstration. Then call to schedule an on-site demo for your entire staff."

- "Will you approve this project today?"

Reinforce the Benefits

People will act in self-interest. Remind them of the benefits that will follow if they take the action you recommend. Here are some examples of benefit statements.

- "Using these lending criteria will reduce loan losses by close to 15 percent. This can really help keep the company profitable. We'll be able to

119

grow quickly into new markets. This can give all of us new opportunities to advance—or retire early!"

I have been a selfish being all my life, in practice, though not in principle.

JANE AUSTEN

- "We'll order based on your selections. You can start the new year with the equipment you need."

- "An on-site demo is a great way to help your management team see how we can help you process information. Less downtime, access to information instantly, and now you can really do target marketing! You can be a real hero!"

- "Your approval means we can start next week. Then we can complete construction in time to move in before October. And the costs can go on the books for this year."

Include Other Information If Needed

You may need to cover logistics, say thank you, or open a question-and-answer session. Just remember, your closing should be no longer than absolutely necessary. A short, to-the-point closing will be more powerful than one that is drawn out. These are some optional elements you may choose to include in your closing.

- Summarize the main points.

- Make recommendations.

- Ask a rhetorical question to leave the audience thinking.

- Use a quotation to reinforce your message.

- Ask for comments.

- Ask for questions.

- Thank the audience or hosts.

Once you have decided how best to structure and develop your information, it is time for one of the most important steps of all. Our own in-depth knowledge and our enthusiasm for our content may lead us to produce lots and lots of content. Now, more than ever, it is important to remember that it really is all about your audience. With that in mind, it is time to edit what we have created.

Edit Ruthlessly

The details of your information will almost always be more precious to you than they are to your audience. Most business presentations would only be improved by ruthless editing. Follow these tips to shorten, tighten, and sharpen the messages in the body of your talk:

- *Time yourself.* You will almost always take longer than you think. Find out how much longer. Now use the tips below to fix the problem.

- *Limit the information about you and your organization.* Your history, your philosophy, your past successes, your current projects, your hopes and dreams—all of these are "all about you." Get to the information that is all about the audience.

- *Cut the information about how you prepared for the presentation.* How you prepared is your past business. The business of the audience now is to hear what you have to say. If you are a consultant and feel a need to justify your fee, limit the explanation of your approach and research. Can you briefly explain what the audience needs to know about your research methods before you report each finding or make a recommendation?

- *Shorten your sentences.* Long, complex sentences often have to be explained or clarified with other long, complex sentences.

- *Limit adverbs and adjectives.* Use nouns and verbs. Eliminate any adverbs and adjectives that aren't necessary. Be ruthless in deciding what qualifies as "necessary."

- *Eliminate redundancies.* Redundancies can occur in phrasing: "We need a qualified expert to identify the basic fundamentals and identify different alternatives that will lead to a new breakthrough." Redundancies also occur when we make the same point twice. Examples, analogies, anecdotes, stories, and jokes that don't add value are redundancies.

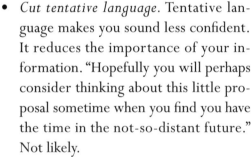

- *Cut slick transitions.* Slick is not genuine. If your presentation flows too smoothly, it can lull your listeners to sleep. Use transitions to link ideas when necessary. Use a pause to separate sections or emphasize a point.

- *Cut tentative language.* Tentative language makes you sound less confident. It reduces the importance of your information. "Hopefully you will perhaps consider thinking about this little proposal sometime when you find you have the time in the not-so-distant future." Not likely.

- *Tape yourself in advance.* Listen for "static." Do you hear "ah," "um," "you know," or "okay" repeatedly? Do you say "actually," "basically," or "simply" when you don't need to? Pause instead.

- *Listen for clichés and eliminate them.* Phrases like "give the green light," "the acid test," "touch and go," "needless to say," and "at the end of the day" should go.

Now time yourself again. Repeat the process as needed.

Summary

How you prepare and organize your content will depend on many factors. But some preparation is absolutely essential. Use the list below to be sure you have done the essentials in organizing your content.

- *A clear and powerful opening and closing.* Make sure your opening earns attention and gives the audience a reason to listen to more. The closing should include a call to action and a benefit to the audience for taking that action.

- *A clear structure.* The structure should support the nature of your content. It should make it easy to follow your thought process or argument. Longer and more complex presentations benefit from clear transitions between sections.

- *The appropriate level of detail.* Consider how much detail your listeners need, want, can handle, and can remember. Then decide how you should best present your information and develop your arguments. Keep in mind the time you have, and allow a little extra for unexpected changes in plan.

- *Knowledge of all protocol issues and a plan to handle them.* Find out who will do introductions. What will be said? Do the right people have the right information? Who will cover logistical information, such as instructions to the audience on the schedule, facilities, refreshments, and any changes in plans?

Make a plan for handling questions. Determine when and how you will handle questions from the audience, and communicate this clearly at the beginning of your talk. Remember that longer presentations will often be more effective if they include intermittent question-and-answer sessions.

> The great enemy of clear language is insincerity. When there
> is a gap between one's real and one's declared aims,
> one turns as it were instinctively to long words and
> exhausted idioms, like cuttlefish squirting out ink.
>
> GEORGE ORWELL

Words That Work

The What and Why of Word Choice

Most listeners much prefer a speaker who is genuine and natural. Choosing the right words will help you sound sincere and conversational. Yet some speakers fall into the habit of using words that come across as pretentious or pompous. Consider the case of Brad Marshall.

Brad Marshall, Wednesday, 9:40 a.m., leaving a voice mail:

"John, hi. Brad Marshall at Company Bee. Here's the update I promised you. Great news! Sales of the WA 2 GO came in way over plan—we even beat the last revision! I want to meet with you and your team ASAP to work on sourcing parts from Asia. I need your help. And the sooner the better! The potential here is huge! We have to act now to lock up the market share. This means a terrific chance for us to work together on something that could pay off big! John, call me. Leave a message. I'm tied up for the next couple of hours, but I want to cover the specifics of what's selling and talk about the pipeline. We have a couple of opportunities that could be bigger than last quarter. I've seen how great your team is, and I'm absolutely sure that if we work together we can make this happen. Those folks at All-Ready There and On the Way won't know what hit them!"

Brad Marshall, Wednesday, 10 a.m., giving a presentation:

"Good morning. Ah, thank you for taking the time out of your busy schedules to join me here today. We made a commitment to you last quarter to significantly increase sales of the WA 2 GO. I am pleased to report that we have exceeded our market objectives, and sales exceeded our specified objectives, even those determined and established as a result of the most recent reassessment. In fact, the objectives were also exceeded by a margin that is, ah, exceedingly gratifying.

"At the present time we believe it is incumbent upon us to investigate alternative and additional potential supply sources for key product components. The opportunities for return on investment, ah, should not be underestimated, as the forecasts predict extremely gratifying results.

"I want to reiterate how very enthusiastic we are about the capabilities and experience of the members of your organization and how convinced we have become that through a well-orchestrated, ah, cooperative effort, successful implementation of these strategies will be accomplished. We believe it will be possible to achieve virtual domination of the market prior to the implementation of effective strategic responses on the part of our competitors.

"At this point in time I would like to entertain your questions and comments."

What happened to Brad Marshall? He fell victim to a common belief that we will be more impressive if we demonstrate more of our vocabulary. Unfortunately for Brad, this is not true.

Simpler Is Better

Except in those instances in which you have a compelling reason to make an alternative choice, select and employ the more succinct, less wordy or verbose method of articulating a particular idea, concept, or connecting phrase

125

in the delivery of the content of your presentation. In other (better) words, rather than sounding like the last sentence, try this: Speak simply.

The simple word is almost always the best word. Simple, straightforward, conversational word choices are usually the best. If you need a longer or more abstract word or phrase for accuracy or precision, use it. But if a shorter word or phrase will do, use that. The following pages will help you avoid some of the more common word choice mistakes that speakers make. The lists are not comprehensive but will help you "tune your ear" so you will be a more natural, conversational, and engaging speaker.

> **Those who run to long words are mainly the unskillful and tasteless; they confuse pomposity with dignity, flaccidity with ease, and bulk with force.**
>
> H. W. FOWLER

Less Is More

The simple language choice is often the best choice. More words do not necessarily make an idea clearer. If a longer phrase has shades of meaning important to your goal, use it. If not, choose the clear and concise short form, as shown in table 10.1.

Fancy or Strong?

Sometimes a "fancy" word has shades of meaning that make it the best choice for your purpose. Use it then. But if you use it just because it sounds impressive, remember that it can also sound stilted, affected, or pompous. This makes you less impressive rather than more. A simpler, stronger word (table 10.2) is then the better choice.

Redundancy

Redundant words or phrases use more words than necessary to get the job done. Redundancy can be used effectively to emphasize or reinforce. But redundancies can sneak in accidentally. Then, rather than making a message stronger, they weaken it with clutter.

Table 10.1 Less Is More

Longer form	Short form
except in a small number of instances	usually
a great number of times	often/frequently
for a brief period of time	briefly
bring to a conclusion	end
direct your attention to	look at
contingent upon	depends on
at this location	here
at that location	there
because of the fact that	because
afford an opportunity	allow/permit
for the reason that	because
in conjunction with	with
in the absence of	without
in the event of	if
in the occurrence of	if it happens
it is often the case that	often
make a decision	decide
if that is/were in fact the case	if
in spite of the fact that	although
in the event that	if
at the present time	now
in the near future	soon
in the direction of	toward
due to the fact that	because
a small number of	few
a large number of	many
a percentage of	some
a high percentage of	most
in many instances	often
in the majority of instances	usually
subsequent to	after
prior to	before
submit an application	apply

Table 10.2 Fancy or Strong

Fancy	Strong
abandon	end, leave
abolish	end, stop
beneficial	good, helpful
benign	harmless
characteristic	typical
cognizant	aware
collaborate	work together
commence	start
component	part
compensation	pay
conceal	hide
contingent upon	depends on
demonstrate	show
deviate	vary, change
disadvantageous	bad, harmful
discontinue	end
disingenuous	insincere
elucidate	explain
encounter	meet
endeavor	try
enumerate	list
envision	see
expedite	streamline
fabricate	make
fluctuate	change, vary
institute	start, begin
ingenuous	sincere
intelligent	smart
judicious	wise
materialize	appear
maximum	most
minimum	least
prior to	before
pursuant to	following
subsequent to	after
utilize	use

Redundancy can occasionally be used to add shades of meaning. *Past history* is redundant because all history is in the past. But *recent history* and *ancient history* increase understanding with added specificity. *Complete opposite* and *diametric opposite,* while redundant, can be used to emphasize the idea of a great difference. Just be aware. Remember: less is more.

Use redundancies both sparingly and consciously. The phrases in the first column of table 10.3 are redundancies. The second column shows a simpler, nonredundant choice.

Clichés

A cliché is a phrase that was originally effective and vivid but has become trite or banal through overuse. It is easy to fall into the cliché habit, but your presentation will lose freshness, a sense of originality, and much of its emotional punch if clichés are overused. Clichés can sound manipulative, even dishonest, when used as an attempt to bolster a weak argument or to excuse bad behavior. "Absence makes the heart grow fonder" is not a legitimate excuse for ignoring an important relationship. And "out of sight, out of mind" is not a good enough reason to pester another person mercilessly.

Use clichés sparingly, and use them when they fit your topic precisely. If the cliché draws attention to itself, it is probably not appropriate.

Sometimes a cliché can be turned on itself to support your meaning. Consider "bedfellows make strange politics" and Oscar Wilde's "Truth is never pure, and rarely simple." Sometimes a minor change creates a humorous allusion to a cliché. Fred Allen's "Imitation is the sincerest form of television" is an example of the amusing use of a minor change. If you are really clever with words you can have a lot of fun with clichés. But if you think you are really clever with clichés, you might want to think again.

Active and Passive Voice

Did your junior high school English teacher criticize you for starting too many sentences with "I"? If so, and if you still hear that teacher's voice when making a decision about whether or not to use "I," this is for you!

129

Table 10.3 Redundant Phrases

Redundant	Nonredundant	Redundant	Nonredundant
absolutely complete	complete	mutual cooperation	cooperation
advance forward	advance	new breakthrough	breakthrough
any and all	any, all	new innovation	innovation
approximate estimate	estimate	one and the same	the same
ask the question	ask	one particular case	one case
assemble together	assemble	one specific example	one example
basic essentials	basics, essentials	one specific reason	one reason
basic fundamentals	basics, fundamentals	only single	only, single
close proximity	close	part and parcel	part
combine together	combine	partial section	section
completely finished	finished	past experience	experience
complete opposite	opposite	past history	history
component parts	components, parts	period of time	period
connect together	connect, join	personal friend	friend
consensus of opinion	consensus, agreement	personal opinion	opinion
continue to remain	remain	plan ahead	plan
contributing factor	factor	plan for the future	plan
cooperate together	cooperate	plan in advance	plan
diametric opposite	opposite	postpone until later	postpone
different alternative	alternative	qualified expert	expert
each and every	each, every	reason why	reason
early in the beginning	early	recur again	recur
end result	result	refer back	refer
entirely finished	finished	repeat again	repeat
exactly identical	identical	retreat back	retreat
experienced expert	expert	resulting effect	result, effect
few in number	few	same exact	same
final conclusion	conclusion	same identical	same
final ending	ending	seems apparent	seems, is apparent
follow after	follow	separate and distinct	separate, distinct
full to capacity	full	single one	single, one
join together	join	small-sized	small
joint partnership	partnership	still remain	remain
large-sized	large	sudden surprise	sudden, surprise
last of all	last	throughout the entire	throughout
main essentials	essentials	true fact	fact
might possibly	might	unanswered question	question
mix together	mix	unsolved problem	problem
more preferable	preferable	very unique	unique

Clichés to Avoid

a bird in the hand is worth two
  in the bush
a finger in every pie
a word to the wise
acid test
armed to the teeth
as high as a kite
at his fingertips
at the end of the day
bite the bullet
bite the dust
by word of mouth
cover your butt
cut and dried
cut to the quick
feet of clay
follow in the footsteps of
give the green light
got a gut feeling
hard and fast
head in the clouds
hold your horses
if it ain't broke, don't fix it
keep our options open
keep your fingers crossed
kill two birds with one stone
line of least resistance
lock, stock, and barrel
long row to hoe
make a long story short
make tracks
needless to say
nip it in the bud
no good deed goes unpunished

no news is good news
no pain, no gain
not playing with a full deck
nothing to write home about
nothing ventured, nothing gained
old as dirt
pack a punch
pass the buck
peel the onion one layer at a time
playing with fire
poetry in motion
pull strings
put it on the back burner
road test
separate the men from the boys
ships that pass in the night
signed, sealed, and delivered
small potatoes
stick to it like glue
stick your neck out
sweep it under the carpet
talking about apples and oranges
the tip of the iceberg
the whole kit and caboodle
there are two sides to every question
there's no fool like an old fool
touch and go
turn back the clock
upset the apple cart
when the cat's away the mice will play
where's the beef?
you can't teach an old dog new tricks
you can't win them all

Some people mistakenly believe that first-person pronouns are not appropriate in business presentations or technical communications in general. This is not true. Unless you have a clear reason for choosing to use the passive voice, use the active voice. First-person pronouns are much more effective than awkward or ambivalent sentences.

An example of the active voice is "I found that . . ."

An example of the passive voice is "It has been shown that . . ."

The passive voice is appropriate when the action itself is more important than the person, persons, or thing that is acting. For example, an agreement is reached, a major change is announced, awards are given, promotions are awarded, restructuring occurs, an initiative is begun.

Technical and scientific speakers tend to overuse the passive voice. With use of the scientific method and the rigor of experimental design, great value is placed on "letting the facts speak for themselves." Personal opinion is less important than data, logic, and intellectual rigor. But many general or business listeners interpret the use of the passive voice as a lack of personal conviction or confidence. When speaking, overuse of the passive voice creates a sense of vagueness, evasiveness, or reluctance to assign or accept responsibility. Even the term *passive* tends to denote neutrality or lack of conviction.

> **The one who loves and understands a thing best will incline to use the personal pronouns in speaking of it. To him there is no neuter gender.**
>
> HENRY DAVID THOREAU

Here are some general guidelines to help you decide when the active voice or the passive voice is your best choice.

- Choose active by habit, passive by conscious choice.

- Do not use passive to avoid using first-person pronouns (I, we, us).

- Do use passive when the action is more important than the actor.

- Do use passive when you want to avoid assigning blame.

Consider the differences between the phrases in table 10.4. The passive voice is used in the first column, the active voice in the second. Notice how the phrases in the second column sound stronger. Also notice that they are shorter!

Table 10.4 Active and Passive Voice

Passive	Active
It is well known that	I know, we know
It has been reported that	Reports tell us
It is widely believed	Many of us believe
It may be worth considering	Let's consider
These rules are outlined in section 12	Section 12 outlines these rules
The changes were observed beginning in in phase 3	The changes began in phase 3
Extra attention should be given to step one	Step one should get extra attention

Positive and Negative Voice

Develop the habit of using positive language. The positive voice will communicate confidence and be more inspiring.

State what you can do, not what you can't. Consider the difference between "I can't comment on that situation" and "Here's what I can tell you about the situation."

Use positive terms. Instead of calling an issue a problem, call it a challenge.

Use the negative voice by conscious choice when you want to emphasize gravity, risk, and danger. Consider the difference between "Wear a seat belt to stay safe" and "There is no way to avoid tragedy when you don't wear a seat belt."

Engage the Senses

Words that engage the five senses will engage your audience. Consider the differences between your responses as you read the words in the first column and those in the second column in table 10.5.

Table 10.5 Engage the Senses

consideration	thunderstorm
alternative	sandpaper
institution	giggle
effectiveness	raspberries
operation	explosion
possibility	diamond
resources	sweat
assessment	starlight
paradigm	chocolate
capabilities	toddler
strategy	bonfire
disadvantage	velvet
organization	espresso
significance	prize

Now consider the sense of emotion or urgency communicated by the words in the first column compared to those in the second column in table 10.6.

Inclusive Language

Inclusive (i.e., nondiscriminatory and nonexclusive) language is language that avoids false assumptions about people regardless of their gender, marital status, ethnicity, disability, and age.

Using gender-inclusive language when speaking or writing in English can be a challenge because of the traditional—and commonly accepted—use of the term *man* to refer to humanity. This practice results in the use of *he, him,* and *his* when referring to a person of unspecified gender. It is also a challenge because of terms used to describe traditionally male occupations, such as *fireman, mailman,* and *chairman.* It can be difficult to always use language that is completely gender neutral. English has traditionally used *he* to refer to individuals when the gender has not been specifically established, but this may inaccurately imply male gender. Switching back and forth between *he*

Table 10.6 Evoke Emotion

conceptualize	hold on
alternatives	watch out
persevere	run for it
utilize	choose
implement	stop
prioritize	danger
improve	fight it out
strategize	show me
consider	hurry
strengthen	jump up
develop	take it
exacerbate	forget it
competitive	go faster
illustrate	wrong

and *she* may be appreciated by some audiences but may sound like too conscious an attempt to be politically correct to others. Yet the repeated use of *he or she* may be awkward. Let's consider some options. We'll use the following sentence as an example:

Each associate must elect his or her withdrawal amount by the end of the month.

Here are ways to avoid that awkward pair of pronouns *(his or her)*.

- Use an article instead of the pronouns. (Each associate must elect a withdrawal amount by the end of the month.)

- Change the singular noun to plural. (All associates must elect a withdrawal amount by the end of the month.)

- Use the second person instead of the third person. (You must elect a withdrawal amount by the end of the month.)

Sometimes simply replacing *man* with *person* can work—but not always. *Personkind* and *personhunt* sound awkward. *Personpower* sounds silly. Would you really want to use any of them? How about *personhole* cover? Or *person-handle?* In recent years, gender-neutral terms have replaced many of those that were more clearly gender specific. Common examples include *firefighter* instead of *fireman, mail carrier* instead of *mailman, flight attendant* instead of *stewardess* or *steward,* and *reporter* instead of *newsman.*

Many cultures are in transition on this issue, and matters are likely to be murky here for a number of years, which means most audiences will be forgiving if you don't get the term just right. But some sensitivity to this issue is generally appreciated. Table 10.7 includes some examples of how you can replace some of the more common gender-specific terms with more gender-neutral ones.

Table 10.7 Gender Neutral Language

Gender specific	*Gender neutral*
businessman	businessperson, manager, entrepreneur, executive
chairman	chairperson, chair
foreman	supervisor, team leader
man-hours	staff hours
repairman	service technician
salesman, saleslady	salesperson
spokesman	spokesperson
waiter, waitress	food server
watchman	security guard
workman	worker

Persuasive Words

A study done some years ago at Yale University concluded that the following words are the twelve most persuasive words in the English language (starting with the most powerful).

- save
- safety
- new
- love
- results
- discovery
- easy
- proven
- health
- guarantee[1]

It's hard to find an advertisement of any kind that isn't sprinkled with these words. Most of them can be found on any box of laundry detergent. But what do *you* think? What words seem most persuasive to you? If you're especially health conscious, the words *health* and *safety* might really work for you. If you need to see evidence that a product or service is for you, then words like *results* and *save* may seem superficial, while *guarantee* and *proven* will make you feel more comfortable. Finally, the listed words are used so often that they may have lost some of their power. Know that they are no guarantee of success and no substitute for a well-organized message with solid evidence to back up your argument or claim.

Jargon and Specialized Language

Every field, trade, and profession has its own jargon—words that are understood in the intended sense by those in that specialty. The existence of jargon and specialized language—language that may have no meaning at all to those outside a particular specialty—creates challenges for the presenter. Within a group, jargon and specialized language streamline communication. When they are understood by all members of the group, they can also help build rapport and foster a feeling of solidarity.

As knowledge continues to increase, more and more specialties continually emerge, and both jargon and specialized language increase accordingly.

Meanwhile, the increasing collaboration between specialists in related fields—and between companies—means that the use of jargon and specialized language presents an ever bigger danger of communication failures. Finally, jargon and specialized language are sometimes used not because they are effective but simply to impress.

The use of jargon quickly confuses those who don't understand what it means. Then, rather than streamlining the flow of information, jargon blocks it. It can divide your listeners and create both confusion and frustration. So, if in doubt, don't use it. If you must use it, define it.

If you plan to use a specialized term that is new to your listeners, think about how you will define it. If the definition itself contains terms the listeners are unlikely to know, you will only have compounded the problem! If you have any doubt about whether defining and using a term will work, experiment with a listener or two before your presentation. And remember, even when you define your terms it is still possible to confuse some people, as Donald Rumsfeld discovered in a press briefing on the situation in the Middle East: "The message is that there are no knowns; there are things we know that we know. There are known unknowns; that is to say that there are things that we now know we don't know. But there are also unknown unknowns; there are things we do not know we don't know. And each year, we discover a few more of those unknown unknowns."[2]

Finally, be aware of your tone of voice when defining a term. If done in a matter-of-fact tone, defining a term for your listeners doesn't sound patronizing. Instead, it demonstrates that your goal is not to impress the listeners or obscure the truth but to achieve genuine understanding. It helps build credibility and trust.

Precision of Word Choice

Using the wrong word can be embarrassing. Having someone in your audience ask, "Did you really mean that, or did you mean this?" can be even more embarrassing. But the trouble can really start when use of the wrong word is not questioned, your true meaning is never understood, and listeners leave without understanding what you meant—or they leave misunderstanding what you meant.

Frequently Misused Words

The list that follows includes some of the words I hear misused most often in business presentations. You can quiz yourself to check that you use them correctly.

Administrate or Administer?

Administer is the verb. *Administration* is the noun.

Administrate has become commonly used as a verb in recent years.

Does usage determine accepted use? You decide. But I recommend using *administer.*

Affect or Effect?

Affect is a verb with two different meanings. It means "to cause a change in," for example, "She believes strongly that an appreciation of the fine arts can positively affect the lives of people of all ages." It also means "to pretend to have," for example, "He affected an interest in ballet until after their fourth date."

Effect is a verb and means "to make happen," for example, "When dishonesty is discovered it can effect consternation and disappointment." It is also a noun and means "a result," for example, "He believes that the effect of his behavior is irreparable damage to their relationship."

Aggravate or Irritate?

Aggravate means "to make worse."

Irritate means "to annoy, bother, make angry, to inflame."

Don't irritate your listeners by using the wrong word. It could aggravate an uncomfortable situation.

Allusion or Illusion?

Allusion means "an indirect, passing, or casual reference."

Illusion means "an unreal image" or "a false impression, a mistaken view of reality."

Example: "In the first stanza of the poem there was an allusion to Shakespeare's Sonnet 18. This gave the illusion that the writer was familiar with the message of the sonnet."

Alternate or Alternative?

Alternate means "every other one in a series." If the series is a series of only two, *alternate* may mean "substitute."

Alternative means "one of two possibilities" and connotes a matter of choice that is not present with alternates.

Example: "The current supplier delivers on alternate days. We recommend you use him as your primary source but still arrange for an alternative in case his ability to deliver is ever interrupted."

Anticipate or Expect?

Anticipate means "to foresee," "to look forward to," or "to act in advance so as to prevent."

Expect also means "to look forward to" but also "to believe to be probable, to presume." Use expect in the sense of simple expectation.

Example: "We expect to meet the deadline because we have addressed all the anticipated difficulties."

Anxious, Eager, or Enthusiastic?

Anxious means "a state of unease or worry."

Eager means "a state of enthusiastic desire or interest."

Enthusiastic means "an intense feeling for a subject or cause," "eagerness, zeal," or "something inspiring."

Anxious has a negative connotation. *Eager* and *enthusiastic* may at times be used interchangeably, but both have positive connotations. Example: "She is anxious because the delay has not been explained, but she is eagerly looking forward to his arrival. The delay is surprising because he was so enthusiastic about coming!"

Compose, Comprise, or Constitute?

Compose means "to make up of parts," for example, "The medley was composed of a series of show tunes." When used this way, *compose* is used with the word *of*. *Compose* also means "to make tranquil or calm," for example, "Compose yourself."

Comprise means "to include, to contain, to be made up of," as in "The winning choral group comprises singers of all ages." *Comprise* is used without the word *of*.

Constitute can be used as a substitute for compose, meaning "to make up." It is best used in the context of politics, as in "to enact, to designate for an office, to appoint."

> Precision of communication is important, more important than ever, in our era of hair-trigger balances, when a false or misunderstood word may create as much disaster as a sudden thoughtless act.
>
> JAMES THURBER

Continual or Continuous?

Continual means "recurring regularly and frequently."

Continuous means "uninterrupted in time or sequence."

Example: "The continuous rapid flow of the river made continual ferry service necessary."

Credible, Creditable, or Credulous?

Credible means "believable or trustworthy."

Creditable means "praiseworthy or honorable."

Credulous means "gullible" or "ready to believe on insufficient evidence."

Example: "In the presence of such credulous jurors, credible witnesses were not necessary for conviction. Conviction in such a case is not evidence of a creditable prosecutor."

Fewer or Less?

Fewer is the comparative form of *few*. It usually refers to things that are counted by units: "fewer barrels of oil."

Less is one of the comparative forms of *little*. It is used to refer to mass or bulk items, as in "less oil."

Imply or Infer?

Imply means "to express indirectly, to suggest or indicate."

Infer means "to conclude by reasoning" or "to deduce from evidence."

Example: "His love of poetry implied a thoughtful and artistic nature. We inferred from his knowledge of the lives of English poets that he had studied them in depth."

Lay or Lie?

Lay means "to place, put, or set." *Lay* and the other principal parts of this verb (past, *laid;* past participle, *laid*) must have an object, for example, "She promised to lay the baby down as soon as he fell asleep," "When setting the table, he laid the salad forks next to the dinner plate," and "We have laid out as many details as possible considering the changing circumstances."

Lie means "to rest or recline, to be in a horizontal or recumbent position, to assume such a position." *Lie* and the other principal parts of this verb (*lay, lain*) are used without an object, for example, "I plan to lie here for another hour. So go away," "She lay on the couch for two hours," and "She could have lain there much longer if the fire alarm had not gone off."

Momentarily or Soon?

Momentarily means "lasting only a moment" or "from moment to moment." It is so often used to mean "soon" that this use is becoming accepted. But save yourself four syllables and use *soon* unless you plan to spend only a moment of your time on the issue.

Orient or Orientate?

Orient means "to determine the bearings of" or "to make or become familiar with a situation." It has become common to use *oriented* to mean placing value or emphasis, as in "She is results oriented."

Orientate means "to orient." Why use *orientate* when the less pretentious *orient* means the same thing? But then, do you really need to use either? Can you find a simpler way to express the thought, such as "She wants results" or "She gets results"?

Preventive or Preventative?

Preventive is an adjective. *Preventative* is an adjective or a noun.

Example: "Preventive maintenance is vital when you need to maximize uptime with all complex systems, and regular preventive maintenance is the best preventative."

Regardless or irregardless?

Regardless of what you might have heard, there is no such word as *irregardless*.

Summary

Even the most important message can be missed or misunderstood if not delivered clearly. Choosing the right words at the right time is a critically important part of presenting a talk well. These guidelines are good ones to follow.

Speak simply. Shorter and stronger words, phrases, and sentences are almost always best.

Avoid redundancy to both shorten and strengthen your message.

Use clichés sparingly and only when they fit your topic precisely.

Make a habit of using the active rather than the passive voice. Use the passive voice only by conscious choice. Overuse of the passive voice can create a sense of vagueness, evasiveness, ambivalence, or reluctance to accept responsibility.

Use the positive rather than the negative voice by habit. The positive voice will communicate confidence and be more inspiring. Use the negative voice by conscious choice to emphasize gravity, risk, or danger.

Words that engage the five senses will engage your audience. Shorter, stronger verbs create a sense of urgency.

Use inclusive language to avoid the impression that you make false assumptions about people based on their gender, marital status, ethnicity, disability, and age.

Use only words, phrases, acronyms, and industry terms that can be easily understood by the audience. If you must use a specialized term, be sure to define it. Be especially careful of this with diverse audiences.

Use the right word. Familiarize yourself with the differences in meaning between similar words, such as anxious, eager, and enthusiastic; compose, comprise, and constitute; imply and infer. Using them correctly prevents confusion or misunderstanding.

> I have a theory about the human mind. A brain is a lot like
> a computer. It will only take so many facts, and then it
> will go on overload and blow up.
>
> ERMA BOMBECK

Rising above the Noise

Make It Meaningful and Memorable

Think back to last weekend. It probably takes some effort to remember specifically how you filled the hours. Do you readily remember all your conversations—everyone you spoke with and what exactly was said—from those hours? Probably not. Now, try to remember any of the commercial messages you were exposed to during those hours. Do you remember any specific television commercials, radio ads, billboards, or messages on food packaging or grooming products? If you are like most of us, you can remember very little. Without conscious thought our minds filter out most of the information our nervous system delivers.

There's good news and there's bad news.

The good news: This filtering is normal and healthy.

The bad news: Your listeners have filters, too. They will filter out most of what they see and hear. They will apply this filter to the information you deliver.

If you make your living communicating with others, it is important to understand this. If you are a team member, a manager, a salesperson, a teacher, a mentor, a leader of any sort—in other words, a speaker—your success is strongly related to your ability to communicate with others.[1] And you need to communicate in ways that make your ideas heard, understood, and remembered by others—others with fully functioning filters.[2]

Filters Allow Us to Focus

Why do we filter information? We filter to focus on what really matters. Without filtering we would be overwhelmed by information and sensation. Background noises, side conversations, lights, colors—even the pressure of our own clothes on our skin—would all be constant distractions. And even if we were able to ignore the truly mundane and retain only facts, statistics, and "intellectual material," our difficulties would not be over. People with superhuman memories, able to recall and recite vast databases of facts and statistics, are often incapable of abstract thought. Without the ability to discriminate, to focus on what really matters, humans cannot make sense of the world around them. They cannot use the information to set or achieve a goal.

> Understanding and managing attention is now the single most important determinant of business success.
>
> THOMAS DAVENPORT AND JOHN BECK

Just because you talk does not mean people will listen and hear you. And even if they listen and hear you they may not fully understand and most probably will not remember much of what you say.[3] The chances are that most of what you say will be briefly considered and then forgotten.

Getting through the Filter

Knowing that your listeners will continue to filter your information as you speak, how can you increase the chance that your information will make it past the filter? How can you get it through to the conscious mind? What are the qualities of information that are not just briefly considered but really "taken to heart"—committed to long-term memory for later use? Information that is committed to long-term memory usually has one—or better, both—of these two qualities: it is somehow familiar and it evokes emotion.

Familiar Information

The human brain operates by making connections, by storing information in overlapping sets and subsets. Familiar information is recognized by the listener as related to something he already knows.

Think of bits of information as people. Our relationships to other people vary greatly. Some of us are members of the same nuclear families—parents, children, siblings. Some are close relations—grandparents, grandchildren, aunts, uncles, and cousins. We have distant cousins. We have friends, colleagues, employers, and employees. Some people are brief acquaintances and some complete strangers.

> The more connections that can be made in the brain, the more integrated the experience is within memory.
>
> DON CAMPBELL

The brain considers incoming information and looks for the right "home" for it. It places new information with the "relatives and friends" of that information, not with complete strangers.

When we hear someone say "It's a lot like" or "That reminds me of," we are listening to a demonstration of the tendency of the human mind to seek similarities and connections. As the poet Robert Frost said, "All thought is a feat of association."

Emotional Information

Emotional information doesn't mean high drama. But it is natural for humans to look for opportunities to experience pleasure and avoid pain. Humans are hard-wired to act to maximize our opportunities for reward and minimize the chances of discomfort. This hardwiring tunes us in to certain frequencies: the sensational, the dramatic, and the expression of emotion by others.[4]

The following pages introduce you to ways to leverage the power of familiarity and emotion when you speak to a group. Using these tools will help your information filter through to your listeners' minds and hearts. You will be a more compelling speaker, and you will greatly increase your listeners' abilities to understand and remember your information. Your listeners will enjoy your presentation more. You will have more fun.

Repetition

Repetition is the simplest way to leverage one of the two keys to long-term memory: the power of familiarity. It is a great way to reinforce information and improve the chance that your listeners will remember what you said.

Nothing new is familiar the first time you hear it. The second time you hear it, it may "sound familiar." The third time, you can welcome it with a satisfying feeling: "Yes, I know that." The fourth time, the response is something like "That must be important if it is being said again."

Now factor this in: not everybody is listening closely every moment. The chances are good that some people will miss some information. They may miss it twice! Many presenters resist repeating or reviewing information because they fear the audience will be bored or impatient. They may not want to repeat or review because it takes time—time they could use to include more information or greater detail. If one of your goals is to have your listeners walk away remembering your most important points, you are much better off limiting the amount of detail and repeating those points at least three times.

How can you do this? The classic approach is to make your points in your opening or content preview, make them again in the body of your presentation, and make them once more when you review or close. But there are many other ways you can use the power of repetition to leverage the human tendency to remember the familiar. Saying something in more than one way, not just more than once, is a great way to reinforce a message.

Transitions

A transition is a device used to move from one section of your presentation to the next. Often, speakers have a sense that transitions are helpful and important, but they can't quite say why. Let's look more closely to understand why transitions matter and how to use them well.

Transitions, like landmarks on a long journey, confirm that you are on course. They show how far you have come and how far you still have to go. They share what the driver knows. They give the children in the backseat the answers to the questions, "Where are we? Why are we going this way? How much longer till we get there?"

Table 11.1 lists six ways transitions can be used to inform your listeners. The examples are from a presentation on gardening.

Table 11.1 Transitions

Transitions tell:	Example:
What you have covered	"So now you know how to prepare the soil."
Why you covered it	"Again, soil preparation is important. It encourages strong and healthy plants."
What you will cover next	"Now let's talk about how to transplant the seedlings into the prepared soil."
Why you will cover it	"Follow these next tips to transplant successfully. Your seedlings will grow like weeds!"
Connections between the two points covered	"Again, remember to think backwards. The type of seedling determines the type of soil preparation."
Connections between the two points and a larger whole	"As with every aspect of gardening, patience is the key. Remember: plan, prepare, plant, and patience. Nature will do the rest."

Transitions can emphasize the connections between the different elements in your talk. They make it easier for the audience to understand how different elements combine to make the "big picture." When you transition by briefly summarizing a just-completed agenda item, you show that you delivered what you promised.

Limit the number of transitions you use. Too many sound verbose or pedantic. Use the types of transitions your audience needs. Here are some tips to help you decide when transitions are valuable.

Transitions Help with Long Presentations

On a fifty-minute flight from Los Angeles to San Francisco I probably don't need to know when I fly over San Luis Obispo. On a five-hour flight from Los Angeles to New York, I remember pulling out the route map in the airline magazine when the captain announced we were over Garden City, Kansas. I wanted to know exactly where we were and how far we still had to go.

A Long Pause Can Be Used as a Transition

Transitions should not be used just to prevent silence. A presentation without pauses is like a paragraph without punctuation (commas, periods, etc.). Just as that paragraph is hard to read, that type of speech makes it difficult to listen to and difficult to understand, assign value to, or respond intellectually or emotionally to. A healthy pause may be the only transition you need.

Try a Brief Question-and-Answer Session at Transition Points

Intermittent question-and-answer sessions can add or clarify information. This helps your listeners better understand the information that follows, which is especially useful in technical, scientific, and educational presentations. Intermittent question-and-answer sessions give highly analytical listeners a chance to clear up any unresolved issues that might otherwise keep nagging at them and distracting them as you move on. The questions you get will give you a better sense of your listeners' concerns. Then you can tailor your information to them. Finally, it can just be a nice change of pace.

Comparisons

Using comparisons is a great way to help listeners understand and appreciate numbers and statistics. Comparisons bring numbers and statistics to life.

Consider these two ways of giving statistics about the size and population of Alaska:

1. Alaska covers 570,000 square miles. It has about 625,000 residents.

2. Alaska covers 570,000 square miles. That is about as big as the twenty-six states east of the Mississippi River combined. Alaska has about 625,000 people—about the same as the population of Milwaukee, Wisconsin—without the suburbs.

Analogies and Metaphors

When we hear "It's a lot like" or "That reminds me of," the speaker is demonstrating the tendency of the human mind to look for similarities and connections. We can use analogies and metaphors to leverage this tendency of the mind. Analogies and metaphors increase understanding by using what is known, which can make our information easier to remember. A well-chosen analogy or metaphor also makes it easier for our listeners to explain our point to a third party.

The Difference between an Analogy and a Metaphor

An analogy is a comparison that shows the similarity between two things in one or more ways. For example, we might compare the brain to a computer or the heart to a pump. The analogy would describe ways in which the two things resemble one another. Analogies can be used to infer that if two things are alike in one respect, they must be alike in others.

A metaphor is a figure of speech used to suggest a resemblance between two things that aren't truly alike. "Life is a journey" and "love is a battlefield" are metaphors. (A simile also points out a similarity but does it more directly. A simile usually uses the words *like* or *as*. "Falling in love is like going to war" is a simile.)

There is some gray area between comparisons, analogies, metaphors, and similes. What's really important is the way they can be used to make your content more understandable and more memorable.

Form, Function, and Feeling

Analogies, metaphors, and similes often point out a similarity in form, in function, or in feeling. A very brief example of each type of similarity follows.

- Form: a network of suppliers

- Function: a corporate whistle-blower

- Feeling: the remark threw a wet blanket on the atmosphere in the room

Analogies, Metaphors, and Similes Can Help Explain Complexity

Using analogies, metaphors, and similes is an excellent way to make complex technical or theoretical information more meaningful to your listeners. Analogies are especially effective. Use an analogy to explain or illustrate a concept when you want to take advantage of your listeners' current knowledge and understanding. Analogies help them understand more quickly and more deeply. Because analogies start with something familiar, they help your listeners feel more comfortable with new information.

Consider the "first mouse–second mouse" analogy used by technology firms. In this analogy, the inventor of the technology—the person who grinds away at the challenges of making an idea a reality—does not reap the biggest reward. The inventor is compared to the "first mouse"—the mouse that gets its head caught in the trap when it reaches for the cheese.

> We hear and apprehend only what we already half know.
>
> HENRY DAVID THOREAU

The engineering and marketing teams that learn from the inventor's mistakes, fine-tune the invention, and successfully bring it to market are the "second mouse." The second mouse stops by after the trap has been sprung. He gets the cheese.

Fresh Analogies, Metaphors, and Similes Work Best.

Avoid clichés; consider creating something fresher using an unexpected similarity in the form, function, or feeling of two otherwise dissimilar things. Effective use of a fresh analogy or simile often needs a brief explanation as to why the comparison was made—why and how the speaker believes the two things are similar. Consider this simile developed and used by Elizabeth Kubler-Ross: "People are like stained-glass windows. They sparkle and shine when the sun is out, but when the darkness sets in; their true beauty is revealed only if there is a light from within."[5]

We see that Kubler-Ross included several devices. In addition to "people are like stained-glass windows" she used "darkness" to mean adversity and disappointment, and "light" to mean a strength of character that includes perseverance and optimism. The listener supplies the understanding, and, because Kubler-Ross established the overriding analogy, the unspoken comparisons honor one's ability to complete the picture.

Carl Sagan, astrophysicist and Pulitzer Prize–winning author, was a master at explaining scientific and technical information in ways that could be understood by a general audience. He knew that "billions and billions" can be hard to fathom. Here is his explanation and illustration of the enormity of cosmic time: "Imagine the fifteen-billion-year lifetime of the universe . . . compressed into the span of a single year . . . it is disconcerting to find that in such a cosmic year the Earth does not condense out of interstellar matter until early September; dinosaurs emerge on Christmas Eve; flowers arise on December 28th; and men and women originate at 10:30 p.m. on New Year's Eve. All recorded history occupies the last ten seconds of December 31; and the time from the waning of the Middle Ages to the present occupies little more than one second."[6]

In the following example, P. J. O'Rourke, writing for readers of the *Atlantic Monthly,* compares the sizes and landscapes of Israel and parts of the Mid-Atlantic states: "Israel is slightly smaller than New Jersey. Moses in effect led the tribes of Israel out of the District of Columbia, parted Chesapeake Bay near Annapolis, and wandered for forty years in Delaware . . . the Lord showed Moses all of Canaan. New Canaan is in Connecticut—but close enough. And there is a Mt. Nebo in Pennsylvania, although it overlooks the Susquehanna rather than the Promised Land of, say, Paramus. Joshua blew the trumpet and the malls of Paramus came tumbling down."[7]

Analogies Help Listeners Grasp Technical and Complex Information

Consider these two analogies, paraphrased from *User's Guide to the Information Age*.

1. *How computers process information.* Computers process information the way people play twenty questions. *True/false* or *yes/no* provide unambiguous responses that let you sort through the information one logical step at a time. That's the foundation of digital communications, where yes/no, or the idea that something is or is not, is the basic unit of information, and yes/no can be expressed in electronic circuits as the binary numbers 0 and 1. Computers can process lengthy strings of yes/no or 0/1 queries almost instantaneously. This is why they can tackle extremely complex problems.[8]

2. *The power of broadband.* To understand the power of broadband, picture a suburban street in midafternoon, where an occasional auto occupied only by the driver ambles along. That's like a low-bandwidth telephone call on analog copper wire. At rush hour, the same street may be bumper-to-bumper with single-passenger cars. There's more traffic, but it's still low bandwidth. Now think of a four-lane interstate. It is crammed with not just single-passenger cars but trucks, buses, and carpools as well. Add a light-rail system running down the highway median. Not only do you have vehicles carrying more people but you also have more lanes, or channels, of traffic integrated into a single transmission path. That's broadband.[9]

Analogies Must Tap an Existing Knowledge Base

Everything may be like something, but is that enough? No. Analogies must do more than just point out how one thing is like another. You must leverage something familiar to the listener. If your listener is familiar with neither component, the analogy won't work.

> Everything must be like something, so what is this like?
>
> E. M. FORSTER

Understanding the existing knowledge base of your listeners, and using your understanding to leverage some existing part of that knowledge base, is the key to using an effective analogy or simile. Like the last example we examined, the next analogy involves broadband, but in a different way. In *Heavy Hitter Selling,* author Steve W. Martin writes for high-technology salespeople who already have a solid understanding of broadband. He uses the concept of low bandwidth versus broadband as the starting point of his analogy. He leverages the readers' existing knowledge of technology to help explain something they may not have considered—the different modes of operation of the conscious and subconscious human mind.

> In computer terms, the conscious mind is like a point-to-point model. For example, a salesperson wants to check her e-mail . . . on the road. Using her laptop, she makes a dial-up connection to the host computer. Her only concern is to get her e-mail, and once she checks it, she disconnects the phone line. This point-to-point connection is similar to the conscious mind . . .
>
> The subconscious mind is more like a broadband connection that is always on, such as a cable modem. The modem has a wider band of data and processes at a higher speed than a dial-up connection. The modem is always on, always receiving information . . . the salesperson always receives e-mail in real time. She doesn't have to dial up a connection.
>
> The subconscious mind retains information that the conscious mind doesn't . . . when your prospective customers say, "Let me sleep on it," they are actually saying, "Let me see if my subconscious mind has any objections since it has some additional information that I don't have right now."[10]

Use a Single Image

More than one image used to support a single idea can cause confusion and reduce the power of the analogy. Consider the confusion of images in this statement: "Our entire industry is facing an uphill battle on a rough playing field in the months ahead. We will have to navigate some stormy seas before we can land this plane safely."

Use the four steps that follow to create your own analogy. Start with the point or topic you want to make, and then introduce the analogy to help explain or reinforce it. Remember that fresh analogies are always more interesting, but you do need to analogize them to something within your listeners' existing knowledge base.

Step 1. State your point. Be brief. Be clear. Edit your point to one sentence.

Step 2. State the basic facts and essential details.

Step 3. Introduce and develop the analogy. Explain why and how this is an analogy, that is, are the two things similar in form, function, or feeling?

Step 4. Repeat the point. Reinforce your position.

> Analogies, it is true, decide nothing, but they can make one feel more at home.
>
> SIGMUND FREUD

When you use analogies, metaphors, and similes well, you will be clearly understood and be more memorable. And referring to information the audience already knows will show you already know something about them. This can help you establish credibility and rapport more quickly.

Storytelling

Stories, legends, fables, myths, yarns, anecdotes, tales, chronicles—humans love stories of all kinds. Long before humans could read or write we told and listened to stories. Stories teach, inspire, caution, and help us remember. They define who we are and who we want to be. The right story at the right time is an extremely listener-friendly way to show an understanding of the listener's needs and concerns.

Use Stories to Influence Others
The skillful use of stories can be enormously helpful in influencing others. In the words of Annette Simmons, author of *The Story Factor: The Secrets of Influence from the Art of Storytelling*,

> Before you attempt to influence anyone, you need to establish enough trust to successfully deliver your message . . . Since you don't usually have time to build trust based on personal experience, the best you can do is tell them

a story that simulates an experience of your trustworthiness. Hearing your story is as close as they can get to firsthand experience of watching you "walk the walk" as opposed to "talk the talk." A story lets them decide for themselves—one of the great secrets of true influence . . . People value their own conclusions more than they value yours . . . If your story is good enough, people—of their own free will—come to the conclusion they can trust you and the message you bring.[11]

Simmons identifies six types of stories that are useful when you need to influence or persuade your audience. These six types of stories are

- "Who I Am" stories

- "Values-in-Action" stories

- "Why I Am Here" stories

- "Teaching" stories

- "The Vision" stories

- "I Know What You Are Thinking" stories[12]

Stories Are a Powerful Management Tool

If you manage others, stories can be a wonderful tool for influencing behavior within your organization. Here's why.

- *Stories have universal appeal.* Stories appeal to very sophisticated as well as less sophisticated listeners. Everyone loves a good story. You will certainly want to choose an appropriate story and tailor the story and how you tell it to your audience. Stories are timeless, not a passing fad.

- *Stories communicate values and traditions.* The stories a company generates tell when customer service is the first priority, when innovation is valued over obedience, when the mission statement is lived or only mouthed. They implicitly teach people how to behave.

- *Stories are natural and powerful training tools.* In teaching people how to behave, stories teach ways to solve problems, when and how to ask for help, or when to make an on-the-spot decision to solve a production problem or satisfy a customer.[13]

- *Stories recognize and reward effort and achievement.* The stories behind the high ratings in a personnel file can be shared to encourage more of the same. Instead of waiting to tell stories when a gold watch is given, or losing both the story and the great performer to a competitor, share success stories. Tell them throughout the organization, any way you can. Then watch them breed more of the same.

- *Stories are fun and memorable.* Tell a good story and it will live for a long, long time. Many of those who hear it told will tell it again, spreading the word for you and learning the lessons of the story again each time they tell it.[14]

Using Stories Effectively

Follow these guidelines when you incorporate a story into a presentation.

- *Keep stories short.* Stories work best when they last less than two minutes. More than that and you risk boring the audience or having them resent the valuable time you take before you "get to the point." It is a good idea to prepare a script of the story, time your delivery, and if over two minutes, edit it to essential details only. The journalist's approach of answering who, what, when, where, and why can help you trim excess detail. Anything else is likely to be a detail that could be cut.

- *Try "clustering" stories.* At times, quickly telling two or three very short stories as examples or testimonials can both make and reinforce a point in a powerful way. The cluster technique is a great way to show that each example is more than an isolated instance, increasing your ability to influence and persuade. Here is an example of the use of three very brief stories that serve to reinforce the ideas in a *BusinessWeek* magazine story on Business Intelligence software:

Get Smart

Business Intelligence software lets companies navigate the oceans of data in their computer systems to better track their operations and ward off problems. Here are ways the software helps:

Data Analysis

After September 11, Las Vegas was empty because customers weren't flying. Harrah's dug into its data with BI software, found gamblers within driving distance, then sent special offers. Within two weeks, its hotels were full again.

Reporting

British Airways used BI software to analyze complaints about lost luggage and found it needed to better advise customers on minimum transfer times so handlers could get their baggage onto connecting flights.

Data Warehousing

Toyota is using BI software to bring its financial, parts, and production data into a central location. With the info easily accessible, the carmaker now takes just a week to close its books at the end of each quarter, down from a month.[15]

- *Consciously choose a current or classic story.* Stories can be current or classic. If you want to make a point about a new issue or show how your subject relates to a changing environment, a contemporary story may be best. The stories above, on Business Intelligence software, are examples of more current stories. If you want to teach an enduring lesson or show that an issue is recurring, a more classic or historical story may work best.

> Nothing serves a leader better than a knack for narrative. Stories appoint role models, impart values, and show how to execute indescribably complex tasks.
>
> THOMAS A. STEWART

In his autobiography *As It Happened,* William Paley, founder of CBS, uses a historical story to make an enduring point. He tells how in the early days of radio in the 1930s, he used the perception of CBS as the underdog to his advantage. It is especially interesting because he recounts the value of telling this story, with its powerful analogy, to persuade advertisers to sponsor programs on CBS.

In the early days, NBC was more prestigious than Paley's CBS. NBC had more money, more people, fancier offices and studios. The perception of CBS as the underdog made it difficult for Paley to persuade advertisers to buy airtime, even though he believed that CBS had better programs. He writes, "It caused me considerable anguish until one day my whole attitude of being the perpetual underdog changed."

Walking one day in New York City, he passed the Capitol Theater, the largest, most luxurious movie theater in town. Across the street he noticed a shabby theater. But the shabby theater had a long line in front! It struck him that people would patronize an ordinary, even shabby, theater to see the best movie. "The analogy struck me so forcibly that I never forgot it . . . for radio, it's what goes into a person's house that counts. The radio listener doesn't know what kind of office I have, what kind of studios I have, he only knows what he hears. And I can forget about all these advantages my competition has . . . I just have to put things on the air that the people will like more."

Paley began to tell that story to potential advertisers. The result? "That story became a very strong point in my being able to persuade advertisers to sponsor programs on CBS. That insight affected me, too, for I became extra careful about spending money on anything in the company that did not affect the product, the program itself."[16]

- *Plan your story.* Use the following steps to plan and edit your story. Then you can tell it well without rambling or missing important details.

Step 1. Tell the story. Start strong. Avoid preambles such as "Now I'm going to tell you a little story that helps illustrate my point." Instead, dive in: "Last summer my best friend, Jack, decided to drive across the country. He set out from L.A. in the middle of July." As soon as you start, the listeners will know you are telling a story. This is the adult version of "Once upon a time."

Step 2. State the point of the story. State it clearly and succinctly. What is the moral or lesson that the story teaches? What is the principle it illustrates? Keep this general. Is it the importance of teamwork? Patience? Perseverance? Creativity? Following the rules? Regular maintenance? The story of Jack might have a concluding point like this: "Now Jack not only gets oil changes at exactly three months or three thousand miles, he uses his dipstick every time he gets gas."

Step 3. Introduce the related topic or issue, and state how the point or principle illustrated by the story applies. If you need approval to fund a retreat for your team, state that the retreat is needed to build team spirit. If you need more time to complete a project, state the importance of patience in achieving the best results. If you want to sell a maintenance service package, state how important regular maintenance is to minimizing the cost of repairs and downtime. In the story about Jack, the related topic could be "Regular inspections and maintenance are absolutely critical with production equipment like yours."

Step 4. Develop the topic or issue at hand. Describe how the retreat will build a spirit of teamwork; then describe how that new spirit will increase productivity back on the job. Explain how you plan to use the additional time to make sure you turn out a quality-tested product and how the quality will help you grab and keep market share. Explain what the maintenance service package will include, describe the problems it will prevent, and estimate the overall cost savings to the potential buyer. Although no mention is made of the story in this step, the information you cover here prepares you to reinforce your point with support from the story.

Step 5. Close the discussion of the issue by using a quick reference back to the story. "So just as regular oil changes now help make sure that Jack doesn't end up in the Mojave Desert with a melting engine, regular maintenance of your production equipment will help it run smoothly, dependably, and very profitably for many years to come."

Finally, one last thought about the power of stories. Just how powerful and memorable can they be?

Can a story be as thrilling as the biggest and most expensive ride in the history of the Sea World Amusement Parks? Here's what James Zoltak, editor of *Amusement Business* magazine says about Sea World San Diego's mega-million-dollar Journey to Atlantis ride: "Story is really what captures people's imaginations, as much as the adrenaline aspects of a thrill ride. Experts I've heard talk about attraction development have said storytelling is one of the most important aspects, right along with ride systems and other effects."[17]

The Journey to Atlantis ride at Sea World lasts six minutes, twenty-three seconds. The story of the lost continent of Atlantis has been told and retold for three thousand years.

Quotations

Quotations make you and your message more credible. When you use a quotation to support your position, that position immediately becomes much more than your personal opinion. Quoting an authority respected by the audience gives you an "expert witness." And you don't have to pay $700 an hour for the help!

Great quotations capture the essence of an idea in a sound bite. A quotation can reinforce your point and make it more memorable. Humorous quotations can lighten a somber mood. Quotations can give a sense of history and hope by showing that a problem has been faced and overcome in the past.

> There are two ways of spreading light: to be the candle or the mirror that reflects it.
>
> EDITH WHARTON

If you aren't a person with a library of great quotations in your memory bank, don't worry. You can find many books of quotations in any bookstore, including collections of quotations from business leaders, humorous quotations, and quotations specially selected for public speakers. Check the resource section in the back of this book for some suggestions for finding that perfect quotation.

When You Use a Quotation

Follow these guidelines to use a quotation most effectively.

- *Be brief.* Less is more. Quote only the key or relevant words or passages. If you need a detailed explanation of the background or context of the quotation, it is likely to be anticlimactic. It may not be the best choice.

- *Get it right.* If quoting directly, feel free to make a written note of the exact words and to read it aloud to the audience. Don't risk forgetting or misquoting. (Remember that your memory is likely to be temporarily unreliable due to the stress of delivering a presentation.)

- *Attribute it accurately.* Give due credit—and give it to the right source. A few years ago the U.S. Secretary of Education attributed a quotation to the wrong Greek philosopher. Can you guess which part of his talk was widely quoted in news magazines?

- *Distinguish between direct and indirect quotations.* If you don't know the original source of the quotation, guess only if you acknowledge you are guessing. If the person you quote is extremely well known to your audience, an explanation of who that person is (or was) is not necessary.

- *Consider sharing the context.* Telling when, where, or why the quotation originated may enrich the meaning. Was the original speaker facing an enormous challenge, showing admirable strength or courage, or speaking from a wealth of experience?

- *"Sandwich"the quotation between pauses.* Pause before you deliver the actual quotation to create anticipation. Pause again after the quotation to let the meaning really sink in.

- *Speak slowly and clearly.* Use the appropriate inflection. Reading a quotation can be the best way to make sure you deliver it accurately.

- *Return to your topic.* Using a key word or phrase from the quotation will reinforce the link between the quotation and your point.

Practice using the three steps that follow to learn to use quotations skill-fully. As Cicero wrote, "The skill to do is in the doing."

Step 1. Supply any needed credit and context.

Step 2. Deliver the quotation.

Step 3. Link the quotation back to the topic at hand.

Here is an example using the three steps.

In a case brought before the Supreme Court, a writer for the *New Yorker* magazine claimed a constitutional right to make up quotations as long as the writer believes they reflect the views of the subject. Although this argument is not accepted by many journalists, it does reflect an acknowledgement of the power of quotations to provide both authority and authenticity. In a previous ruling on the case, Federal Appeals Judge Alex Kozsinski wrote, "An article devoid of [quotations], one that consists entirely of the author's own observations and conclusions, generally leaves readers dissatisfied and unpersuaded as well as bored."[18] If you want to increase your ability to satisfy and persuade your listeners, using a quotation—and using it well—is a great strategy.

Humor

The ability to use humor well is a wonderful asset for business speakers. It can help the speaker make a point, connect with listeners emotionally, and lighten the mood. Humor creates a sense of community. But humor can be risky. When an attempt to be funny fails, it can fail in a big way. It can fall flat or, worse, offend or alienate your listeners.

A joke is a very serious thing.

WINSTON CHURCHILL

Dr. Richard Wiseman of the University of Hertfordshire designed an experiment to determine the World's Funniest Joke. Ten thousand volunteers from eleven countries were invited to judge jokes and to contribute their own. From over forty thousand jokes and two million ratings, here is an abridged version of the one elected the World's Funniest Joke.

Two hunters are out in the woods when one of them collapses. He doesn't seem to be breathing and his eyes are glazed. The other guy takes out his phone and calls emergency services.

He gasps, "My friend is dead! What can I do?" The operator says, "Calm down, I can help. First, let's make sure he's dead." There is a silence; then a gunshot is heard. Back on the phone, the guy says, "Okay, now what?"

You probably smiled or chuckled after reading the hunter joke, but is it really the funniest joke you ever heard? Chances are that it is not. Most of us have been reduced to helpless, breathless, doubled-over laughter at some point in our lives. And most of us, when trying to relate the humor of the moment to others later, have been reduced to saying "Well, I guess you had to be there." Why is that? It must be possible to examine the nature of humor and to come to some conclusions about what makes something tickle the human funny bone.

> Examining humor seriously is like dissecting a frog. There's nothing funny about it, and the subject dies in the process.
>
> ROBERT BENCHLEY

Wiseman said the hunter joke appealed to men and women, to young and old, and across different cultures. "Many of the jokes submitted received higher ratings from certain groups of people, but this one had real universal appeal," he said. "[Jokes] sometimes make us feel superior to others, reduce the emotional impact of anxiety-provoking situations or surprise us because of some kind of incongruity. The hunters joke contained all three elements."[19]

Understanding your audience is very important. According to Wiseman, the study showed "fundamental differences in the ways in which males and females use humor. Males use humor to appear superior to others, whilst women are more linguistically skilled and prefer word-puns." And Wiseman concluded that from culture to culture, people have "fundamentally different senses of humor." The study found that Americans enjoy marriage-mocking jokes and that both Americans and Canadians preferred jokes with a strong sense of superiority because a character either looks or is made to look stupid. People in France, Denmark, and Belgium are especially fond of offbeat surreal humor. Europeans also enjoy jokes that involve making light of anxiety-provoking topics such as sickness, death, and marriage. People from the Republic of Ireland, the United Kingdom, Australia, and New Zealand most enjoy jokes involving wordplay. Wiseman advised, "Humor is vital to communication and the more we understand about how people's culture and background affect their sense of humor, the more we will be able to communicate effectively."[20]

Ted Cohen, professor of philosophy at the University of Chicago, explains that when we tell a joke, we presuppose something in those who listen—some knowledge, belief, familiarity, or prejudice—that will supply the background needed for the joke to succeed. Whether very simple or very complex, the joke will always require the audience to supply something. When that something is supplied simultaneously by members of an audience, a community is created—a community of people joined by the understanding of what they share with the joke teller and with each other.[21] Let's see how this works. Here's an example.

> There's nothing like a gleam of humor to reassure you that a fellow human being is ticking inside a strange face.
>
> EVA HOFFMAN

What did the Dalai Lama say to the hot dog vendor? "Make me one with everything."

To "get" this joke, considerable knowledge is needed by the listeners if they are to supply what is missing. They must have an understanding of two interpretations of the word *one,* some knowledge of Eastern religious philosophy, and familiarity with a common expression for ordering a hot dog with all the available condiments.

I first heard this joke in a business context: that of a software marketing executive expressing the need of large organizations to combine the information in many different databases into one integrated system. Additional levels of complexity and meaning are now added to the line "Make me one with everything."

Information management professionals will respond to this joke by supplying these additional, more specialized, meanings. Part of their enjoyment of the joke will come from the recognition of the need they share with others who struggle with the same integration challenges. As Cohen explains, "One of the things accomplished when a joke succeeds is the creation of a community of people enough like one another to be laughing at the same thing."[22]

This joke also introduces another aspect of humor, one identified by many students of humor: much humor has a basis in pain or discomfort. Attempts to integrate databases can be painfully difficult. So in this context the humor serves to lighten the mood as well as create a sense of community among the listeners.

> If you can't make it better, you can laugh at it.
>
> ERMA BOMBECK

Jokes we find really funny often are funny for more than one reason. This complexity can add to our enjoyment even as it makes it harder to pinpoint the reason. Here's the joke from the Wiseman study that Americans found funniest.

A man and a friend are playing golf one day. One of the guys is about to chip onto the green when he sees a long funeral procession on the road next to the course. He stops in mid-swing, takes off his golf cap, closes his eyes, and bows down in prayer. His friend says: "Wow. That is the most thoughtful and touching thing I have ever seen. You are truly a kind man."

The man then replies: "Yeah, well, we were married 35 years."[23]

Notice how this joke is multidimensional. It uses the unexpected, tickles the American fondness for marriage-mocking, touches on our underlying anxiety about death, and requires that we fill in the unspoken with our own familiarity with golf fanatics.

To learn more about the nature of humor and, most importantly, more about how to use humor effectively in a presentation, see the Top 10 Guidelines for Using Humor.

The Top 10 Guidelines for Using Humor

10. *Use humorous quotations.* Many books of humorous quotations are available. Finding and using one related to your point is one of the best ways to safely incorporate humor. And if a joke falls flat, at least you aren't the only one responsible.

9. *Use humorous analogies.* Analogies often appeal to the shared knowledge that creates the sense of community mentioned by Ted Cohen.

8. *Be cautious about using humor aimed at an individual or group.* Aristotle taught that all humor was at the expense of someone. Be very careful not to offend an individual, members of a group, or a person who may have sympathy with such an individual or group. It is safest to avoid this type of humor.

7. *Make it quick.* The more you draw out a joke, the more you raise the expectations of your audience. Get to the punch line quickly. People need to see the humor themselves. The slow buildup of expectations can make them feel manipulated. (Wiseman's study found that 103 words was the ideal length for a joke.)

6. *Then pause to let the laughter happen.* Laughter is contagious, and humor works best when people laugh together out loud. Stop after a funny line. Let people enjoy the moment. Don't stifle the laughter by talking again too soon.

5. *Make it relevant to the topic at hand.* Telling a joke just to "warm up the audience" can smack of manipulation. Instead, choose humor that makes or supports a point from your presentation. Even if not everyone thinks it is funny, at least the audience will see the point, which means you haven't wasted their time.

4. *Use a touch of self-directed humor.* Poking fun at ourselves and taking ourselves lightly can create the impression of extreme confidence. It can demonstrate a willingness to learn from our mistakes and to consider the ideas and opinions of others.

3. *Avoid too much self-deprecating humor.* Reciting a list of your mistakes can make you seem like a slow learner. Avoid humor so consistently self-deprecating that the audience begins to believe that you have a low opinion of yourself.

2. *Be sensitive to the pain often inherent in humor.* Much humor has a basis in pain or discomfort. If you are asking listeners to "smile through their tears," consider whether the humor is appropriate. If the audience is likely to be highly sensitive, or the pain is too great or simply too recent, the attempt at humor may seem insensitive and in bad taste.

1. *Use humor that is funny to the audience in general, not to just a few members.* Consider whether or not audience members have the background to fill in the necessary information to see the humor. If their experience or culture makes it unlikely that they will "get it," then don't use it. If the humor depends on familiarity with a quirk of language or knowledge of a historical event significant to only one group of people, it may not work well with a culturally diverse audience.

Summary

In this world of information overload we have all learned to filter out most of what we hear and focus only on what matters to us. This means that most of what we say in most presentations will be briefly considered by our listeners and then forgotten. What is remembered after the presentation ends? Information that has one or both of these two qualities:

1. It evokes emotion in the listener.

2. It is somehow familiar, that is, it is somehow connected to something the listener already knows.

The rhetorical tools covered in this chapter have stood the test of time for making information more compelling and memorable. Using them will help you and your message rise above the white noise of information overload.

Repetition is the simplest way to leverage one of the two keys to long-term memory: the power of familiarity. It is a great way to reinforce information and improve the chance that your listeners will remember what you said.

Transitions can leverage the familiar by repeating or referencing an important point. They can emphasize the connection between different points. They make it easier to understand how different points combine to make the big picture.

Stories and anecdotes tap into your listeners' emotions and help them recall similar or related experiences. Stories are a powerful way to influence and persuade. When remembered and retold by listeners, they carry your message to a wider audience. The points or lessons of the story are made again and again.

Comparisons, analogies, metaphors, and similes take advantage of the familiar. They leverage your listeners' current knowledge and understanding. They help you present new, complex, or conceptual information in ways that can be understood. And because they start with the familiar, they can make your listeners more comfortable with new information. Using comparisons is a great way to help listeners understand and appreciate numbers and statistics.

Quotations add to your credibility by showing that your point is more than your personal opinion. They can give a sense of history and hope by showing that a similar problem has been faced by others. Humorous quotations can help lighten a somber mood, put problems in a different perspective, and give your listeners a sound bite to remember and repeat.

Humor taps into some unspoken but shared knowledge, emotion or even pain to create a sense of community among you and your listeners. It changes the pace, lightens the mood, and helps present you as human.

These and many other creative ways of presenting your content can help you rise above the noise of information overload. Understanding your listeners and using your creativity to evoke emotion and leverage the power of the already familiar will make your content more meaningful, memorable, and enjoyable.

Thinking is more interesting than knowing,
but less interesting than looking.

GOETHE

Can You Picture It?

Visual Aids That Really Are

Good visual aids can increase audience attention, understanding, and retention.[1] Just hearing information involves only one of the five senses; the use of visual aids adds one more. This creates a richer overall experience. The old sayings "Seeing is believing" and "A picture is worth a thousand words" testify to the value of visual aids.

Yet we have all sat through presentations in which the visual aids were so ineffective that they didn't really deserve the name. They were boring. They were too simplistic to add value. They were too detailed to process. They couldn't be seen.

You wouldn't inflict that type of punishment on your audience, would you? Never! At least never again.

What should you do? When should you use visual aids? What kind and what medium should you use? What information belongs on a visual aid? What design principles should you follow?

To answer these questions, let's first consider when you should use visual aids and when it is better not to use them. The guidelines below will help you make wise choices.

Do use visual elements when your goal is to

- Stimulate interest

- Focus attention

- Illustrate hard-to-visualize information

- Help explain relationships

- Help assign value

- Evoke emotion

- Reinforce your verbal message

- Help the audience remember

- Help the audience explain a point to others

When a visual element accomplishes one or more of these goals, it has earned the right to be called a *visual aid*.

Do not use visual elements to

- Present simple ideas that are easily stated verbally

- Cover many ideas on one slide

- Impress your audience with quantity of detail

- Prove how many PowerPoint features you can use

- Serve as detailed speaker notes

- Serve as a script

- Avoid interaction with the audience

When a visual element—a chart, graph, photograph, and so on—cannot be removed without harming comprehension, it is *germane*. If you need to reduce the number of visual aids in a presentation, test them for germaneness.

Visual Aids Are Not Speaker Notes

The dos and don'ts above should lead to this conclusion: your speaker notes are very unlikely to make good visual aids and vice versa. If your notes are comprehensive, they will probably include more detail, or different forms of detail, than should be included on a visual aid. If you choose to use your slides as your only speaker notes, you must be ruthless in editing out those things that should be communicated only verbally. These include reminders to you about how you want to deliver certain information (for example, repeat something slowly or ask a rhetorical question) or reminders about how to handle logistical or facilities issues (for example, when to show a slide, when to turn the lights back on, or when to call for a break). These things belong in speaker notes, not in visual aids.

Here's another reason for separating your notes from your visual aids. You learned in chapter 6 that the normal stress of delivering a presentation can cause a cortisol-induced memory lapse. There is really no way you can be absolutely sure you will remember everything you want to say or do without consulting speaker notes during your presentation. So use notes. Chapter 9 gives you all you need to know about creating good notes. In chapter 15 you will learn all you need to know about using notes with confidence.

Choose the Best Type of Visual Aids

If you decide to use visual aids, the next question is, What type should I use? Your choice will be based on the topic, the venue, the availability of equipment, and your own preferences. Often the choice is obvious. But if you have some flexibility, you may want to consider the options in table 12.1.

When you have decided what type of visual aid to use, you will know what type of work is needed to get them ready. Whether you do all the preparation yourself, have help from others in your organization, or recruit outside expertise, keep the possible disadvantages of your chosen type in

Table 12.1 Visual Aid Choices

Option	Audience size	Advantages	Disadvantages
Computer-generated slides used with computer projector	Varies with size of screen available	Have a professional appearance Are an indication of technical expertise Can hyperlink to other documents or Web sites Allow use of electronic photos Allow for hidden and embedded slides to manage level of detail Are relatively easy to revise and reorder	Require computer and computer projector (or equivalent) May require a darkened room Equipment difficult to troubleshoot
Computer-generated overhead transparencies	Upper limit around 50, but varies with screen size	Can appear professional Indicate preparation Are easy to reorder, can change selection Are easy to write on to elaborate Are easy to transport	Changes require new transparencies Can be time consuming to create Require overhead projector May require darkened room Fan may be loud
Photo slides	Upper limit around 50, but varies with screen size	Provide realistic, accurate images Provide specific details	Can be difficult to reorder or return to previous slide Can appear dated
Handmade or copied overhead transparencies	Upper limit around 50, but varies with screen size	Are easy to create, easy to change Are easy to reorder, can change selection Are easy to write on to elaborate Are easy to transport	Can appear messy or unprofessional Copied photos can include details so small as to be difficult to see Require overhead projector May require a darkened room Fan may be loud

Software demonstrations	Varies with size of screen available	Demonstrate applications, functions, and options available Can be adapted to individual audience needs Demonstrate speed, ease of use	Detailed interfaces can make focusing attention difficult May require a darkened room
Videos	Varies with size of screen available	Show movement, provide sound Provide changes of pace and sensory input	Require video or computer equipment, screen large enough for audience Can be expensive to produce
Multimedia productions	Varies with size of screen available	Create and support a professional atmosphere Demonstrate thoughtful preparation Demonstrate investment to produce and deliver Appeal to multiple senses	Can be time consuming and expensive to produce Require extensive equipment and expertise to produce Can overwhelm audience
Write-on boards, flip charts	Upper limit around 20	Support a casual atmosphere Allow spontaneity Allow capture of audience input Support a collaborative atmosphere	Require legible handwriting Require good spelling skills Can be time consuming Can indicate lack of preparation Are inappropriate in formal environments
Prepared flip charts	Upper limit around 20	Are easy to create Are relatively easy to transport Can be easily interchanged Support a casual atmosphere	Can be inappropriate for formal environments Can easily show wear and tear

mind. Do everything you can to minimize or eliminate potential problems each type might present.

Computer-Generated Slides

Computer-generated slides are the most common choice for visual aids in business today. They give tremendous flexibility and convenience in both design and use. But with this flexibility come choices that can be confusing. So let's take a look at some of the principles of slide design. Many of these design principles can and should be applied to other types of visual aids as well.

Before we discuss the principles of good slide design, it is worth mentioning that many companies and organizations have a design template to follow. The template is generally well designed, creates a consistent look, and usually includes the company's logo and signature colors for a professional look. Presentation software always includes a number of standard templates. Use of a standard template may eliminate the need to concern yourself with many of the principles we cover. But if you can choose the design or your look (or when you have the freedom to choose from among a variety of templates), consider whether or not your own design or the template adheres to the slide design guidelines that follow. First, some basic design principles.

Color

Color can be a powerful addition to your visual aids. Used well, it can clarify, increase and accelerate understanding of your information, and increase emotional impact. Use color to highlight important information, to establish hierarchies of information, and to group related points. Color can make your message look more professional and polished. It should be used to achieve these goals, not just for decoration.

Contrast Is Vital

Color contrast is one key to a good slide. And simply using different colors may not be enough to give you the contrast you need. When the value of two colors (the relative darkness or lightness) is about the same, the line between the background and the text can be hard to see. The text may look fuzzy around the edges or even seem to move or vibrate. A good way to check if the values of colors are different enough to work well together is to look at them in gray scale. If the contrast is not easy to see in gray scale, it may not be easy to see in color.

Use a Deep Green or Blue Background

Given a choice of environments, people gravitate toward green and blue. The most coveted real estate in the world offers views with both. Even in major cities, those who can afford them choose views of parks, rivers, lakefronts, oceans. Green and blue ultimately sustain life on earth. Pulitzer Prize–winning scientist and conservationist Edward O. Wilson calls this human affinity for the natural world *biophilia*.[2] He explains that humans evolved in similar landscapes. Rich green foliage and grasslands, blue water, the contrasting color of flowers that indicated fruit to follow, and the red and yellow of ripe fruit meaning the wait was over—we still prize these elements. Landscape designers use them in the design of parks and open spaces. We plant and nurture them in our yards and gardens: the foliage on trees and shrubs contains rich, deep greens; yellow, white, pink, red, and lavender flowers are strong and bright contrasts against the green. These are pleasant contrasts that appeal to the eye, help us relax, and help us recharge our batteries to face the world again. Deep green or blue backgrounds leverage this human preference.

Avoid White Backgrounds

For the same reasons that deep green or blue backgrounds are a good choice, white backgrounds are not. Looking at a series of slides with white or very light backgrounds is like staring at a snowfield on a sunny day—*not* easy on the eyes! Light backgrounds are great for printed material but not for a lit screen.

Use White or Yellow Text

White as the basic color and yellow for emphasis is a common and effective choice. Very light shades of other colors can work well, especially if they are not just lighter shades of your background color. Be sure to avoid colors that don't provide enough contrast with your background.

Color Vision Deficiency

People who have color vision deficiency (color blindness) cannot distinguish certain colors. Estimates of the percentage of the population with color deficiency in some form range from 6 to 20 percent of males (most common are estimates of between 8 and 12 percent) and $\frac{1}{2}$ of 1 percent of females. Red/green color blindness is by far the most common form, about 99 percent of cases, and causes problems in distinguishing reds and greens. Blue/yellow color vision deficiency is rare. Total color blindness (seeing in only shades of gray) is extremely rare.[3]

A simple way to address this in your visual aids is to minimize the amount of red and green you use, especially if they have the same value. See the resources under "Color Vision Deficiency" for more information about this issue, including links to software you can download to check your images and correct them for viewing by a person with color vision deficiency.

Text

The following guidelines will help you use text effectively when designing slides. Many of the principles can be applied to other types of visual aids—overhead transparencies, flip charts, chalkboards, and whiteboards—as well.

Text Must Be Large Enough to Be Read Easily

The size of the text you use can vary with the size of your screen and the size of the audience. Generally accepted guidelines are at least 30 points for titles and at least 20 points for text.

Clean and Simple Fonts Work Best

Arial is a top choice for slide fonts. It is a sans serif font, meaning it is clean and simple with no little artifacts at the end of the character points. It also has a rather extended font family—Arial Narrow, Arial Black, Arial Rounded

MT Bold (fig. 12.1). This gives you the choice of adding variety when you need it without creating an entirely new look. It works well across platforms. But remember that even within the same font family, more than two varieties of text can become a distraction.

Avoid Using All Capitals

All capitals are harder—hence slower—to read. They also make it difficult to read acronyms (e.g., ASAP).

Figure 12.1 The Arial Font Family

The Arial family

This is Arial, a clean and simple sans serif font.
This is Arial italicized.
This is Arial Narrow.
This is Arial bold.
This is Arial Black.
This is Arial Rounded MT Bold.

Moving Beyond Text

Why is a picture worth a thousand words? Pictures increase attention. They wake up and invigorate a listener's brain by shifting the mode of sensory input from audio to visual. They make a point come alive in the listener's mind. They can communicate subtleties that are difficult to put into words. They are also a great way to create an emotional response. And they increase the listener's familiarity with a point and reinforce it by repeating it in a visual way. (Remember: two keys to creating a long-term memory are to evoke emotion and to leverage the listener's familiarity with a point or topic.) For those who learn well visually, they can be the most powerful and effective part of your presentation.

Graphics

Charts and graphs can help you present data so members of your audience can understand and interpret it more easily. Studies have shown that both understanding and retention go up when more than one sense is used to receive a message.[4] Using graphics can also help hold listeners' attention just by creating a change of pace.

Business-office software packages have built-in graph creation tools. These graph creation tools will meet the needs of most presenters most of the time. You can find examples of charts, advice on the best kind of chart to use to present your data, and examples to look at in your presentation software, word processing software, and spreadsheet software.

Many different kinds of charts and graphs are used in specific fields and for specific purposes. In addition, specialized graphing software programs are available for technical and scientific specialties. (See "Visual Aids" in the resources section in the back of this book.)

You can also use built-in graphing tools to create a basic graph and then add other visual elements, such as lines, text boxes, or arrows. Another option is to import a graph from another software package. For more on how to use charts and graphs to illustrate your data, check under "Visual Aids" in the resources section in the back of the book.

No matter what kind of chart or graph you use, the guidelines that follow will help you make the most of it.

Title

The title of the graph should provide an interpretation of the data. The title alone should help the audience understand the point the slide makes. Rather than "Year-to-Date Sales Results," the slide should say "Sales Up 30 Percent Year-to-Date."

Axes

It is important to set the scales of the axes to be appropriate to the data being shown. Also, make sure that axis labels indicating the values along each axis are big enough to be clearly read when the graph is displayed. If the axis labels are not clear, the graph may be misinterpreted because the differences in the data are not clear to the audience.

Colors

The background color and the color of each data block or line must provide enough contrast for visibility. All colors should also be consistent with the overall color scheme of the slides. Consider any symbolic meaning of colors. Red may mean "in the red" for financial services audiences. Would it be appropriate to use an organization's logo or trademark colors?

Depth

Consider moving from a two-dimensional graph to three dimensions. This option works best with bar, column, and pie graphs. When you add a third dimension to data blocks, they have a more solid and tangible look. With more than about three data blocks a 3-D graph can begin to look too busy, making it harder to understand. You can find 3-D graphs among the choices of standard graphs in basic software packages.

Labels

Use data labels to add emphasis or precision to the values on a graph. Each label should be placed close to the data point. Labels work best at the end of bars or columns, above data points on a line graph, or outside the sections in a pie graph. The type should be large enough and have enough color contrast to be legible. Keep the labels consistent in style throughout the graph.

Legends

Use a legend when you have more than one element on a graph. The legend connects a data element to a color on the graph. It makes the graph easier to understand.

Tombstones

You may choose to use a brief summary statement, sometimes called the tombstone (what the audience should remember when this slide is "dead and gone"), at the bottom of your slide. The tombstone can reinforce the title or add a further explanation or interpretation of the data. For example, with the title "Sales Up 30 Percent Year-to-Date," the tombstone might be "Every region contributed to increase."

Tables

Tables are sets of columns and rows that hold and organize data. A table shows the data without interpreting it. Tables are useful for raw data and allow the audience freedom of interpretation. In presentations, which are generally used to persuade and convince rather than simply to inform, tables are used less frequently than graphs. You may want to include a table to show the thoroughness of your research and the richness of the data and then use a graph to interpret the data for the audience.

Tables are often difficult to read, so keep tables to a reasonable size. No more than six rows and six columns is a good rule of thumb, but table size should always depend on the audience's ability to see the screen. If you choose to interpret the data in a table without adding a graph, it helps to highlight the most important cells for the audience. You might change the background color of the important cells, change the text by changing the color or making it bold, or both. Making your column and row headings bold helps the audience read the table and find pertinent data more easily.

Presentation software packages have built-in table creation tools, and tables can be imported from other software packages as well. When you import, always test your slides on the same presentation equipment you will use for your presentation to make sure the imported table translated accurately.

Photographs

Photographs are now the most popular images used on presentation slides. They give you a lot more options, precision, and subtlety. Photos, especially those of people, can evoke strong emotional responses. Members of your audience will process photos quickly, using more emotion and less logic, than when processing text or spoken words. Keep this in mind if using a photo in an emotionally charged environment.

You can take a digital photo yourself, find one on the Web, purchase a stock photo, or import one from one of the many software packages that provide them. Search on the Internet under "stock photos" for a wide variety of resources.

Fresh images are usually best, but a familiar photo used in an unexpected way can be a great method of introducing a new idea or adding humor.

Resolution matters for clarity of the image. For presentation slides, aim for a minimum of 640 by 480 dpi (dots per inch). Converting a high-resolution photo using a graphics program can reduce the file size and save disk space. This helps keep your presentation file to a size that will run quickly.

Clip Art

Most presentation software contains clip art. But many people have used these images in a lot of presentations. Unless the standard clip art is absolutely perfect for your need, use something fresher. And speaking of fresh, avoid dated-looking photos and images. That photo of a businesswoman in her 1980s power suit with the little silk bow tie and the wing-tip pumps can make you look dated. You can find more original and updated images free on the Internet or in clip art software packages. (See the resources section under "Visual Aids" for Web site addresses.)

Be careful about the colors of a clip art image. They must provide enough contrast with your slide background color to be seen well. Avoid black clip art unless you are using a very light colored background; it is hard to see black on top of most colors.

Animation

When using a graph or a table, you may want to animate the graph or table elements so that they appear on-screen one at a time. This helps you manage the attention of audience members. Animation can eliminate the need to use a pointer when using more complex slides. But be judicious—don't use every animation effect in your software package in the same series of slides. Keep it simple.

Working with Images

Once you have an image—chart, graph, photo, clip art—in your presentation slide, you can make some changes to the image that will make it even more effective. Here are some of the most common changes.

Sizing

The image should be big enough for all the important details to be seen by everyone in the audience. When you combine an image and text on the same slide, consider which, if either, you want to be dominant. Size them accordingly. Leave enough space around the image and text so they don't crowd one another or cut one another off. You can change the size of an image by selecting it and then dragging the expansion handle at the corner of the image. When you use the corner handle to size an image you keep the aspect ratio (the ratio of width to height) and do not distort the image. Try putting the image inside a text box if you want to easily move it around the face of the slide to position it just right. You can modify the text box to create a frame or to hide it to "float" the image on the background.

Cropping

You can crop out the unnecessary parts of an image. Find the cropping function within the function for formatting images. Check the size of the image before setting the cropping distances from each edge so that you can crop out just the right amount on each side in just a few tries.

Color Choice

Some clip art allows you to change one or more of the colors used. You can do this to increase the contrast with your background color or to create a more pleasing look. After you have inserted the clip art, select it and then select the format function.

Brightness

The brightness of an image affects how good it will look on the screen you use. You may need to make the image brighter to project a good image. If possible, check your photos using the same projector and room lighting you will use for your actual presentation. To adjust the brightness, use the brightness setting found in the format function. If checking before the presentation is not possible, experiment with adjusting the brightness as you finalize your presentation slides. Then you will be prepared to test the photos and adjust the brightness as you set up for your presentation.

Simplicity versus Detail

Consider the design of traffic signs. They usually have just two high-contrast colors: white letters on deep green, black letters on goldenrod, white letters on red. They have large letters; clean, spare fonts; one or two words. An extremely simple graphic might be used: a round-headed stick figure walking, two bold lines merging, two bold lines crossed. Their simple, distinctive shapes—triangles, octagons, rectangles—are easy to recognize and understand. Traffic signs have enough information to guide drivers and absolutely nothing more—nothing to distract them.

Let's also consider billboards: one large picture, just a few words with huge letters. Billboards communicate just one idea.

Is a traffic sign or a billboard a good model for an ideal slide? Must your slides be that simple to be good? Absolutely not. Here's why.

Very few ideas you will talk about are going to be as simple or familiar to your audience as the messages on traffic signs or billboards. Simple traffic signs and billboards are a good way to remind people of concepts they already know, especially when they are driving by at forty miles an hour, watching the traffic around them, listening to their favorite CD, and talking to a customer on the phone (or two children in the backseat). They are not a good way to communicate new material, more complex information, or the differences between two or more ideas or products. A "traffic sign" approach to slide design won't help your listeners see an emerging trend. It won't give them the subtle details that will help them make a fully informed decision. It won't help them

> Everything should be made as simple as possible. But not simpler.
>
> ALBERT EINSTEIN

185

choose between two emotionally charged options. If you are going to use a slide the way it should be used—as a *visual* tool to *aid* your listener in understanding and remembering important information—you probably need to design something that demands and deserves more conscious attention than a traffic sign.

Yale professor and guru of visual presentation of information Edward Tufte is a severe critic of the oversimplified design of many electronic slides. He points to oversimplification as a major cause of the slide overdose that far too many presenters try to pour down the throats of listeners. This oversimplification, he believes, is encouraged by electronic slide software, specifically PowerPoint. He explains that the typical PowerPoint slide shows about forty words and can be read in about eight seconds. He states, "With so little information per slide, many, many slides are needed. Audiences consequently endure a relentless sequentiality, one damn slide after another."[5]

Tufte believes strongly that complexity, detail, and the showing of information side by side—not in sequence—are often necessary to achieve understanding. Especially when presenting statistical data and complex technical information, more detail often means greater clarity and understanding. The side-by-side presentation of information is what makes it possible to explain relationships, compare and contrast, and assign value.

This makes sense. But it also raises a question. Why do the presentation software templates (and most presentation training guides) recommend slides that are so simple? I think this is a well-intentioned response to too much unnecessary detail. Too many presenters use slides that are so complicated, filled with so much text and so many graphics, they become not just hard to understand but often hard to see or read.

Finding the Right Visual Balance

The visual presentation of complex information in an understandable way is a real challenge. To make a slide understandable you must find the right balance between the needed detail and the clearest possible design. Both text and graphics must be large enough so your listeners see them clearly. Expecting listeners to understand information they can't see is like trying to teach a cow to sing: you get frustrated and the cow gets mad (or vice versa).

Presentation software has many features that can be used to create slides that are as simple or as detailed as you need. Learning to use these features will give you the control and flexibility to design in ways that go beyond the standard templates. Many fields—finance, technology, mathematics, and the different branches of science—have other software specifically designed to help communicate specialized and complex information effectively. If you are presenting highly specialized information, you may want to check out some of this software.

The Advantages of Detailed Slides

More detail on slides makes it necessary to move more slowly through these slides. Moving more slowly gives listeners a chance to understand and digest the more complex information. Aim to combine more detailed slides and a slower pace with intermittent use of simpler slides (or no slides at all). This creates the kind of changes in pace that will keep your audience more attentive. When you choose this approach be sure you use the tips in chapter 15 on using visual aids effectively.

I do not recommend that you deliberately create complicated or detailed slides. Your slides, like the rest of your presentation, should be made as simple as possible. Do not include words, graphics, or even colors that don't aid listeners' ability to understand and remember your information. But don't worry if you include details or complexity that is essential to your message. Include detail if it is germane. Just make sure your listeners can see it.

Now that you know there is really no reason to put everything you want your audience to hear on visual aids, let's reinforce this point by introducing the Law of Visual Aid Supply and Demand.

The Law of Visual Aid Supply and Demand

The Law of Visual Aid Supply and Demand states, "Every added visual aid reduces the importance of the others." (This is probably the least-obeyed law in the world.) Far too many presenters show far too many slides—slide after slide after slide. First they insult the listeners' intelligence. Then they bore, then they numb, and then they lull. Part of the solution is to recognize that sometimes one more complex or detailed slide is needed, not twelve simpler ones. Part of the solution is to recognize that slides are not your speaker notes. Part of the solution is to remember that you can and should speak without slides at least part of the time. And part of the solution is to remember that there are many other ways to help create pictures in the minds of listeners: use an analogy, tell a story, describe something using gestures, have the listeners close their eyes and picture it.

Summary

A visual aid should be visual. It should aid your listeners in understanding and remembering your information. The best visual aids are germane to your content, that is, they cannot be removed without harming understanding.

Choose the best visual aid for your message, your audience, and your speaking venue.

Visual elements—charts, graphs, photos, clip art—should be chosen carefully. Charts and graphs can be made using many different software programs. The most popular word processing, spreadsheet, and presentation software all have examples and guidelines to follow when choosing and designing a visual aid. More specialized software for disciplines such as science, mathematics, and medicine is available as well.

Colors of the background, text, and visual images should be chosen with your audience in mind. Consider both legibility and aesthetic appeal when choosing a text style and size: generally, the simpler and bigger, the better.

13

You Look Marvelous!

What to Wear, Where

You are your first visual aid. Your appearance will speak to your audience before you do. It will be an important part of the first impression you create, an impression that will either support or detract from your ability to influence your audience. Whether or not you believe your audience *should* judge you on your appearance, they will. It is important to understand this and to dress and groom yourself in ways that will support your message.

Business attire is much more varied than it was in years past. Different organizations, industries, and geographic regions all can have different dress codes. Now more than ever, your choice of what to wear is influenced by the type of presentation, your knowledge of your audience and their expectations, and the venue or setting.

Know Your Goal

An important question to ask is this: Are you coming to represent *your* position, company, or industry, or are you coming to fit in with *theirs?*

If you are approaching another company's management team about a joint venture, dressing as they do can help create a feeling of shared identity. If you want to establish your credentials as a banker, you may need to dress for the expectations your audience will have for a banker. If you develop software, the expectations will likely be different. If you are a creative artist, they will be different again. If you are an interior designer presenting your ideas for a new boutique hotel, why not show the audience your understanding of how well-chosen colors, textures, and accessories create a look with your personal ensemble? If you are seeking funding to continue excavating a Wari village in the Andes of Peru, wearing the latest Italian silk suit will probably raise some questions about where the funds are going. But ripped and dirty field clothes will not show respect for the audience and occasion.

Some reasonable compromise between highly formal and extremely casual is usually needed. If you aren't sure about the right choice, or if you just aren't that interested in fashion, get some advice from someone you respect. Many companies offer the services of fashion consultants who can assess your looks, help you update them, and work with you to put together a wardrobe that can serve as your "business uniform."

What Is Business Attire?

A conservative, well-cut suit with a neatly pressed shirt or blouse is the standard attire for ordinary business presentations. In most business environments, a woman's suit can include either slacks or a skirt, although a skirt of modest length is the more conservative choice. Hose should be worn with skirts, and conservative, well-polished shoes with heels of no more than two inches complete the look.

If you are unsure of how formally you should dress, ask the organizers of the event. If you are still unsure, dress more formally rather than less. Dressing slightly more formally demonstrates respect for the occasion and for the audience and can help establish your credibility.

Women have a great variety of choices. Choose what is appropriate for the occasion and attractive without being too revealing or suggestive. Avoid sleeveless dresses or blouses; they do not create an impression of strength.

A traditional, more conservative, view is that darker shades of blue and gray are the most appropriate suit colors for men and women. Solid-color or subtly patterned shirts and blouses and conservative ties or scarves complete the traditional look.

A less conservative view is that women can and should wear more striking colors. Jewel-tone suits or jackets—ruby red, sapphire blue, emerald green—can be appropriate and attractive when the garment is conservatively styled. More vibrantly colored men's shirts, and ties that  closely match the shirt, can also be appropriate. These richer and brighter tones should be chosen to complement skin tone and hair color.

Both men and women should choose accessories that are conservative and limited. Avoid distractions for yourself and your audience. Jewelry should be minimal, conservative, and of good quality. More than one ring on each hand is distracting. If worn, earrings, necklaces, and bracelets should be discreet.

What Is Business Casual?

"Business casual" is an oxymoron to some people and a mystery to most others. It can have many different meanings. It changes from company to company and even from one department to another. Do whatever you can to discover the specifics of what "business casual" means for the occasion. Think about your goals and the expectations of your audience. Dressing just slightly more formally than your audience will give you an air of authority without appearing out of place.

Clean, well-pressed, and well-fitted clothes are a must. If wearing a knit shirt, choose a collared shirt such as a polo or golf shirt rather than a simple T-shirt. Well-pressed khaki or navy blue pants are generally a better choice than jeans. A cardigan sweater lets you complete an outfit and remain comfortable in an air-conditioned room.

Again, women have a great many choices. Choose clothing that is simple and well-fitted, comfortable and not too revealing. Avoid extremes of color or style. Bare arms or legs are distracting and do not give a message of strength; consider pants if a skirt and hose are not appropriate. Avoid sandals, open-toed shoes, and athletic shoes unless you are speaking poolside or courtside. Accessories should remain reasonably conservative and limited to avoid becoming distracting. Costume jewelry may be appropriate but should still be minimal and of good quality.

Personal Grooming for the Business Environment

Hair, makeup (if any), and hands and nails are important parts of your overall appearance. Following these guidelines will enhance the impression you make.

Hair

Your hair should be clean and styled in a conservative and flattering manner. If you have had the same hairstyle for several years, get an honest and objective opinion about it. Extremely long hair on women as well as men can be distracting. If you decide to make a change, invest in a good cut. And do so a week before your presentation. This will give you time to get used to the new you. If youth is desirable in your field, consider coloring gray hair. Consult a professional hairdresser for an opinion on color. Lighter colors are generally recommended.

Don't let your hair cover your eyebrows or hang in your face. People need to see your eyes and your facial expressions. Continually brushing or tossing aside your hair is extremely distracting. Men and women should use hair spray if needed. Beards and mustaches should be neatly trimmed. They should not cover your lips.

Makeup

Makeup should be used to enhance you, not hide you or re-create you. As with your hair, you may decide to update your look. Free makeovers are available at the cosmetic counters in reputable department and specialty stores and can be a great way to get suggestions on how to update your look. Explain your purpose to the makeup artist, or choose an artist with a look you find appropriate.

Stay with subtle colors that work well with both your skin tone and the outfit you plan to wear. If you tend to perspire, avoid makeup that can melt and run. Powder can help prevent shine for men as well as women. If you will be speaking under bright lights, more makeup may be appropriate. Bright lights tend to wash out your natural color. If you are speaking on television, ask if a makeup artist will be provided and how much time you should allow for your makeup session.

Hands and Nails

Your hands should be clean and your nails well manicured. If you polish your nails, clear or conservative polishes in peach, pink, and bronze tones are best. Men should not use nail polish unless it is customary among the men in the audience. Avoid having extremely long nails or extreme differences in the length of your nails. Avoid very dark or very brightly colored polish. Do not use stencils, patterns, or rhinestones on your nails if you want to be taken seriously.

Finally, before your presentation begins, ask a colleague to give you a quick once-over just to make sure that buttons are buttoned, zippers are zipped, static electricity hasn't left one trouser leg attached to your shin, and so on. You have enough to think about!

Summary

Whether or not they should be, your dress and overall appearance are important sources of nonverbal information. Your listeners will make quick and often subconscious judgments about you based on the visual clues you give. If the initial judgments are positive, you will find a more receptive audience. If the judgments are negative, it can be very hard—even impossible—to overcome the unfavorable impression.

Your goals should affect your choice of clothing. If you want to emphasize similarities between you and your listeners you may want to dress as they do. If you want to be seen as an expert, then more formal dress or clothing that identifies you as an expert in a particular field may be appropriate. If you are in doubt about what is appropriate, ask ahead of time. If still in doubt, dress more formally rather than less. Conservative choices that do not distract the audience from your message are generally best. Neatness and cleanliness are a must. Your clothes should be clean, well fitted, and in good condition. Your skin, hair, and nails should also be clean and well cared for. Your appearance should show self-respect as well as respect of your listeners and of the occasion.

PART THREE

DELIVERING YOUR
PRESENTATION

You can do a lot of observing just by watching.

YOGI BERRA

Your Body Speaks

The Power of Nonverbal Delivery Skills

The ability to communicate with fellow human beings makes us what we are. Inventions such as writing, the telegraph, the telephone, e-mail, and electronic slide presentations have contributed immeasurably to our ability to communicate with our fellow human beings. As helpful as all these modes of communication are, try to imagine how difficult our lives would be if a worldwide virus of the vocal cords took away our ability to talk to one another. What would you do?

Chances are you would quickly resort to pointing, demonstrating, nodding yes, or shaking your head no—in short, putting to use any experiences you have had playing charades!

We all know that we can use these methods if we need to. But we probably don't pay much attention to how much we do use these methods because we can! These ways of communicating are actually much more than just alternatives. They supplement, reinforce, emphasize, soften, and add subtle but powerful meanings and shades of meanings to our communications.

We use them every time we speak. Our dialogues are rich with them and much richer because of them. We need to use these nonverbal means of communication to deliver a complete presentation. They matter. But while we have a great deal of formal training in the complexities of spoken and written language, we have very little conscious awareness of our use of body language.

Let's look at how nonverbal communication can replace words. But even more importantly—at least unless that epidemic vocal cord virus really does occur—let's look at how it can change, supplement, support, or contradict those carefully chosen words you use when speaking to a group.

We all know language itself can be divided into nouns, verbs, objects, pronouns, prepositions, and so on. Let's look at some of the categories of nonverbal communication.

The Varieties of Nonverbal Communication

Nonverbal communication can be divided into two major categories: prosody and paralanguage. *Prosody* refers to the qualities of voice and vocal delivery that change the meaning of the verbal communication used. Volume, inflection, tone, rhythm, and pacing are examples of prosody. Humor and sarcasm are largely dependent on prosody.

Paralanguage refers to communication apart from the verbal communication. Paralanguage changes or supplements the meaning of language. Paralanguage itself can be divided into two categories: vocal and nonvocal.

Vocal paralanguage can be heard but can't be found in the dictionary. Laughter, crying, sighing, grunting, snorting, and giggling are all examples of vocal paralanguage. Nonvocal paralanguage is often referred to as body language. Variations in posture, gestures, facial expressions, and eye contact patterns are all nonvocal paralanguage. Obvious examples include slouching, waving, smiling, and winking. More subtle examples include slightly raising eyebrows, narrowing the lips, and turning slightly to avoid facing someone straight on. Proxemics—the use of space (for example, how close we come and how we position ourselves in relation to others)—is another aspect of body language.[1]

Prosody and paralanguage are commonly referred to as nonverbal delivery skills when used as part of your delivery of information in a presentation.

The normal challenge and stress of speaking to a group will often affect your ability to use these delivery skills naturally and effectively. When you become the salient object, things feel different. You become self-conscious, hyperaware of your body. The fight-or-flight response battles with the knowledge that you must stay where you are and speak—and deliver a monologue! The body reacts instinctively. It searches for ways to feel more comfortable. You may stiffen or shift your weight. You may put your hands in your pockets and keep them there or hold them together in front of your stomach for many minutes at a time in an instinctive move to protect your vital organs. Your eyes may look away from your listeners or move so quickly that you never focus on anyone. This instinctive response reduces the feeling of danger by eliminating the direct look that can escalate into a confrontation.

Awareness of how *your* body responds to this self-consciousness is the first step to returning to more natural, conversational uses of body language. Practice and feedback—video feedback is by far the best—are both needed to become truly skillful in delivering your message well.

Consistency between the verbal and nonverbal parts of your message is the key to looking natural, comfortable, and confident. It is an important part of establishing credibility in the minds of listeners. This is especially true when you are speaking to people who don't already know you well. Remember the fundamental attribution error from chapter 4? The bottom line is this: to be most effective, *how* you say something needs to be consistent with *what* you say.[2]

The irony is that most people need to learn how to act natural when in front of a group. If this seems silly, think about what it takes to practice a specific sports skill until it become natural, comfortable, and fluid. Then think of how it takes less energy and effort to use the skill as you get better. Now think of the power you have when you master it. The physical components of speaking to a group, of using your nonverbal speaking skills to support your message, are no different. But there is one big difference between learning to use nonverbal communication effectively and learning a sport.

Learning to use nonverbal communication doesn't involve learning anything new! You won't have to build new muscles or stretch them in new ways. You won't have to improve your hand-eye coordination. You won't have to spend hundreds of dollars on equipment, either. You will simply be reminding your body of what it does when you aren't self-conscious. And because the skills aren't new it doesn't take years to master them. It just takes consciousness, reminders, and practice. When you start to use your regular, everyday nonverbal communication habits when speaking to a group, you will have regained the ability to speak in a natural, confident, and comfortable way.

How Important Is Good Nonverbal Communication?

Good nonverbal communication, the kind that supports your verbal message instead of contradicting it or distracting your listeners, is very important. But it is not a substitute for good content. Content that is clear, well organized, and tailored to your audience is the foundation of any successful presentation. But good content is not a substitute for good nonverbal communication, either. If your nonverbal content undermines your verbal message, you will not succeed in winning over the minds and hearts of your listeners. You need to "say it like you mean it."

> A word, a look, an accent, may affect the destiny not only of individuals, but of nations. He is a bold man who calls anything a trifle.
>
> ANDREW CARNEGIE

Understanding and using the nonverbal delivery skills described on the following pages will help you look and sound more natural, confident, and comfortable. You will communicate confidence and honesty. Your genuine self—the self so apparent in your frequent dialogues with others—will work for you!

Good Nonverbal Delivery Skills Stop the Downward Spiral

Remember the downward spiral from chapter 2? You learned that when you worry about other people noticing your anxiety you become even more anxious. Again, remember the concept of fundamental attribution error. You sense that listeners who don't know you well will make an error in judging your knowledge, ability, or conviction if they notice signs of nervousness as you speak. That anxiety also causes more anxiety.

These are reasons why having good nonverbal delivery skills is so important. When you use these skills, you hide any residual anxiety you feel. No one will be able to tell that you don't feel as comfortable and as confident as you look and sound! Just knowing this will help reduce your anxiety. When you know that others cannot see or hear your anxiety, the downward spiral loses a lot of strength. It is likely to fizzle out like a hurricane over the desert. You will be able to let go of much of your anxiety. As you master the use of these skills you will be able to focus more easily on what you want to say, and on how best to say it, at this time and to this group.

These changes won't take place overnight. Your body, drawing on all its Stone Age wisdom, will protest when you ask it to stop protecting its vital organs by clasping both hands in front of its stomach. It will protest when you ask it to stand balanced and tall instead of shifting back and forth, getting ready to run. It will even protest when you ask it to finish a point, stop, and take a deep breath: "I'm standing here *totally* exposed, *greatly* outnumbered, and you want me to *relax? Are you crazy?*"

Practice, coaching, and video feedback are the fastest ways to learn to integrate good nonverbal delivery skills with your spoken content. Even if you've been making presentations for years you should invest time and energy in having an unbiased coach work with you. Some of the most experienced speakers actually have very poor delivery skills. These ineffective behaviors have become habits over the years. They may have served to make the speaker feel more comfortable when he started making presentations. That doesn't mean they work well. But who's going to be the one to tell the CEO that he annoys everyone when he stands onstage constantly "washing" his hands?

Steel and Sparks

The two types of nonverbal delivery skills are "steel" skills and "spark" skills. Using both is the secret to looking, and becoming, comfortable and confident.

Let's take a closer look at how you can use each skill to deliver a natural and energized presentation. To do this we will look at how each skill is used in the most common and natural type of human communication: dialogue. This awareness will be the foundation for applying the skills when delivering a monologue.

Steel Skills: A Closer Look

Steel skills are the foundation of your delivery style. The three steel skills are eye contact, pace (including the pause), and posture. These skills communicate strength, confidence, honesty, and relaxation. Master the steel skills to communicate with authority and composure.

Eye Contact

What are your immediate responses to these phrases?

- A steady gaze
- She looked me right in the eye

And to these?

- She looked down at her feet
- Shifty eyes

Steady eye contact is one of the most important body language skills. It is a powerful way to communicate confidence and honesty. Let's look at how we use eye contact when engaged in unselfconscious dialogue.

When the eyes say one thing, and the tongue another, a practiced man relies on the language of the first.

RALPH WALDO EMERSON

In one-on-one conversations, and when speaking in very small groups, most people naturally look each other in the eye. The speaker shows a desire to "connect with" the listener. He also observes the listener's reaction—does she understand, show confusion or concern, agree or disagree?

In front of a group, this usually changes. Shifty eyes are the norm for unskilled speakers. And then comes the bad advice: "Look at the back wall.

Look at their foreheads. Pretend they are in their underwear. Imagine them naked."

To establish and maintain effective eye contact, try the suggestions in table 14.1 instead.

Table 14.1 Eye Contact

Strong eye contact communicates confidence, honesty, and interest in your listeners.

Here's how:	*Here's why:*
Begin and end your presentation by sweeping the audience with your eyes.	This honors your natural tendency to check the situation over and gather people together.
During the rest of the presentation, look one person in the eyes while you deliver a point—a phrase or sentence. Aim for approximately three to six seconds of eye contact before moving on.	You communicate confidence, honesty, interest in your audience but not aggression. You can watch for listeners' reactions, read your audience, and respond.
Look at people in all parts of the audience—front, back, sides, the third balcony.	All the listeners will feel more involved and valued. Knowing you will see them helps keep them looking at you!
Use a seemingly random pattern, and avoid focusing a disproportionate amount of time on "decision makers."	You will avoid falling into obvious patterns and will avoid being perceived as giving someone preferential treatment.
Look at people when speaking. If you need to break eye contact to think or to check your notes or visual aids, stop talking—pause and breathe—while doing so.	You avoid the "data dump" syndrome, encourage yourself to take appropriate pauses, and increase the strength of your connection with your audience.
Learn about and honor individual and cultural preferences for varying lengths of eye contact.	You avoid appearing evasive, insensitive, or overbearing. You establish rapport and respect.

A direct stare is typical of the most out-and-out aggression . . . A professional lecturer takes some time to train himself to look directly at members of his audience . . . Even though he is in such a dominant position, there are so many of them, all staring (from the safety of their seats) that he experiences a basic and initially uncontrollable fear of them . . . He has all his intellectual worries about the qualities of his performance and its reception . . . but the massed threat-stare is an additional and more fundamental hazard for him.—*Desmond Morris in* The Naked Ape

Pace and Pause

When engaged in dialogue, we usually speak at a pace that is relaxed, measured, and varied with our emotion and level of enthusiasm. Our natural speech

patterns are much like music. Variations in tempo, pace, and the frequency and length of the pauses—the "rests"—communicate varying degrees of emphasis and a wide range of emotions.

Some of us speak more quickly, some at a slower, more measured pace. Our own thinking styles and cultural differences are reflected, as is the nature of our content. But we all vary our pace, our tone, and the frequency and length of our pauses.

Pauses are punctuation in speech. Pauses are commas, periods, colons, and semicolons. They are the indentations at the beginning of new paragraphs and the white space at the end of a chapter. We wouldn't think of writing a memo, much less a story, without using punctuation.

The challenges—intellectual, emotional, and physical—of speaking before a group can combine to rob us of the natural timing we use so skillfully when in dialogue with other people. The release of adrenaline that is part of the natural stress response will often cause us to speak more rapidly than we normally do. And I have heard people say, "The faster I talk the sooner I get to sit down!"

Your listeners need time to process the information you deliver. They need to think about what it means to them. Pausing gives them opportunities to do this. It gives them time to experience the emotional response your information brings—to feel the excitement, the enthusiasm, the concern. To keep your great natural timing, try the tips in table 14.2.

> The notes I handle no better than many pianists. But the pauses between the notes—ah, that is where the art resides.
>
> ARTUR SCHNABEL

Posture

Your listeners will begin to assess your confidence well before you begin to speak. From the moment they first see you, the way you hold your body suggests to them how you feel about yourself and your information. Fortunately,

Table 14.2 Pace and Pause

Pausing and pacing your rate of speech help you speak naturally and comfortably.

Here's how:	*Here's why:*
Slow down—consciously. If you wonder whether you are speaking too fast, you are. If you never thought about this, you probably are speaking too fast.	Adrenaline (and the desire to sit down) makes you speak more quickly. Slow down to sound more natural, genuine, and comfortable.
Slow down more.	Your listeners can process and appreciate your information. Remember, it is not what you give them that matters; it is what they get. Don't drown them.
Punctuate your speech with frequent pauses of varied lengths.	Pauses are your commas, colons, semi-colons, periods, indentations, and white space. They add meaning, emphasis, and interest.
Breathe deeply when you pause. Use longer pauses to exhale. Feel yourself relax as you exhale. Then breathe again.	You need oxygen. Breathing when you pause gives you something productive to do during pauses. This makes it much easier to eliminate the static of extraneous filler words.
Banish "static" from your lines of communication. Eliminate fillers such as "ah . . . um . . . you know . . . actually . . . like."[3]	You sound more confident and knowledgeable. You have time to breathe. You avoid annoying people who tend to count "ums."
Pause and breathe when you "take care of other business," for example, check your notes, change your slides, let your listeners read your slides, let listeners take notes.	You seem confident, relaxed, and in control. You create anticipation for your next comment. You communicate concern for the needs of your listeners.

Talking is like playing on the harp; there is as much in laying the hand on the strings to stop their vibrations as in twanging them to bring out their music.—*Oliver Wendell Holmes Sr.*

good posture is not exotic. It doesn't take years of practice. You can do it right now: practice every day, and use it for a variety of reasons throughout your presentations.

If you are walking to the front of the room or onto a stage or speaking platform, keep your head up and your shoulders back. If you are seated where your listeners can see you before you begin to speak, whether in a chair onstage or behind a table as a panelist, remember that you are already communicating to them. When seated, sit upright, hands resting in your lap or, if at a table, on top of the table.

Developing the habit of maintaining a relaxed, nondefensive, confident posture is the first way you will master the symptoms of the fight-or-flight response. Many mind-body disciplines, including yoga and the martial arts, teach the importance of posture. Good posture increases both confidence and the ability to relax (table 14.3). It opens your chest and lungs so you can breathe deeply. This gives your body and brain the oxygen they need to help you perform at your best.

Spark Skills: A Closer Look

Spark skills add energy, enthusiasm, and variety to your style. The four spark skills are facial expressions, voice, gestures, and movement (including the use of space). How you use the sparks skills can vary greatly with the nature of your content. Master the spark skills to keep the audience attentive and engaged.

Facial Expressions

Facial expressions can often transcend cultural norms and cultural differences. Infants respond to facial expressions long before they understand the meaning of words. Throughout life humans continue to "speak" with and "listen" to facial expressions when communicating with words and sentences.

Facial expressions are not unique to humans. Many animals use facial expressions to communicate a variety of messages, but humans can communicate a richer and wider variety of meaning than any other species. When

Table 14.3 Posture

Good posture will communicate confidence, energy, openness, and relaxation.

Here's how:	*Here's why:*
Stand with your feet several inches apart. Balance your weight evenly over the arches of your feet. Keep your legs and knees relaxed.	Your stance is balanced, strong, but not overly aggressive. You take full advantage of your height, increasing your personal presence.
Stand tall. Hold your head high and your shoulders back. Lift your torso.	You appear confident and energetic. You open your diaphragm for easy breathing.
Stand firmly. Avoid shifting or rocking back and forth.	You look both confident and relaxed. You will find more effective ways (gestures, movement) to dissipate your natural energy.
Stand facing the entire audience, no matter where you are on the speaking platform, with your toes pointing to the middle of the back wall. This will put you in the best position to be seen by the majority of the audience.	You can establish eye contact with any member of the audience—all listeners will feel included. You will reduce the likelihood of moving too frequently in an attempt to see all sections of the audience.
Rest your arms at your sides when not gesturing purposefully. Avoid "protecting your soft underbelly" with locked arms or wringing hands.	You will look more confident, relaxed, and nondefensive. Your hands and arms will be free to use in appropriate gestures.

Our posture says a lot about our inner life. If we appear hunched over, it is probably because we are inwardly collapsed. If we strut about with our chest sticking out and our nose in the air we are undoubtedly posturing, parading our inflated sense of self. Our bearing and our gestures contain valuable clues about our emotional state—it is hard to lie with the body.—*From* Living Yoga, *Edited by G. Feuerstein and S. Bodian* we engage in dialogue, even on the phone, our faces communicate a wide range of emotions.

Many adults have become quite skilled at not using facial expressions—of cultivating the ability to maintain a poker face or display only those emotions we believe are socially acceptable. We hide our feelings behind a mask of "professionalism." Over time, this can reduce our natural tendency to allow our facial expressions to support our spoken messages.[4]

When you make a presentation, self-consciousness, intense concentration on content, and fear may reduce your natural tendency to communicate freely using facial expressions. When this happens, you often won't look as if you really mean what you say. This inconsistency between the verbal and nonverbal messages can be very disconcerting to your listeners. It can interfere with your ability to communicate confidence, honesty, enthusiasm—or any other emotion supporting your message. It can strongly affect your listeners' subconscious assessment of you and your material.

A conscious awareness of the importance of facial expressions, and of your own individual, natural facial expressions, is the key to using them to help create the look and feel of dialogue with your listeners (table 14.4).

Voice

Variety is the key to a voice that is both natural and conversational. Variations in tone, pitch, pace, and volume create the sound and feeling of dialogue. Tone is vital; changes in tone often completely change the meaning of our words.

> A man's style is his mind's voice. Wooden minds, wooden voices.
>
> RALPH WALDO EMERSON

If you have not heard your voice except on your own answering machine or voice mail message, it's time to do so. Record yourself speaking for at least several minutes. (Using a tape recorder is fine, but using a video camera to capture the relationship between your voice, your face, and your

Table 14.4 Facial Expressions

Varied and natural facial expressions communicate sincerity and reinforce your message.

Here's how:	*Here's why:*
Use a variety of appropriate facial expressions throughout your presentation.	Your expressions will support your content. Your message will be presented more consistently. You will communicate confidence and honesty.
At times, show your emotion rather than telling it. A big, warm smile does a better job of saying "I'm delighted to be here" than the words do without the smile.	You will encourage people to look at you and increase their ability to stay focused on both your verbal and nonverbal messages. You will evoke more emotional responses and improve your listeners' ability to remember.
Smile frequently, unless the mood is extremely sober or somber. Anxiety can make us smile less frequently than we might otherwise.	A smile communicates warmth, good humor, and relaxation. And it can be contagious, improving the mood and receptivity of your listeners.
Increase your conscious awareness of the variety and power of facial expressions. Watch television with the sound off. Use language to describe the emotions the actors and actresses communicate. Then recreate the expressions looking in a mirror.	You will develop a better understanding of how much is enough and how much is too much and will feel more comfortable using facial expressions.

The human face is really like one of those Oriental Gods: a whole group of faces juxtaposed on different planes; it is impossible to see them all simultaneously.—*Marcel Proust*

other body language is even more valuable.) Your voice should sound different when it is recorded than it does while you are speaking.

We hear through our bones, not just our ears. Bones are a good conductor of sound. Added to and blended with what we hear through our ears, the sounds we hear through the bones of our body are different from what others hear. A recording device picks up only the sounds that travel through the air and, even electronically reproduced, will give us a sound closer to what others hear. Once you are used to the difference, listen closely for pitch, tone, modulation, and rate of speech. Work on any issues you find by repeating the same sentence or short paragraph over and over until you achieve the desired result.

Although deeper, richer tones are appropriate for most speaking events, a monotonous voice is deadly. Our natural dialogue tends to be greatly varied in modulation, pitch, and even the rate of speech. Research has shown that when we speak louder, as we do when trying to be heard over a din, we also tend to speak with purer, more musical tones. This happens regardless of musical ability or training. Researchers believe it may be caused by unconsciously trying to capitalize on the emotional qualities of music to capture our listeners' attention.[5] Confidence in your material helps you speak naturally but is no guarantee of a voice that communicates with confidence and energy. Get to know your voice, and practice making any changes you know will improve it.

The voice is a wind instrument. You supply your voice the fuel it needs when you breathe frequently and deeply. This means pausing—which may take some effort at first but will give needed variety to your pace of speech.

To add variety to your voice, try the tips in table 14.5.

Gestures

I have had literally hundreds of clients ask, "What should I do with my hands?" The simple answer is that you should do exactly what you do (with a few notable exceptions) when speaking one-on-one or in a small group. The problem with this answer is that most of us don't know what we usually do. We use gestures naturally and unselfconsciously when engaged in dialogue with others. Because our gestures are so natural, we use them without much conscious awareness. The heightened self-awareness—being the center of attention—makes us question our gestures. The sense of vulnerability that comes with delivering a monologue will often cause us to be overly self-protective with our gestures. Most inexperienced speakers will clasp their hands in front

Table 14.5 Voice

Variations in your voice support both your content and your emotional tone.

Here's how:	*Here's why:*
Breathe deeply before you speak and when you pause between points.	You will have the breath you need to produce the sound you need and to maintain a strong voice.
Speak with enough volume to be heard easily by everyone in the audience.	Your message can be heard. You sound confident.
Ask for feedback on your volume. If you think you might need a microphone, you do. A cordless microphone is the simplest type to use.	You can speak naturally, without straining. A cordless microphone gives you freedom of movement and reduces the danger of tripping on a cord.
Vary your volume.	You will make it easier for your listeners to pay attention.
Increase your volume at times.	You will communicate importance, urgency, and confidence.
Decrease your volume at times.	You will create a feeling of intimacy, of a secret being shared. People may listen more closely.
Vary your tone.	Your voice will support your content and emotion.
Use higher tones at times.	You will communicate excitement, enthusiasm, or energy.
Use lower tones at times.	You will communicate gravity and conviction.

There is no index of character so sure as the voice.—*Benjamin Disraeli* of their chest, stomach, or groin. It's no coincidence that this places them directly in front of our "soft underbelly" to protect our vital organs.

While this served our ancestors as protection against threats to their life, it doesn't help us to relax, to look confident, or to take advantage of gestures to help us communicate with our listeners.

Gestures can be subtle and effective at the same time . . . for most of us, the more subtle a gesture is the more persuasive it is.

ANNETTE SIMMONS

Gestures have purpose. They help illustrate, emphasize, and punctuate our speech. Author and storyteller Annette Simmons explains, "gestures can add meaning to your story, intensify your message, and create a stage upon which your story is played . . . to increase the intensity of emotion, to intentionally send an incongruent message, or just to have a bit of fun."[6]

If you really can't remember using any specific gestures, ask yourself these questions.

- Have you ever nodded your head to say yes or shaken it to say no? Have you ever held up your hand, palm out and fingers pointing up, to signal some-one to stop? If so, you've used what researchers call symbolic gestures.

- Have you ever pointed a finger to show someone that something is "over there" or "that way"? If so, you've used indicative gestures.

- Have you ever noticed yourself emphasizing a point by "chopping" the air, holding your hand in a fairly rigid position as you move it up and down? This is an example of a motor gesture. Motor gestures are usually re-peated several times, but they often don't have any obvious relationship to the content of the speech.

- Have you ever noticed that when you are having trouble finding the right word, using gestures can help you remember it? Drawing small circles in the air with your hand or using your hand to mimic the way an object may be used or held can help you access your vocabulary, or lexicon. These are lexical gestures. Studies have shown that when speakers are prevented from using their hands, they take longer to access words or even fail to come up with them at all.[7]

Most of us have a very low level of awareness of our own repertoire of gestures and can be uncomfortable gesturing when in front of a group. To increase your comfort, increase your awareness of your habits. For the next few days, observe your behavior when you speak with enthusiasm or urgency or to instruct or explain.

Table 14.6 Gestures

Gestures—both subtle and expansive—add meaning and increase understanding.

Here's how:	*Here's why:*
Observe your gestures as you communicate with others.	You will become more aware of your own gestural habits and repertoire. You will be more comfortable gesturing in front of a group when acting naturally.
Observe the gestures others use when speaking.	You will discover what works well for others and may expand your repertoire.
Use a variety of gestures.	You will avoid looking mechanical, stiff, or overly repetitive.
Use subtle gestures of the head and upper body as well as of the hands and arms.	You will be more natural and persuasive. You will increase the understanding and emotional involvement of the audience.
Use more expansive gestures of the whole arm and body.	You will look confident and energetic and will tend to project your voice.
Illustrate objects, images, and concepts with gestures.	You will help your audience visualize and understand your material.
Avoid gesturing continually with just the hands and wrists.	You will avoid looking like a dolphin.
Drop your arms to rest when not gesturing with purpose.	You will look more relaxed and open. You will avoid nervous hand clasping, hand wringing, or other distracting habits.

Gestures and facial expressions do indeed communicate, as anyone can prove by turning off the sound on a television set and asking watchers to characterize the speakers from the picture alone.—*Peter Farb*

Finally, remember that recent research provides a growing body of evidence that using gestures may help speakers access their vocabulary more easily and quickly—one more excellent reason not to keep your hands in your pockets or clasped behind your back!

Table 14.6 contains suggestions on using gestures.

Movement

How long can an average person remain interested in looking at a statue? Probably not as long as you will be speaking.

Standing still, especially if you're partially hidden by a lectern or table, does nothing to help you connect with your listeners. It increases the feeling of separation and therefore reduces any similarity between the monologue you must present and the dialogue of daily speech. To help keep the attention of the audience and to show confidence, natural and purposeful, energetic movement is an important skill to master.

> Things in motion sooner catch the eye than what not stirs.
>
> SHAKESPEARE

Movement allows you to minimize the distance between you and members of the audience. It demonstrates comfort with your environment. It can also demonstrate a sense of ownership of the space available to you, implying a sense of ownership and command of your material and the occasion.

Movement does not mean pacing. But like pacing, it helps you relax, burn off adrenaline-induced energy, and think more clearly.

Of course, movement is not a skill to use in front of a camera during an interview or video teleconference. Then your other skills must be tapped to communicate energy, confidence, and ownership.

Whenever possible and appropriate, choose or arrange your venue so that you can move freely—and safely. Table 14.7 provides additional tips.

Reading Your Listeners' Body Language

A good working knowledge of body language requires not just an awareness of what you do but also of what your listeners do. You know that your true feelings will tend to "leak" into your communications through your body

Table 14.7 Movement

Movement—purposeful but intermittent—both increases attention and communicates authority.

Here's how:	Here's why:
Use most of the space available to you at some point during your presentation.	You communicate a sense of ownership of the venue and of the occasion, indicating confidence and authority.
Move intermittently; punctuate your movement with periods of erect and evenly balanced posture in one place.	You avoid the impression of nervous pacing yet reap the benefits of increased audience attention.
To move, establish eye contact with an individual in the audience; move toward her while speaking to her.	Your movement has purpose; continued eye contact keeps your movement focused and intentional.
Vary the direction, pace, and distance of your movement; match your movement to the nature and tone of your content.	Your movement will visually support your message. You will move more naturally and avoid inconsistency between your spoken and visual messages.
Move at a natural pace—avoid slow, ponderous, or lethargic movement.	Unnaturally slow movement looks self-conscious and tentative. A quicker, more natural pace is more confident.
Avoid overly aggressive or invasive movement. Generally maintain at least four feet of "social" space between you and your listeners.	Listeners will feel involved without feeling threatened or singled out.

When I rest my feet, my mind also ceases to function.—*J. G. Hamann, quoted in* The Songlines *by Bruce Chatwin* language. So will the true feelings of your listeners. Increasing your ability to read body language is an excellent way for you to evaluate whether or not you are communicating effectively with your listeners.

Interpreting body language is an art, not a science. Individual habits, cultural differences, even the temperature in the room can all affect body language. Be flexible in your interpretations of the body language of others.

Watch your listeners as much as possible during your presentation. What you learn from their body language may help you tailor your material more effectively; recognize when you need to clarify, explain, or offer to stop and answer questions; and help you deliver at the right pace.

> As I grow older I pay less attention to what men say. I just watch what they do.
>
> ANDREW CARNEGIE

Remember that body language is always open to interpretation. Crossed arms may mean a listener is chilled, not defensive. Listeners might be reacting to one of their own thoughts. But you will always learn more about your listeners by looking at and talking to them rather than anything else in the room!

Table 14.8 lists some common components of body language and their likely meanings. It can be used to raise your awareness of your listeners' needs during your presentation.

Here's a tip for using body language to eliminate the awkward moment that can occur at the close of your presentation. If the audience seems uncertain that you have finished, don't shrug and say something like "That's all I have." Instead, pause. Drop both arms to your sides. Say a firm "Thank you." It will be very clear that you have finished. Hold your ground. Even if there will be no question-and-answer session, don't rush off. Standing a few seconds will mean you finish on a note of confidence.

Table 14.8 Interpreting Body Language

You will discover what works well for others and may expand your repertoire.

This body language:	*May mean this:*
nodding head	understanding, agreement
shaking head	disagreement, dissension
head cocked to one side	thinking, considering, possible skepticism
narrowed eyes, furrowed brow	thinking, analysis, evaluation
rolling eyes	"that is obvious," "that is impractical," "that is stupid"
rubbing of eyes	suspicion, doubt, disbelief, tiredness
coughing, clearing throat	nervousness, preparation to speak
deep sighing	boredom, impatience, disinterest
light sighing	thoughtfulness, interest
hands in front of mouth	embarrassment, lack of confidence, reluctance to speak
smiling	confidence, friendliness, enjoyment, politeness
smirking	smugness, condescension
leaning back, slumping, turning away	disinterest, detachment
hands chest height, forward, hands open with palms up	seriousness, sincerity, emphasis
counting points on fingers	organization, logic, confidence
steepling of fingers	self-confidence, strength
pointing	singling out, aggressiveness
wagging finger	pedantry, warning, disagreement
arms crossed in front of chest	judgment, resistance, defensiveness
arms open with hands below chest, palms up	helplessness, plea for help, plea for consideration
hands in pockets	relaxation, reservation, lack of involvement
one hand above head	emphasis, differentiation
two hands above head	success, triumph

Summary

Nonverbal communication is a critical component of a successful presentation. Our body language speaks to our listeners even before we say our first word.

The fight-or-flight response is a natural reaction to the stress of public speaking. It often causes us to behave in cautious and defensive ways. These behaviors can increase our nervousness by interfering with our ability to release tension. They can also make us look and sound as if we are not confident or knowledgeable. Using the seven nonverbal delivery skills the same way we do when relaxed, unselfconscious, and confident is the key to great delivery.

Delivery skills can be divided into two groups: "steel" skills and "spark" skills. The three steel skills are eye contact, pace/pause (the pace of speech and use of pauses), and posture. Steel skills are the solid foundation of your delivery style. They communicate strength, confidence, honesty, and composure. Master these steel skills to communicate with both calmness and authority.

Spark skills add energy, emotion, and variety to your style. The four spark skills are facial expressions, voice, gestures, and movement. The use of spark skills can vary greatly with the nature of your content, environment, and purpose. Master your spark skills to keep the audience attentive, engaged, and emotionally involved.

Recognizing and understanding the meaning of your listeners' body language is a great tool for modifying your presentation to meet their needs.

Man is a tool-using animal. Weak in himself and of small stature . . .
he can use tools, can devise tools . . . Without tools
he is nothing, with tools he is all.

THOMAS CARLYLE

Tools of the Trade

Using Notes, Visual Aids, Lecterns, and Microphones

When you use tools such as notes, visual aids, lecterns, and microphones during a presentation, you add one more layer of complexity to all the tasks your mind and body are already doing. Used incorrectly or unnecessarily, they will not only not help you get the job done right, but they can interfere with your presentation and do real damage to your efforts to get results. But used when you need them and when managed well, they can be enormously helpful both to you and to your audience.

One of the major challenges you will face at first is using good nonverbal delivery skills when you also use these tools. A number of questions may come up:

- How can I maintain good eye contact with members of the audience when I use notes or slides?

- Will I lose the attention of the audience if I pause to change a slide?

- How can I create a sense of dialogue if I'm standing behind a lectern?

- Can I still move around the speaking platform if I use a microphone or notes or slides?

For the answers to these and many other questions, keep reading.

Using Notes

When planning a presentation, most people realize that it will be difficult for them to remember everything they plan to say and to say it in the best order. There are three typical responses to this problem. One is to create detailed slides to serve as speaker notes. The second is to write a script for the presentation. The third is to try to memorize the script. Each of these approaches creates new problems.

Putting all (or even most) of the information you want to cover onto slides almost always results in awful slides. They will take too much time to create. They will be too complex for listeners to easily read, understand, or remember.

> **Our memories are card indexes consulted and then returned by authorities whom we do not control.**
>
> CYRIL CONNOLLY

Reading a script word for word will sound stilted and will foster overdependence on the script. It will be almost impossible to create rapport with the audience or to make on-the-spot changes.

Memorizing the script and reciting it from memory will cause many of the same problems as reading the script. Since memory is unreliable under stress, the speaker becomes extremely vulnerable to memory loss. Memorizing is also just plain inefficient. It's a terrible use of the speaker's time.

The solution is to use notes with skill and without apologizing. Would you apologize for coming to a meeting with an agenda, for making a list to take grocery shopping, or for bringing a trail guide and a compass when hiking in the mountains? Of course not.

Know that when you check your notes you are not cheating. You are demonstrating that you "plan your work and work your plan." You are well organized. You have more sense than to spend your valuable time memorizing your presentation. Checking your notes demonstrates your commitment to giving your audience full value. And, even better, it is possible to demonstrate all these points and not remain behind a lectern. The following method for checking notes is worth practicing until you can do it with confidence and comfort.

1. Walk to the front and center of the speaking area or platform, leaving the lectern off to the side or behind you. Cover a few points in a conversational manner. You will know when you are close to finishing a point and need to check your notes for the next one. Finish the point you are on with a confident tone and demeanor.

2. Do not start the next sentence. Instead, pause to let the audience think about the completed point. Turn, walk briskly to the lectern, and face your notes straight on (rather than leaning toward them from a distance or looking at them over your shoulder while your body faces the audience).

3. Read your notes until you have all the information you need. Really read—do not rush. The more deliberate you are, the more confident you will look and the more likely you will be to actually see the notes. This may sound simplistic, but many people who first try this during a seminar say "Can I try that again? I looked, but I didn't really see anything." The second time they try it they say "That really works!"

4. Look up, and then talk. When you know what you want to talk about next, look up and make eye contact with a member of the audience. Walk toward that person as you begin to talk about the next point.

What's the secret to doing this with perfect confidence? Separate each action. Don't talk when you are walking or reading. Look up first, move away from your notes, and then speak. Allow the pauses to create expectation in the minds of your listeners. With just a little practice this technique will become easy to use. Now you never have to worry about leaving out something important again!

Using Visual Aids

Imagine you have made the investment in time and money to travel to a major industry conference. You have arrived at the first presentation, hoping it will be very valuable. The speaker's first words are "Before I begin, I want you to know that this entire presentation is available on our Web site."

You will probably wonder if you should have come! Still, chances are you will stay to listen, hoping the speaker will add insights, develop the ideas in the presentation more fully, or otherwise just entertain you. But if the speaker asks for the lights to be turned out, turns his back on the audience, faces the screen, and begins to read his slides aloud, you'll be very disappointed.

Let's make sure you never do *that* to your listeners. A closer look at the experience just described will help you do a much better job when you use visual aids.

One of the first facts to know about using slides is this: if you turn off the lights, the audience will sleep. Here's the quick explanation of what happens. The full explanation, including why it happens, is in the sidebar below.

Darkness causes the body to produce melatonin, a hormone that helps make us sleepy. But do you really want to encourage your listeners to sleep during your presentation or even to get drowsy? If not, leave the lights on.

How bright must the light be to inhibit the production of extra melatonin? The threshold is that of ordinary fluorescent lighting. Maximum inhibition of melatonin production occurs after exposure to intense light for one hour.[1] In other words, bright light helps keep us wide awake. Obviously, keeping the lights on fully will not be possible if you are using visual aids such as slides that require a dark room to give the images enough contrast to be seen clearly. So what are your options?

First, do everything you can when designing your visual aids so that they can be easily seen in a room that is dim but not completely dark. All the design principals discussed in chapter 12—high contrast, simplicity, large and legible fonts—will help you do this.

Second, the more lumens your projector puts out, the better the image will be in a partially lit room. Find out how bright the projector will be. If you have a choice, request the brightest projector available. Most newer projectors have at least 1,000 lumens, enough to allow the room lights to be kept on at least part of the way. If you can't get a bright projector, find out if you can vary the lighting in the room. Many times it is possible to turn off the lights in the front of the room while the lights in the middle and back of the room stay on. This increases the visibility of your slides without plunging the room into darkness.

If all else fails, have frequent "light breaks." Can you design your presentation so you have intervals without slides and turn the lights up during those intervals? Holding intermittent short question-and-answer sessions is a great way to do this. Encourage your listeners to go outside into the sunshine on breaks.

Finally, consider telling your listeners about the effects of darkness and of the resulting melatonin doses they receive. If they understand the importance of getting out into bright light on breaks, they are more likely to do it. If the worst happens and somebody falls asleep, nobody will think it was just because of you or your subject matter!

Using visual aids well can be the difference between a ho-hum presentation and a really great one. The tips that follow will help you use your slides to add real value and maintain the audience's focus, so vital to a truly powerful presentation.

Nature's Night Moves

Our ancestors lived till morning by sleeping at night. Most of us sleep at night. Human "night owls" are relatively rare. Perhaps many were removed from the gene pool by giant hyenas and saber-toothed tigers!

In many nocturnal predators, the retina of the eye has a special reflective membrane called the *tapetum lucidum* or "bright carpet." This membrane acts almost like a mirror at the backs of their eyes. It bounces light back through the light-sensitive cells in front of it, giving the cells twice the chance to absorb available light. This reflection of light is the cause of that spooky night shine in the eyes of pet cats and dogs.

Giant hyenas and saber-toothed tigers had tapeta lucida. Lions, tigers, and coyotes have them. The minimum light needed for vision by animals with tapeta lucida can be as low as one-seventh of that needed by humans.[2]

Nature evened the playing field by giving tapeta lucida to many animals that are the natural prey of night predators. Deer have tapeta lucida. Wildebeests have tapeta lucida. Jack rabbits have tapeta lucida. And all these prey animals have eyes on the sides of their head, not in the front. This eye placement gives them a much larger field of vision.

Humans have no tapetum lucidum, so we can't see well in the dark. Eyes in the front of our head give us a relatively limited field of vision. That's two strikes against us! So what did nature do for us? Nature designed us to stay home at night.

Located in the geometric center of the human brain, behind the eyes and above the tip of the brainstem, is a small cone-shaped gland called the *pineal gland.* Melatonin is the principal hormone secreted by the pineal gland in humans and animals. When darkness descends, the pineal gland increases the production of melatonin. Melatonin makes us sleepy.

Melatonin gained popularity as a sleep aid a number of years ago. It may do much more. Studies are looking into its roles in the body's immune response, sexual maturation and reproduction, cardiovascular function, thyroid and adrenal function, and body temperature—more reasons to get enough sleep.

Tips for Using Visual Aids

Decide who—or what—is the center of attention. Are you the center of attention or are your slides? Really think about this. If your slides are intended to visually aid you in the delivery of your message, they are secondary. Can you have the screen put to one side, angled so everyone can see it? If you can, do so. If you can't (and often the screen is stationary or can't be moved between speakers), then work to ensure you don't become "the invisible voice in the dark corner."

Pause when you introduce a new slide. Sometimes you will use your slides as notes. Sometimes you may forget what slide is coming next until you see it. This is *not* a problem. You should almost always pause after introducing a new slide. Do not talk. Let the members of your audience do what they are there to do: look, think, and learn. This is especially important if the slide is designed to be read. Don't chatter on about the slide without letting the audience read it first. Doing this creates a distraction: what do you want them to do—read or listen? They can't do both well at the same time, so pause. Pause long enough for the audience to take in the visual information visually. An exception to this rule occurs when you have a complex slide that needs an immediate explanation. Another exception is when you are using a quick barrage of slides to create a special impact. But unless you have a very good reason not to pause, pause. Breathe. Think about what you want to say. And let the slide do its work in silence.

When is it time to begin speaking? Wait until at least half the members of the audience look away from the visual aid and back to you. Now they are ready to listen.

Add value. Interpret, explain, and personalize the information on the slides for your audience. You are the expert. What can you tell them that the slide does not already say? Why is the information important to them? If you have nothing else to say, you might as well have sent them the slides by e-mail or left them on your Web site or not have come at all!

Start and finish your presentation without a slide. If you are speaking at a breakout session at a conference, you may want to have the first slide on the screen as the attendees take their seats. This is one way of helping them make sure they are in the right place. But after that, turn it off. When you start front and center, just you and the audience, you make a much better first impression. You look more confident, more conversational, more interested in the audience than in your own information. Often the information on the first slide is redundant. Do you really need the slide competing for the audience's attention as you open your presentation?

Use slides intermittently. Remember the Law of Visual Aid Supply and Demand: every time you add one more slide, all the other slides become a little less important. Less is more with slides. So use them only when they really do visually aid the listeners' ability to understand and remember your point. If they aren't needed, don't use them. Punctuate your presentation with periods of no slides—just one human being talking to others. Then, when you do use a slide, it will provide variety, get more attention, and make a stronger impression.

Using Pointers

Sometimes, a pointer can be extremely helpful. If you need to locate precise points on a complex diagram or find a particular number on an unavoidably long list, a pointer can be useful. But too often pointers are used to give the speaker something to hold onto—something that, if waved, keeps anyone around at a safe distance.

Do you really need a pointer? Can you design your slides to make using one unnecessary? If your slides are simple and clear and the graphics and text are large enough to be seen easily, you will not need a pointer.

Try a Verbal Pointer

Can you use a verbal pointer? Try simply telling the audience where to look and what to focus on. Examples of this technique might include

- "Let's look at the numbers for January."

- "Notice the intersection of the two lines. That is where we started seeing a net profit."

PowerPoint Tips

PowerPoint has several functions you can use during your presentation to increase the impact of your slides. Use the tips that follow to deliver your message with added expertise and comfort.

BEFRIEND YOUR B KEY

If you use Microsoft PowerPoint slides, the B key on your computer's keyboard is a great tool for managing the use of slides in a way that effectively directs the attention of your audience where you want it. Using it allows you to deliver just a visual message, just a spoken message, or both at any time. Try this:

- Open a PowerPoint slide presentation. Click on the small screen icon to choose Slide Show format.
- Press the B key once to blacken the screen. Press it again to return to the slide you were on.

Use this simple function to manage your delivery with slides. Darken your screen between slides to cover information that doesn't need visual support, to cover a tangential point, or to answer a question from the audience. Open and close your presentation with a dark screen to give a strong message that you, not your slides, are the expert. This adds to your credibility, communicates confidence and authority, and increases your ability to quickly establish rapport with your audience.

NAVIGATE WITH NUMBERS

Do you need to return to a particular slide but don't want to take the time to go to slide sorter and then select it? Try this:

- Open a PowerPoint presentation and click on the small screen icon on the lower left of your screen to choose Slide Show format.
- Key in the slide number.
- Hit enter. The slide will appear.

Print a hard copy of your slide sorter before your presentation. You will have a handy display of all your slides, complete with the corresponding slide numbers. Bring the copy with your speaker notes. You can glance at it, find the slide and slide number, and enter the number. Now you can navigate quickly to return to a slide or jump ahead. This saves you the awkward steps of scrolling through your slides or going back and forth between Slide Sorter and Slide Show while your listeners wait. It adds to your comfortable, confident delivery.

For other tips that will help you navigate through your PowerPoint slides, right click your mouse when in Slide Show format. Select Help from the drop-down menu. Spend a few minutes getting familiar with your options. You will be able to navigate like a pro.

Consider a speaker taking his listeners through two consecutive slides:

"The pie chart—the one on the left—shows the percentage of market share for the five leading providers at the beginning of the year. We are in blue. Our 27 percent was respectable but certainly not a clear leadership position.

"Now take a good look at the chart on the right. Comparing it to the first shows the progress we made in increasing market share in just the last nine months! Still in blue, we have 37 percent! We are now in second place!

"But here's the exciting part! Let's look at where we'll be if we continue to grow at this same rate for the next nine months. This slide shows our projected market share by the beginning of the third quarter next year. We're still in blue. If we maintain our pace we'll have over 50 percent of the market!"

Old-fashioned wooden pointers, and even telescoping metal pointers, can be difficult to manage when you're not using them and can look pedantic or authoritarian. If you must use a pointer, don't swing or flourish it, and don't hit the screen with it. Put it down when you don't need it.

Consider a laser light pointer if you use a large or elevated screen. Use the pointer only when you need it; then turn it off. You don't want to have the little red light moving all over the screen or shining in the eyes of people in the audience. Be aware that holding the light steady on one very small part of the screen is difficult. If you are at all shaky, the light will dance around for the audience. Laser pointers work best when used very briefly to circle or pinpoint the detail being discussed.

Using Lecterns

A lectern distinguishes the speaker from the audience, immediately establishing him as the center of attention. It communicates authority and helps to establish the impression of expertise. But it serves another, less obvious, purpose as well. At times, the lectern is the shelter that a frightened public speaking animal retreats to. Yes, it holds your notes. But so would the slender music stand musicians use to hold their "notes."

A lectern in the front of the room is like a tall and sturdy tree trunk in an open field—the tree trunk to hide behind when feeling vulnerable, ex-

PowerPoint Pointer

PowerPoint has a function that gives you the advantages of using a pointer without having to add another piece of physical equipment to your presentation tool chest. If you decide to use this function, practice with it before your presentation until you can use it easily and comfortably.

A Word about A and E

If you use Microsoft PowerPoint slides, the A key on your computer's keyboard will give you a "pointer-on-demand." Try this:

- Open a PowerPoint slide presentation. Click on the small screen icon to choose Slide Show format.
- Press the A key once. A small pointer will appear on the screen. You can control the pointer with your mouse. When you are done, press the A key again to remove the pointer from the screen.
- Now, right click your mouse. Select Pointer Options from the drop-down menu. Click on Pen. Your pointer arrow will turn into a small pen icon. But wait, there's more!
- Select the color "ink" you want in your pen. Drag your mouse to draw on your slide. This can be useful for circling an area of the slide, underlining for emphasis, and so on. But use this tool selectively— your goal is to direct attention and increase understanding, not to impress the audience with your artistic ability (or even with your proficiency with PowerPoint).
- You can erase what you drew by pressing the E key.

posed, or threatened. Landscape architects understand this need. When designing parks and other spaces used for public gatherings, they break up the open ground with trees, boulders, gazebos, pergolas, and other structures. These are the spots where people gather. A landscape is more aesthetically pleasing and we humans are more comfortable when we are in easy range of such shelters—just in case.

The problem with lecterns is that when you stand behind one it becomes a barrier between you and the audience. If this suits your purpose, as in a formal setting with firmly established protocol, then use the lectern. But if you want to eliminate the barrier, as you might if addressing potential business partners, it may be wiser to speak without a lectern or to use it only to hold your notes (as described in the lesson on using notes).

Consider Your Relationship with Your Audience

The key question to answer when deciding whether or not to use a lectern is, What relationship do I want to have with my audience?

Do you want to be seen as an expert? If your goal is to communicate power and authority, to establish yourself as an expert, to in some way emphasize the differences between you and the members of your audience, speaking from behind a lectern is a visible way to reinforce the differences.

Do you want to be seen as a partner? If your goal is to connect with your audience, to eliminate obstacles, to remove barriers, then speaking without a lectern will create an atmosphere that is more democratic and more cooperative.

If your goal is some combination of these (and it often is), review the lesson on using notes. It will give you tips for speaking with notes and using the lectern without staying behind it during your entire talk. You and your listeners can have the best of both worlds!

When You Use a Lectern

Check the height of the lectern. The audience should be able to easily see your face and your gestures. If in doubt, call ahead and arrive early to check. If you are less than about five feet six inches tall, you may want to ask for or bring a small, sturdy platform to stand on. Step aerobic platforms, available at sporting goods stores, are ideal.

Check the lighting. Make sure that the area around the lectern is well lit from external sources. Lecterns with lights that shine up on your face can make you look like a Halloween mask.

Check the front of the lectern. Lecterns that have the hotel name plastered across the front can turn your talk into an advertisement for sleeping rooms and restaurants. If you are doing a great deal of speaking in hotels, you may want to bring your own version of a "presidential seal" to cover the advertisement on the front of lecterns.

Using a Microphone

Using a microphone can be the difference between being heard and not being heard. And if you can't be heard, don't bother to speak.

You are likely to encounter three types of microphones. (A fourth, less common type is a headset microphone.) The type you use will depend in part on the type of event, the technology available at the site, and the budget of the event.

1. Fixed microphones are attached to a lectern or a stationary stand. These are the most limiting.

2. Hand-held microphones are just that. Most are now cordless.

3. Lapel microphones are also cordless, and the head of the microphone is small enough to clip to your lapel, blouse, or tie. Wearing slacks, trousers, or a jacket with a pocket will make it easier to find a secure spot for the battery mechanism (often about the size of a deck of cards).

A lapel microphone is your best choice for most presentations. It is easier to use than a hand-held microphone and leaves your hands free to gesture, change your notes or slides, or work with the keyboard of your computer. It gives you the greatest freedom of movement, allowing you to take full advantage of the space on your speaking platform. Even if you speak from behind a lectern, it keeps the microphone the same distance from your mouth at all times, regulating your volume and preventing volume fadeouts. Most venues have lapel microphones available on request. If one is not available, consider renting one for the occasion.

When you use a microphone,

- Locate any on-site sound technician. Ask for information about the microphone or sound system.

- Ask the sound technician if you will turn the microphone on and off or if he will do it remotely before and after you speak. If you will be responsible for this task, find the on/off switch and test it. Keep your microphone off until just before your presentation begins. Switch it off again when you are done. If for some reason your microphone must be kept open (in the on position), be very, very aware of what you say and do at all times.

- Conduct a sound check before the audience arrives. Any echo will be greater when the room is empty. Rely on the sound technician for advice or an adjustment later.

- Test the microphone placement for the best sound. The head of the microphone should usually be about six inches from your mouth, pointing at your chin.

- Make sure you attach the lapel microphone where you won't brush it with your hand or sleeve.

- If you are using a hand-held microphone with a cord and you intend to walk around the speaking platform, loop the slack of the cord in your free hand. This may take a bit of practice.

- Ask the sound technician about any potential problems with feedback. They may be eliminated if you stay behind any speakers located in the front of the room.

- Go lightly on the "exploding consonants" such as *p* and *t*. They can make an annoying popping sound if overemphasized. Avoid habitual and audible sniffing and clearing of your throat.

- Never wear a lapel microphone into the rest room.

Summary

When you know how to use notes, visual aids, lecterns, and microphones skillfully, you have less to worry about. Your increased comfort and confidence will be communicated to your listeners.

Notes show thoughtful preparation and a determination to stay focused and give your listeners all the information they need. They are also insurance against the memory loss that so often follows a rise in your cortisol level. Mastery of the pause is the key to using notes well. Feel free to check your notes as often as you need. When you pause long enough to really read, you will look more confident and need to check less often. Resume talking after you have reestablished eye contact with a member of the audience.

Visual aids should increase your listeners' ability to understand and remember your information. You should add value by explaining, interpreting, personalizing, and reinforcing the message on a visual aid. Pausing after you introduce a new visual aid is a great way to let the visual aid do the work it is designed to do. Eye contact with the audience while you speak maintains your focus on the audience.

Lecterns in a formal setting communicate authority by clearly separating you from the audience. In less formal settings this may work against you. If your goals include establishing a sense of your authority or expertise, or if the venue or protocol requires a lectern, plan ahead to make sure it is positioned appropriately, is the right height, and is lit properly. If your goal is to create a democratic and cooperative environment, you may want to step away from the lectern to speak. You may return to it to check your notes or change your slides.

The microphone should always be tested ahead of time. If possible, practice with it to make sure you don't fade in and out or produce annoying feedback. Whenever possible, use a clip-on cordless microphone to give you freedom of motion and freedom from cords. To avoid possible embarrassment, remember to turn off the microphone when not in use.

If one talks to more than four people, it is an audience; and one cannot
really think or exchange thoughts with an audience.

ANNE MORROW LINDBERGH

Can We Talk?

Moving from Monologue to Dialogue

Monologue is an inherently unnatural form of communication. We
learn to speak using dialogue. We know from chapter 5 that the turn-taking of everyday conversation is the basic form of spoken human communication. We learn to speak by exchanging words—at first just one, then
two, then phrases and sentences—with our caregivers. Child-development
expert and author John Bowlby, whom we first met in chapter 3, tells us
that dialogue develops between a mother and her infant in the first few
weeks of the infant's life. The fact that this happens quickly and naturally and
is enjoyed by both the mother and baby is evidence that the turn-taking of
conversation is an innate element of human nature.[1]

So dialogue is the natural form of human spoken communication. It is
also important to recognize that it is by far the most practiced. Monologues
are much, much rarer, more often absent entirely from the training and practice we receive in our formative years. As we acquire social skills, the importance of listening, asking questions, and responding to the verbal and

nonverbal messages of others is continually emphasized. We become practiced and skillful at dialogue. But we seldom, if ever, need to communicate more than a brief paragraph without comments, interruptions, questions, or some other type of contribution by at least one other person. We receive little, if any, training or practice in organizing and verbally delivering subject matter of any quantity in monologue form.

In chapter 5 we discussed two other elements of dialogue that are missing from monologue. Grounding and entrainment, both of which are vital components for connecting with your listeners, are missing when you deliver a monologue. No wonder presentations can be such a challenge to both prepare and deliver. And no wonder returning to a dialogue format, even briefly, can be such a welcome change for you—and for your listeners.

Here is another insight into our discomfort with speaking to groups. In his book *Grooming, Gossip, and the Evolution of Language,* Professor Robin Dunbar shares observations and conclusions about the strong human predisposition toward dialogue in small groups. He tells how this behavior can be seen at parties and receptions.

Dunbar describes how conversations progress comfortably between two, three, and four people. But when a fifth person joins the small group, the situation tends to get awkward. Even when members consciously try to involve all five (or more) people in the group, the attention level and interest in the conversation will start to wane. Two people will strike up their own conversation. Soon, they drift away and start their own group. Dunbar observes, "This is a remarkably robust feature of human conversational behavior, and I guarantee that you will see it if you spend a few minutes watching people in social settings."[2]

Involvement Helps Hold Your Listeners' Attention

The strong human preference for communicating in groups smaller than five can help explain more than a speaker's discomfort when communicating to large groups. It helps explain why maintaining the attention of listeners can be such a challenge. Listeners are much more likely to stay attentive when they feel involved, even more so if they have the opportunity to actively participate. When the average level of participation is low, as in a group larger than four, people may naturally look for ways to become more actively involved. At cocktail parties they can start a new conversation and begin to form a new small group. During presentations, they may start side conversations with their neighbors!

It is difficult to keep quiet if you have nothing to do.

ARTHUR SCHOPENHAUER

The skillful speaker understands this and looks for ways to incorporate the "look and feel" of dialogue into a presentation. When you create interaction with your listeners or even just change the pace and rhythm of your presentation to create the look and feel of dialogue, you will be glad you did. A large body of research shows that when listeners feel involved, they learn more, remember more, and are more likely to consider new points of view. When listeners feel involved, they are much more likely to be persuaded. The benefits of creating interaction far outweigh the risk you may feel when you temporarily give up complete control.[3]

Sometimes you will be able to engage your listeners in true dialogue. Actual (although limited) dialogue is created when you ask your listeners to answer a question out loud, to voice an opinion, or to share information. It also takes place when your listeners ask questions or make comments. But what if either the logistics or protocol limits the dialogue? What if the situation makes it impossible?

At these times you can create the look and feel of dialogue in other ways. This will help the audience stay focused and attentive, and you will find it easier to build rapport. Creating the look and feel of dialogue is especially important as the pace of life increases and attention spans decrease accordingly.

None of these methods for creating the look and feel of dialogue is difficult to use. Trying one or two in your next presentation will convince you how easy it is to incorporate them and of how well they work. With a little practice you will look and sound more natural, confident, and comfortable. So let's learn how to create the look and feel of dialogue for more effective presentations.

The Look and Feel of Dialogue

You can create the look and feel of dialogue many ways. Following are four ways that often work well.

1. Tell the audience a little-known fact or a late-breaking piece of news.

2. Tell a story or share an anecdote.

3. Do something to change the pace of your presentation.

4. Ask audience members to do something that requires a change in the direction of their thinking.

   Let's look at some examples of each of these.

Tell the Audience a Little-Known Fact or a Late-Breaking Piece of News

Let the audience process this information and respond emotionally. Here are some specific suggestions with examples.

- *Give a little-known fact.* "Studies show that companies that increase customer retention by just 5 percent can increase bottom-line profits by as much as 50 percent."

- *Share the latest news.* "This morning, Global Air made an offer to buy Air Express."

- *Make a startling or shocking statement.* "Look around your table. Within seven years, one of you will be dead."

- *Share a startling statistic.* "How pervasive is the information revolution? Worldwide, 62 percent of the people alive today have never used a telephone."

Tell a Story or Share an Anecdote

For more about the value of stories, and about how to tell stories well, see the information on using stories in chapter 11. Try these types of stories:

- *Share a common experience.* "Last week, driving home from the store, I looked in my rear view mirror and saw flashing red lights."

- *Relate an experience shared by members of the audience.* "As I entered the parking lot this morning, it seemed very full. I didn't want to drive to the top of the parking garage, so I considered the valet parking."

- *Share a "learning moment."* "Last night I drove my fourteen-year-old son, Matt, and three other boys on his basketball team home from a practice. As I listened to them, I realized that every one of them is expecting his parents to buy him his own car when he turns sixteen! Including Matt!"

Do Something to Change the Pace of Your Presentation

Changing the pace creates a more conversational rhythm. Giving the audience a chance to gather information using a new sense (seeing, hearing, touching, even smelling or tasting)—or using a sense in a new way—is usually a welcome change. Here are some suggestions for changing the pace.

- Use a long pause.

- Use a barrage of statements or facts.

- Do a demonstration.

- Use a series of quick questions.

- Pass out samples.

- Show a single, powerful visual aid.

- Show a short video.

- Use a barrage of visual aids.

- Use a prop.

- Use a series of short statements.

Ask the Audience to Do Something Intellectual or Physical

Ask the audience to think, imagine, or remember. Ask them to take some immediate action or try some behavior. This will increase their intellectual involvement and often their emotional involvement as well. Here are some suggestions.

- Ask a rhetorical question followed by a long pause.

- Ask the audience to recall an experience.

- Ask the audience to imagine an experience.

- Tell the audience to turn to the next page of your handout.

- Ask for a show of hands.

- Tell the audience to stand up.

- Tell the audience to look around.

- Tell the audience to make a note of an important point.

As effective as these techniques can be, real dialogue will always be the most powerful way to both connect with and learn from your audience. When time, protocol, and your goals allow it, engaging in dialogue with members of the audience will allow you to connect with them most effectively.

Real Dialogue Is the Most Powerful Form of Interaction

Real dialogue is the key to effective communication. Here are ways you can encourage dialogue with your listeners.

Welcome Questions at Any Time

When you open your presentation, tell the audience that you will welcome questions at any time. Give them specific directions as to how to let you know they have a question. For example, "As we go through this information, let's discuss any questions you have. Whenever you have a question, please raise your hand. I'll call on you to ask the question as soon as I finish the point I'm on."

Hold a Question-and-Answer Session

When you open your presentation, let the audience know that you will give them a chance to ask questions. Tell them when this will be and how long it will last. Encourage them to make a mental or written note of their questions when they come up so they will have them ready when the question-and-answer session begins.

Hold Intermittent Question-and-Answer Sessions

If you will speak for longer than about twenty minutes, consider holding brief question-and-answer sessions intermittently. This is a great way to answer questions while they are fresh in the minds of the listeners. This also helps clear up any confusion that might make it difficult for the listeners to understand the information to follow. (Do this only if you feel you can keep control of the timing of the sessions and get back to your remaining information.)

Ask the Audience Members to Share Comments

Asking the audience for comments and insights can be combined with the question-and-answer sessions or be done apart from them. This is especially valuable when you are sharing information without positioning yourself as an expert. Consider arranging a way to capture the information that is shared. One good way is to ask for a volunteer who will record the comments of others.

Break the Audience into Small Groups to Share Ideas

A wonderful way to get the audience members involved when you have a larger audience is to have them share ideas in small groups. A group size of five to eight people usually works best to generate a variety of ideas without becoming unmanageable. Then have a spokesperson from each group report the best ideas back to the larger audience. Clear directions and time limits are crucial if this is to work successfully.

Ask the Right Kind of Question at the Right Time

Have you ever been in the audience when a speaker asks a question that is followed only by an awkward silence? Asking questions to get the audience members more involved, to learn more about their thinking, or just to change the pace can add a lot to a presentation. But when a question falls flat, so can the atmosphere in the room. The confidence level of the speaker usually falls, too.

Simply using an open-ended question (a question that cannot be answered with a yes, no, or very few words and is designed to elicit a longer response such as a description or explanation) is not the answer. Here's why.

When people are just listening, not engaged in conversation, their brains focus activity in certain areas. When listeners make the mental shift from listening to preparing to speak, their brain activity shifts also, and the blood flow supplying oxygen to the brain shifts as well. Another shift takes place when listeners actually begin to speak. These shifts take time, just as a car must slow down to turn a corner, round a curve, or otherwise change direction.[4] A speaker who moves too abruptly from a monologue to a request for a response from the audience is inviting an awkward silence.

An awkward silence can be filled in many different ways. Here are some of the steps a speaker can take, along with the pros and cons of each.

- Answer the question herself.
  Pro: This fills the awkward silence.
  Con: It fails to generate any interaction.

- Call on someone specific.
  Pro: This may increase the chances of getting a response because someone is put "on the spot."
  Con: It can easily cause pity, resentment, and anxiety among listeners because someone is put on the spot. ("Poor thing. What a jerk *that* speaker is. *And I might be next!*")

- Rephrase the question to be easier to answer.
  Pro: This could increase the chances of getting an answer.
  Con: It is still possible that nobody will answer, increasing the awkwardness. When a question is rephrased to be easier to answer it can become a leading question; the speaker risks sounding manipulative or pedantic. For example, "How many of you would like to work fewer hours and make a lot more money?"

- Pause, wait, and let the tension build.
  - Pro: Someone will probably (eventually) be unable to bear the silence and speak.
  - Con: Nobody wants to sit through an awkward silence until it becomes unbearable.

The Engage-by-Stage Four-Stage Questioning Model

If you want the benefits of interaction but want to avoid awkward silences and the problems that can follow, the Engage-by-Stage four-stage questioning model for moving from a monologue into dialogue is the answer. Using the Engage-by-Stage model gives people a chance to move from a listening mode into thinking mode, and then on to a speaking mode, without awkwardness. Each stage of the model corresponds to a specific type of question. Asked in a specific order, the questions give listeners a chance to get in touch with their own thoughts, organize those thoughts for speaking, and volunteer to speak when they feel ready.

The model in use is invisible to listeners. With just a little thought, you, as the speaker, can use it seamlessly. It's actually fun to use, and the result is real dialogue between you and your listeners. Let's go through a brief explanation of how the model can work for you.

Stage 1: Ask a Rhetorical Question

Ask a question that is clearly rhetorical. Nobody should feel the need to speak. After the question, pause. Allow time for thought. Observe the reactions of your listeners.

An example might be "Think back. What was the best vacation you had in the last five years? What made it good?" Pause and look around the room. Watch for reactions (e.g., smiles, closed eyes, sighs). This type of question gets people thinking, remembering, and calling to mind the specifics they will need to participate as you move on.

Stage 2: Poll with a Show-of-Hands Question

As the only answer needed for your next question, ask for a show of hands. Get a rough count of the response. Is it half the group? More? Everybody? Report the results to the audience to establish a sense of shared experience and interest.

Here's an example: "With a show of hands, how many of you can think of more than one reason that that was such a good vacation?" Put your own hand up to model the response you want. This demonstration of the desired response can jump-start the participation. Pause and count the hands as they come up. Watch for positive facial expressions, nodding heads, and other signs of thoughts and memories coming to mind.

This show-of-hands question helps to narrow, focus, and refine the thinking of your listeners. Raising their hands increases their involvement. Now they are not only mentally engaged but also physically involved—all in a safe environment. No one person has been singled out, but the show of hands creates a sense of community—many members of the group have things in common. Now you and the group are ready for the next step.

Stage 3: Ask a "Closed" Question

A "closed" question is one that can be answered very briefly. The usual response is a yes, a no, a number, or a single word or short phrase. This answer is easy for the listeners to supply, especially since they have had time to think. It also is very low risk. It doesn't take much time to organize in their heads. It doesn't demand that the listeners respond articulately or eloquently. It simply breaks the ice and gets them talking out loud. An example might be "Who went with you on that vacation?"

Take several responses so several people have a chance to speak. Probe briefly if necessary or desired; now that they have spoken you may ask a question to clarify a response. For example, if one of the answers to the question above is "My family," you might ask "Which members of your family?" This is the beginning of the real dialogue. When you have had several responses, summarize them. What do the responses have in common? Is there a common thread that should be clarified? An example of a summary might be "It sounds like most of your best vacations were taken with just your spouse." This summary also serves as your transition to the next step.

Stage 4: Ask an "Open" Question

An "open" question asks the speaker to interpret, elaborate, to describe in further detail, to explain not just the "what" but also the "why." More information is shared, and more opportunities for dialogue emerge. Members of the audience will often discover a shared experience or opinion. Differences of opinion surface and lead to more dialogue in the form of questions and explanations.

An example of an open question might be "What advice would you give to someone planning a vacation with a spouse?" You can go back to the listeners who responded to a question in stage 3, or you may choose to allow anyone in the group to respond. And people will respond! You have already created an atmosphere that is safe and participative. You have given the listeners time to think about their own experience and learn that others have shared similar experiences.

Resist the temptation to overcontrol the responses you get. Some of the responses may not be what you anticipated, but a free flow of dialogue will almost always give you many bits of information you will find pertinent and useful. You can incorporate this information into your presentation, selecting the points that support the message you want to deliver.

What are the goals of your presentation? For example, if one of your goals is to present a set of guidelines for having a successful vacation, you might incorporate information from the dialogue with your listeners in this way: "It sounds like a willingness to plan activities you can share is a real key to keeping everyone happy. We also heard how important it is for vacationers to be willing to try something new. Like Kristin discovered with scuba diving, sometimes things you are reluctant to try can be a lot of fun. And because Kristin agreed to take the diving instructions, she and Bill found one more thing they like to do together."

In his book, *Shepherding a Child's Heart,* Tedd Tripp writes, "Communication is not monologue. It is dialogue . . . The finest art of communication is not learning how to express your thoughts. It is learning how to draw out the thoughts of another."[5]

Once the dialogue has begun, you need to use your own good judgment in managing it. How long will you let it go on? How many people do you want to hear from? How much detail do you want from each person? How will you manage the dialogue if different speakers disagree? How will you summarize the information you get? How will you return to your topic? When you do, how will you incorporate what you have learned?

The answers to these questions depend on the situation. But you may be surprised by how easy it is to manage the dialogue. You will often handle it the same ways you would if you were managing a meeting.

Try using the Engage-by-Stage four-stage questioning model in a meeting. Polish the skill of using it to begin and manage dialogue. Your meetings will become more participative. You will quickly become skillful at asking the appropriate questions, probing effectively for needed details, and guiding the conversations to productive conclusions. And the skills will transfer easily to a more formal presentation environment.

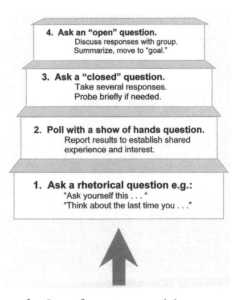

Your keys to success with the Engage-by Stage four-stage model are

- Choose your questions thoughtfully.
- Stay open to audience responses that differ from what you expect.
- When you need to, probe for additional information.
- Listen closely to the dialogue for information that supports your presentation goals. Incorporate this information as you summarize the dialogue

and return to discussing your goal topic, that is, the topic you planned to cover and the points you planned to make.

Practicing and using the Engage-by-Stage four-stage questioning model will give you both the skill and the confidence to move smoothly and comfortably from monologue to dialogue. You will have another great way to make your presentations more interactive, more relaxed, more informative, and more fun!

Summary

We learn to speak using dialogue. The turn-taking of conversation is the basic, and by far the most practiced, form of human communication. Monologue is unnatural and seldom practiced. This can add to our discomfort when we make a presentation and it can also make it difficult for listeners to stay interested and attentive.

Participation is the key to intellectual and emotional involvement. Skillful speakers understand this and work to create opportunities for dialogue with members of the audience. When this is not possible, they will incorporate verbal tools that help create the "look and feel" of dialogue.

Four excellent ways to create the look and feel of dialogue are these:

1. Tell the audience a little-known fact or a late-breaking piece of news.

2. Tell a story or share an anecdote.

3. Do something to change the pace of your presentation.

4. Ask audience members to do something that requires a change in the direction of their thinking.

When it is possible to involve members of the audience in actual dialogue, the skillful speaker will do so. Using the Engage-by Stage four-stage questioning model is a great way to stimulate dialogue.

Honest disagreement is often a good sign of progress.

MOHANDAS GANDHI

Meeting of the Minds

Answers to Questions on Questions and Answers

Answering questions can be the best part of your presentation. Even if your presentation has been a monologue until now—perhaps because of the size of the audience, nature of the material, time restrictions, or established formal protocol, having a question-and-answer session will put you in a dialogue with your audience. You will have the opportunity to communicate in the way that you have used virtually every day of your life. You are already an expert at this.

A question-and-answer session is a wonderful opportunity to discover differences and work toward understanding and agreement. The audience members can share their thoughts with you. You will learn about their concerns, add details they want, explain in more depth, and have the chance to eliminate confusion or misunderstanding.

> A clash of doctrines is not a disaster—it is an opportunity.
>
> ALFRED NORTH WHITEHEAD

Why Doesn't It Feel Like an Opportunity?

The same intellectual and emotional challenges that you have faced up until now still exist. And since you have given up some of your control, they may be magnified. You may worry that you can't predict all the possible questions, so you can't possibly be prepared with all the perfect answers. You may also assume that since you are giving the presentation, thereby setting yourself up as an expert, the audience will expect you to have all the answers. Any concerns you have about losing credibility, failing to convince, or simply exposing yourself as less than a total expert may contribute to your anxiety. These are normal concerns, but are they justified?

Remember: a presentation is a chance to share, not an oral exam. Your job is to share what you know when you make a presentation and to learn what the audience still needs to know when you handle questions. Many questions you will be able to answer on the spot. Some you may need to research. Sometimes you will refer the questioner to another source, explain why the question can't be answered, or state when in the future it can be. But let's first look at how you can minimize your anxiety by being as prepared as possible.

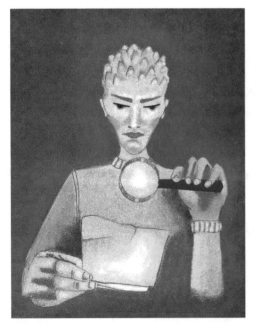

You Can Prepare for Most Questions

Most sources of information—instruction books, user manuals, Web sites—have a section for FAQs (frequently asked questions). This is because most questions are FAQs—and FAQs can be anticipated. Many of the questions you are likely to be asked can also be anticipated. In most cases you have been asked to speak because you know at least as much about your topic as the audience does.

With a little bit of thought, and a little bit of detective work, you can be extremely well prepared for most questions you will be asked.

What's the first step? Revisit the thinking you did when you started to work on your presentation. Reminding yourself about your listeners—their needs, interests, concerns, and even quirks—will help you anticipate their questions. Let's look again at the questions we considered in chapter 8. Do you know

> We can't cross a bridge till we come to it, but I always like to lay down a pontoon ahead of time.
>
> BERNARD M. BARUCH

- Who will attend? What are their names? Job titles? Job responsibilities?

- What are their ages? Genders? Levels of education? Cultural backgrounds?

- What do they believe they need? What challenges do they have?

- What problems do they need to solve? What limitations do they have?

- What are their attitudes about your subject? Your organization? You?

- What do they know? How familiar are they with the issues? How much technical understanding do they have? What concepts will you need to explain? What terms should be used, defined, or avoided?

- How important is the topic to your audience? How much do they care? What emotions do they have around this topic or issue? Why do they feel this way?

- What are the costs to them in terms of money, time, effort, risk? Are they able to pay the costs? Are they willing to pay?

- What special considerations exist? Does your audience have any unusual needs? Do you need to take their history into account? Are some topics taboo?

- Who makes the decisions? What decision-making power do they have?

- Who influences the decisions? What power of influence do they have?

Based on your answers to these questions, brainstorm a list of the questions you might be asked. What would the most supportive members of your audience want to know? What would the most sophisticated and knowledgeable listeners ask? What would the most skeptical person ask? What would the least informed or knowledgeable person ask? Write down each question.

Have others brainstorm questions for you. Two people brainstorming is better than one. Different perspectives help tremendously in thinking "outside the box." You might be too close to your own subject to anticipate some of the simplest questions.

This should give you a good foundation for thinking about and preparing your answers. But you can do more. Play detective. Do your homework. Contact a few members of your audience. Ask if they have any particular concerns they would like addressed or any questions they want answered.

If you can't talk to audience members in advance, think about others you can contact. Who is likely to have similar interests, concerns, and challenges? What do they want to know? When you answer these questions you should have a very comprehensive list of possible questions.

Easy Questions and Hard Questions

After you generate a list of possible questions (or even while you are making your list) you will probably notice two kinds of questions: easy questions and hard questions. Let's briefly cover a few points about answering the easy questions. Then we can spend more time where you need to spend your time: planning how to handle the hard ones!

Easy Questions

Easy questions are questions you can answer easily. The answer is not confidential or proprietary information. It is not controversial, and most of the audience will likely understand and agree with the answer. Often, your biggest challenge with this type of question is to be brief. Remember that not everyone is likely to want all the details. If you aren't sure how much detail is needed, find out how much the questioner wants and needs. This is not the time to demonstrate the breadth and depth of your knowledge. It is time to give the questioner the information he needs (if possible) and move on to the next question.

Hard Questions

Hard questions can be difficult to answer for many different reasons. Perhaps you don't know the answer. Perhaps it would take a great deal of time to answer completely, or perhaps a complete understanding would require more knowledge or special training than members of the audience have. Perhaps the answer is controversial. Perhaps the information is confidential or proprietary. Perhaps the question is unclear. Perhaps the questioner is hostile or argumentative or is using the opportunity to relate a horror story about an experience he had with your company. Perhaps the questioner just enjoys demonstrating the extent of his knowledge and seems unlikely to stop talking in the foreseeable future.

Below you will find a model for framing your answer. This model gives you three distinct steps to follow when answering a hard question. When you follow these steps you will greatly increase your chances of giving an answer that will satisfy the person who asked the question, other listeners, and you. As you become more skillful in using this model you will be able to think of excellent answers to hard questions while you still have an audience—not in the car on the way home.

Before you frame your answer in a clear, strategic way you must pause and think. This is the most important thing you can do when answering challenging questions. It will do more to determine whether you respond clearly, appear truly knowledgeable, and create the impressions of both confidence and honesty than anything else you can do. In many cases it will be the difference between success and failure.

Why Pause and Think?

Listening to a question, formulating an answer, and delivering the answer out loud are different intellectual tasks. PET (positron emission tomography) scans of the brain show that blood flow in the brain shifts to different locations for each of these tasks.[1] This takes time. Beginning to speak too soon means you are trying to do all of these intellectual tasks at once. When you do this, no one part of the brain is getting all the oxygen it needs for peak performance. The quality of both your content and your delivery is likely to suffer.

And do you really want your listeners to hear your "first draft"? Would you send a prospective client an e-mail document with all the revisions available for him to see? If you start your answer without pausing to organize your thoughts, you will be sending out a very rough draft. Without taking a few seconds to choose your words, you may need to backtrack or rephrase what you said. You may need to take more time to explain, qualify, or even apologize. But although pausing before you begin to answer sounds logical, even obvious, it isn't always easy.

Your instinct will most likely be to begin your answer immediately. You will initially feel uncomfortable with the silence of the pause. You may assume, often subconsciously, that an immediate response demonstrates knowledge while a pause sounds as if you don't know the answer. If you make these assumptions and respond immediately, you will cheat yourself and your audience out of the best possible answer. You will be much less likely to follow the model for framing your answer and much more likely to say something you will regret.

Will pausing give the impression that you don't know the answer? The opposite is true. When you pause, keeping your body language confident and nondefensive, you appear thoughtful and confident. The impressions you create are these:

- I am honoring you by carefully considering what you have asked.

- I am thinking about how best to respond to meet your needs.

- I am comfortable being here.

- I do not feel like this is an oral exam but rather an opportunity to share information and understand one another's positions.

- My answer will be worth the short wait.

Frame Your Answer

After you have paused and thought, frame your answer using these three steps:

1. Demonstrate that you understood the question; find common ground.

2. Give information to support, clarify, or supplement your content or position.

3. Restate your belief, opinion, or recommendation or an important point.

Let's look more closely at each step.

Demonstrate That You Understood the Question; Find Common Ground

Responding with "I understand what you mean, but . . ." does *not* demonstrate understanding. This well-worn phrase will sound like you *assume* you understand, you disagree, and you can't wait to have the floor back. Let's look at some better options. Your good judgment (exercised while you pause to think) will help you decide if, when, and how to choose from among these options.

Clarify the Question
Do everything you can to be absolutely sure you understand what the question means to the questioner. Do what you would do in a dialogue. If you aren't sure, ask. Ask for a brief explanation, for the context of the question, for a missing essential detail. Ask before you answer the wrong question.

Encourage More Information
When you need more information but aren't sure what question to ask, use body language and verbal cues to encourage the questioner to continue or expand on the question. A pause with raised eyebrows is usually enough for the questioner to realize you want and need more information. "Tell me a

bit more about what you are thinking" encourages the questioner to give more information. This extra information will often help you get to the heart of the matter.

Mirror the Question

Repeat the question using the questioner's exact words. This is especially helpful if you think he may have misspoken. Keep your voice neutral—you don't want to sound sarcastic. Mirror the question only to check for or to demonstrate understanding, not to stall for time. If you need more time to think, pause.

Paraphrase the Question

Paraphrasing (stating the question in your own words) demonstrates how well you understood the question. Paraphrasing gives the listener an opportunity to clarify the question if you have not understood it correctly or fully. It is a way to ground the exchange of information—to check for common understanding of the message before you continue. When paraphrasing, avoid beginning with "So what I hear you saying is" (which may make you sound as if you just took a night class on how to communicate with your adolescent). A simple "Do you mean . . . ?" or "Let's see if I got that right . . ." will serve you better.

Repeat the Question

Repeating the question is a good option if you feel confident you understood the full meaning *and* if some members of the audience may not have heard the question the first time. But don't repeat the question just to gain time to think. That technique is more tricky than honest. Pause instead. Don't rush. As long as your body language remains confident and nondefensive you will appear thoughtful, as if you are choosing from among your many options.

Find Common Ground

What can you and the questioner agree on? For example, if the question lets you know a customer is balking at the price you quoted, you can agree on the fact that "Price is certainly an important consideration in your decision."

Sometimes the only common ground is "This is a really tough issue, and we both definitely have strong feelings about it!" But finding some common ground is a great way to immediately create a feeling of working *with* the questioner, not against him.

When you have finished with any of these options, you are ready to deliver the substance of your answer.

Give Information to Support, Clarify, or Supplement Your Content or Position

The next step involves the substance of your answer. Let's look at some of your options for framing an answer.

Add Information

What else does the questioner want to know or need to know? What details are needed? Give the additional information as succinctly as you can.

Clarify or Correct Understanding

Shades of meaning, an interpretation of a point, or even a different interpretation of the meaning of a word can cause confusion or a mistaken assumption. When a listener asks a question that implies he misunderstood your point, you have the opportunity to clarify or correct it.

Being able to share information that may contradict or rebut that of the questioner without causing conflict can make all the difference in how both you and your information are received. A very simple technique can help you do this.

What is the message you get as soon as you hear "I understand what you mean, but . . . "? The message, especially if the speaker speaks quickly and vehemently, is "You're wrong!" Not only do you feel a lack of understanding, you also feel negated—publicly.

When you answer a question, try using *and* instead of *but*. Just substituting *and* for *but* eliminates the negation. As a speaker, you appear openminded and nondefensive.

Listeners are much more likely to really listen than to immediately start concentrating on how to prove their point.

You can make your response even more effective by using phrases such as "I agree with much of that and . . ." or "I appreciate that point and . . ." or "I respect what you're saying and . . ." This simple change can help you create a positive and cooperative environment, even in very tough situations.

Restate Your Belief, Opinion, or Recommendation or an Important Point

Even well-intentioned questions can pull you off course. As you finish your answer, reset your course by repeating an important point. This is a great way to refocus yourself and the audience on the content and purpose of your presentation, not on the last question.

Repetition is one of the keys to long-term memory, so use this opportunity to repeat a key point you want the audience to remember.

Answering Questions

While you pause before you begin your answer, first decide if you *should* know the answer. Just because someone asked you a question doesn't mean that you are obligated to know the answer. Is the answer within the scope of your expertise, or is someone else better qualified to answer the question? Second, decide if you should answer the question at all. Some questions are so unrelated to the topic that answering them would waste the time of the rest of the listeners. Some questions don't have an answer. The answer may be impossible to state definitively. It may be a matter of opinion. It simply may not be known yet. It may be confidential or proprietary. Only after you consider these possibilities are you ready to respond to the questioner. Let's look more closely at your options.

When You Don't Know the Answer

If you believe you should know the answer but don't, you can offer to find out and then get back to the questioner. If you choose this option, get the questioner's contact information. Choose this option only if you really are the best source of an answer.

If the answer is not within your scope of responsibility or expertise, say so. Refer the questioner to another source for the answer. The best source may be another person, a reference document, or even an Internet search.

Another option is to ask the rest of the audience. It may be appropriate to say something like "Can anyone here answer that question?" or "Has anyone here had that issue come up?" If you choose this approach, be prepared. You might not agree with the answer. You might get a long-winded volunteer and have to manage the length of the answer. But it may also be a great way to get the audience involved.

> Teach the tongue to say:
> I do not know.
>
> MAIMONIDES

Questions Unrelated to the Topic

Some questions are unrelated to the topic, only superficially related, or so specific to the questioner that to spend time answering them would waste the time of the rest of the listeners. When you get this kind of question, it is your responsibility to redirect the group back to the topic at hand. Try saying something like this: "I know that may be a concern as well, but right now we need to stay on task. Come up after we finish if you'd like to discuss that issue. In the time we have left I need to answer as many questions directly related to our topic as I can. What other questions do we have?"

Confidential and Proprietary Information

If the question involves proprietary or confidential information, say so. But don't say just "No comment." This sounds too abrupt and evasive, as if you have something to hide. Instead, tell the audience what you *can* say, and let them know if and when you will be able to say more. It might sound something like this: "I can't answer that question because the information is proprietary. I *can* say that we are aware that a number of customers have needs in that area. We're excited about the opportunities those needs

> Questions are never indiscreet, answers sometimes are.
>
> OSCAR WILDE

257

present to us. I can also say that we hope to have an announcement about that issue before the end of the third quarter. So stay tuned!"

Questions That Have Already Been Answered

Be willing to repeat information you have already covered. If one person in the audience missed some of the information you covered earlier, the chances are great that other members of the audience also missed it. Don't begin your answer with "As I said earlier." This can sound defensive or accusatory. Instead, make a mental note of information needed. Could you present it in a more attention-getting or memorable way the next time?

Occasionally, one audience member may repeatedly ask you questions about information you already covered. If answering these questions would clearly not be a good use of time for others in the audience, you may choose to offer to meet with the questioner after your talk or to send him the information. Then move on to give others a chance to ask questions.

Hostile and Argumentative Questions

When asked a hostile question, maintain eye contact and a friendly or neutral expression as you pause to think. Resist the natural impulse to look or walk away from the questioner. Again, be sure you pause before speaking. Blurting an answer will make you look defensive or panicky. The pause will make you look calm and thoughtful.

To answer a hostile question, follow the three steps for framing an answer. Again, these are the steps:

1. Demonstrate that you understood the question; find common ground.

2. Give information to support, clarify, or supplement your content or position.

3. Restate your belief, opinion, or recommendation or an important point.

To become really prepared to answer tough and hostile questions, become familiar with the logical fallacies listed in chapter 18. Many tough and hostile questions, and all trick questions, contain a logical fallacy. When you can recognize the fallacy you can respond much more easily, confidently, and effectively. A questioner who asks hostile questions is less likely to do so when it is clear that his own faulty thinking will be clearly and publicly exposed. When you respond calmly and logically, you can defuse a potentially damaging situation. This is a powerful way to increase your credibility with both the questioner and the rest of your listeners.

There is nothing more exhilarating than to be shot at without result."

WINSTON CHURCHILL

The Controlling Questioner

A controlling questioner may attempt to dominate by shouting his question without regard for protocol, ask multiple questions, or attempt to draw you into an argument.

If the questioner attempts to dominate by shouting a question, try this. Look him in the eye and calmly say, "Please remember that question. Let me answer the other (or others) and I'll get back to you shortly." Then turn away and proceed with the answer you choose. This action will reinforce the protocol and your authority and will show respect for the other listeners. Get back to the questioner when it is appropriate to do so.

If one questioner insists on asking multiple questions, be firm. Answer what you think you should and then say something like "I want to answer the questions of as many people as possible. Who else has a question?" Look away from the controlling questioner as you speak, and make eye contact with other listeners as a way of inviting their questions.

If the questioner attempts to draw you into a discussion that is inappropriate for the situation, you may need to take the question "off-line." Try something like this: "It's going to take more time than we have here to discuss that with

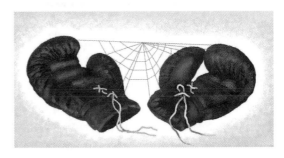

you. I really need to know more of the specifics of your situation. Right now I need to answer as many questions as I can in the time we have. Come up when we're finished here and we can talk about it one-on-one." Then make eye contact with someone else as you ask, "Who has another question?"

Technical Questions

Nontechnical people often complain that technical people give too much information and too many details when asked a question—"I asked him what time it was, and he told me how to build an atomic clock!"

Providing more information than is wanted or needed not only frustrates a less technical questioner but also wastes time. It reduces the number of questions that can be asked—and answered—in the limited time available at a presentation or meeting. Yet a specialist or technical presenter, understanding the many variables that can complicate an issue and wanting to be precise, thorough, truthful, and helpful, often finds it very difficult to know when to stop. So how does a technical presenter know how much is enough and when it becomes too much?

In *Effective Communication Skills for Scientific and Technical Professionals*, author Harry E. Chambers suggests that the technical speaker ask the questioner for guidance. This helps the speaker resolve the "how much detail?" dilemma before he begins the answer. Giving the questioner specific choices about the level of detail wanted can help solve this problem. Paraphrased from Chambers' book, the options might sound something like this:

The secret of being a bore is to tell everything.

VOLTAIRE

- "It would help me to know how best to answer that question if I understood more about how you will use the information. Can you tell me more about your need or concern?"

- "I can give you a detailed explanation of the research project. That will take about ten minutes."

- "I can give a basic understanding of the design and approach, and tell you how to get more information if you need it."

- "I can give you a brief overview, and then answer your specific questions."[2]

If time and protocol allow, the speaker can also offer to answer individual questions after the presentation, give information such as business cards and e-mail addresses so the questioner can follow up, or allow the rest of the audience to have input on how much time—and interest—they have.

> Involve others in determining the level of detail they require by asking them—before you start your response to their original question.
>
> HARRY E. CHAMBERS

Questions from Top Executives

Top executives are likely to ask two types of questions: extremely high level or very precise and detailed. Honeywell chairman Larry Boswell, in discussing the importance of execution, explained why these questions are used: "It's not just getting things done. It's understanding the things that are necessary to be in place in order to get things done. Fifteen years ago the CEO could be a high-level strategist and spend the rest of his time visiting customers or going to Washington dinners. That's not the case anymore. You certainly have to be a strategist, but you better make sure you're involved in the orchestration, the implementation of strategy, as well. If you don't, and it doesn't succeed, you're toast."[3]

The high-level questions are often the questions that have to do with the larger organizational strategy, while the precise and detailed questions address the orchestration, implementation, and specifics of the expected results. Here's an example of a high-level question: "What do you believe are the implications of this reorganization in light of our emphasis on R&D?" An example of an extremely precise question is this: "How would the key numbers change if that interest rate rises by 2 percent?"

While it would be wonderful if you could have all the answers on the tip of your tongue, you can't. No one can. But being able to answer in a way that shows you have considered the high-level strategy issues will demonstrate that you have basic business sense. This will likely do more to enhance your credibility than being able to give vast amounts of detail or even being able to answer every detailed question on the spot. This is doubly true if the questions are hypothetical. Showing you have considered various approaches and options related to organizational strategy demonstrates flexible thinking and open-mindedness. And if the detailed question is hypothetical, especially when it requires that you "crunch numbers" to provide a specific answer, the questioner is often willing to wait for the math to be done.

A key part of preparing for an executive presentation is to thoroughly think through the types of strategic and implementation challenges related to your topic.

Body Language Matters

Even the best answer loses credibility if answered in a defensive or evasive way. And even answers that may not completely satisfy a listener are more easily accepted if answered in a straightforward and confident way. While no substitute for knowledge of content, your behavior when answering a question is an important part of the total message you communicate. An awareness of what the body tends to do when under stress and the knowledge of how to manage your body so it supports your content are important parts of delivering your overall message. If you don't have this awareness, any feelings of anxiety or stress will show in your body language. With an awareness of how to use your body to communicate confidence and sincerity, your body language can enhance the credibility of your content. And knowing you will look and sound confident will again prevent the downward spiral of anxiety and allow you to relax and think clearly.

The body language to use when answering questions is the same body language you should use during the rest of the presentation. The nonverbal delivery skills introduced in chapter 14—eye contact, pace, posture, facial expressions, voice, gestures and movement—will all serve you well.

Don't Change Styles Now!

Maintaining a consistent style when you move from delivering planned information to answering questions is a critical part of communicating a natural, honest approach. If your style changes drastically between the different parts of your presentation, the listeners will wonder which of the styles is the "real" you. This naturally raises a question about your credibility—if you were "real" only part of the time, when were you real and when weren't you? And what were your intentions when you were *not* real?

Use Body Language Purposefully

Let's look at some specific ways you can use the nonverbal delivery skills from chapter 14 to enhance your credibility and help defuse some otherwise awkward or difficult moments.

Pause and Breathe

Earlier you read how important it is to pause before you begin an answer. Be sure you remember to breathe while you pause. Holding your breath will make you feel and look tense. And don't exhale audibly. You don't want to sound like you are sighing as you think about what to say.

Maintain Eye Contact

Eye contact is extremely important when answering questions. Maintain eye contact with the questioner as he speaks. Even if looking away feels more comfortable, it will almost always give the impression that you are not really listening. And maintaining eye contact gives you the chance to notice any subtle facial expression or body language that gives clues about the questions behind the question. If you absolutely must look away to think, look back and reestablish eye contact with the listener before you begin speaking. Don't deliver your answer to the floor, wall, or ceiling—deliver it to the questioner. If the answer is very brief, you can maintain eye contact with the questioner throughout your delivery. If the answer is lengthier—if it lasts much more than about ten seconds, it is very effective to look at others in different parts of the audience as you continue with your answer. Here's why.

Too much eye contact with the questioner can become uncomfortable for both parties. It will also weaken your connection with the rest of the audience. Others may be interested in the answer and should be included.

Some members of the audience may not be as interested and will tend to drift away mentally, but eye contact will help them stay attentive.

End the Answer with Confidence

When you have moved your eyes off the questioner and have begun to include others in the answer, you can choose whom you want to have eye contact with as you finish your answer. Generally, it is a good practice to look back at the original questioner as you conclude your answer. This allows you to check for facial expressions and body language that communicate understanding and acceptance of your answer. In presentations that aim to educate or inform the audience you may want to ask, "Does that answer your question?"

Ending the Answer to a Hostile Question

In situations where the questioner is argumentative or even hostile, you can choose not to look at the questioner again as you complete your answer. Although subtle, this is a powerful way to reduce the chances that the questioner will ask another question or try to embroil you in an argument. You are giving a strong message that the topic has been dealt with and that you are ready to move on to the next question. A powerful democratic dynamic exists in most question-and-answer sessions. Most listeners, even those who would like to ask more than one question, generally accept that other listeners must also be given a chance to ask questions.

Ending the Question-and-Answer Session

Keep track of the time while answering questions. If you need help with this, ask for it. Find someone—the moderator, the host, or even a member of the audience—who will keep track of the time and let you know several minutes before your time is up. Then let the audience know you have time for just one or two more questions. You may want to invite further questions, one-on-one, after the presentation.

Use the Power of Repetition for a Strong Close

When the time is up, you have one final opportunity to reinforce the most important points you covered. Use it. Don't just thank the audience. While nice to do, it doesn't take advantage of the chance you have to further your cause. Instead, repeat your close. Once again, briefly state the actions you would like the audience to take. Be as specific as possible. Repeat the benefits they can expect if they do as you recommend. Then stop and hold your ground. Don't dash away as if you are thrilled to be finished. Stand in place for a few seconds. Enjoy the applause.

Summary

Answering questions can be the best part of your presentation. Question-and-answer sessions start a dialogue with your audience. In many ways you are already an expert at this. You will learn the most when you are in a dialogue.

The audience members can share their thoughts with you. You will learn about their concerns, add details they want, explain in more depth, and have the chance to eliminate confusion or misunderstanding.

To make the most of a question-and-answer session, brainstorm a list of possible questions. You can then identify which can be easily answered, which need to be researched, and which may need to be referred or deferred. A presentation is a chance to share, not an oral exam. Your job is to share what you know when you make a presentation and to learn what the audience still needs to know when you handle questions.

The three-step model for framing your answers can be used for planning answers to anticipated questions and for thinking on your feet as you respond to unanticipated questions.

Use body language that communicates confidence, honesty, and a sincere desire to share information with the audience.

Conclude your presentation by restating the close of your prepared remarks, and then stand in place for a few seconds. Enjoy the applause!

18

Peace rules the day, where reason rules the mind.

WILLIAM COLLINS

Something Isn't Right Here

Self-Defense for Trick and Hostile Questions

The ability to recognize fallacies is an immensely important skill for speakers in highly visible, controversial, and high-stakes situations. A fallacy is an argument that sounds convincing but is essentially flawed. Fallacies are usually born from an attempt to persuade through nonlogical means but can be caused by careless thinking.

Many tough questions, and especially trick questions, contain logical fallacies. Professional interviewers, including business and financial analysts, often are highly skilled at asking questions that contain fallacies. These questions can sound persuasive and can be very difficult to answer convincingly if you can't recognize and expose the logical flaw.

Similarly, when our listeners ask us tough questions, any fallacies in our own arguments are vulnerable to exposure. We can make an argument that sounds persuasive but that might be wrong for any number of reasons. Our "facts" might be wrong or incomplete. Our information may be correct, but we can be wrong about what we have inferred and concluded. We may use words carelessly. Or we may use words in clever ways in an attempt to influence our listeners in an illogical way.

A familiarity with the most common fallacies makes us less likely to commit them unconsciously. If the possible rewards of using fallacies to persuade your listeners outweigh the risks, you may choose to use them. But if you are going to risk leaving yourself open to having your own faulty thinking exposed in a public forum, you should at least do it consciously.

It is terrible to speak well and be wrong.

SOPHOCLES

An explanation of the logical fallacies often found in tough questions asked at business presentations follows. Each fallacious argument is identified, defined, and then used in a sample question similar to one you might hear at a presentation. The first six fallacies include not only sample questions but also sample answers that debunk the fallacious argument.

To practice handling tough questions, try constructing the answers to the remaining sample questions yourself. Remember to consider the tone of your answer as well as the content. As you construct your answers it will be helpful to refer to the three-step model for framing your answers that was introduced in the last chapter.

Common Fallacious Arguments

Learn to recognize these common fallacious arguments (here couched in question form) and you will be much better prepared to respond to tough questions from the audience.

Begging the Question

Begging the question is also known as assuming the answer or circular reasoning. This fallacy occurs when a proposition is used to prove itself. It may sound as if the speaker is giving a reason for something when she is simply restating it. In more formal terms, when the premises in an argument for a proposition contain the proposition itself, both are equally doubtful. In recent years it has become common for the phrase "begs the question" to be mistakenly substituted for "raises the question," but these two phrases actually have very different meanings.

Question: "Since the best way to improve customer satisfaction is to inspect the finished products twice, can't we try doubling the number of inspections on the finished product?"

Logic is the art of making truth prevail.

JEAN DE LA BRUYERE

Answer: "We sure don't want defective products leaving the factory. But the cost of producing a defective product remains even if we catch it before it is shipped. Let's consider ways to reduce the number of defects happening."

Loaded Question

A loaded question includes an assumption as an attempt to damage the position of the other party. This sidetracks the argument. It can antagonize others by making them feel manipulated or bullied.

Question: "Since the marketing department has repeatedly demonstrated incompetence, who on the development team is going to write the press releases?"

Answer: "The development team will have input on what should be included in the press releases. The folks in marketing were definitely challenged by the timing of our competitors' last release and by budget restraints. They are very talented and dedicated people who make a huge contribution to customer awareness of what we can offer, and they will have continued responsibility for press releases."

Swinging the Big Stick

Swinging the big stick is more formally known as the argument from adverse consequences or the appeal to fear. The threat of harm is used to advance the speaker's position.

Question: "How can we not raise our prices? If we don't raise prices, we won't make any money this year. No raises, no bonuses, and no job security next year."

Answer: "We will need to look at ways to improve the bottom line. One idea would be to analyze whether a drop in prices would increase sales volume enough to increase the bottom line. Another would be to look for ways to cut expenses."

Slippery Slope

The slippery slope fallacy assumes that if a first step is taken, a disastrous and inevitable set of consequences will follow. These consequences are presented as the reason for not taking the first step. The slippery slope assumes an inability to make exceptions, set limits, or make decisions on a case-by-case basis.

Question: "Do you really think this is wise? If we fund this project, pretty soon we're going to have every engineer working on his or her own idea, no matter how unlikely it is to ever generate revenue, and then key projects will never be completed!"

Answer: "We have to establish criteria for funding, including potential payoff. We can make this kind of judgment call, just as we do every time we approve a budget."

C Cubed

C cubed—the confusion of correlation and causation—is also known as the fallacy of false cause. It assumes that because two events happened together—in time, in place, or to the same person or group—one must have caused the other.

Question: "When the stock markets peaked, our national murder rate dropped more sharply than in any of the last thirty-five years. So how can you argue with the fact that prosperity decreases violent crime?"

Answer: As happy as I am with the drop in crime then, I'm even happier that we haven't seen an increase in the violent crime rate in the last few years, in spite of drops in the markets. Some sociologists attribute the drop in violent crime to a change in policing policies in major cities. Some think it is due more to the aging of the echo boom generation and the resulting drop in testosterone levels! There are probably many factors that contribute to any significant change."

Non Sequitur

Non sequitur is Latin for "it doesn't follow." A non sequitur is an error in logic made when the conclusion of an argument simply fails to follow from its premise or premises.

Question: "Why should we worry so much about maintaining market leadership? We have by far the best quality products. Our users love us!"

Answer: Our quality has been a huge factor in getting—and keeping—our market leadership. Recently we have been hearing more customers begin to question our pricing. They say that several of our competitors have products that work well for them and that their prices are about 20 percent lower than ours. Let's talk about how customers make buying decisions."

Straw Man

The straw man fallacy is used when a person attacks an argument different from and weaker than the opposition's best argument. This is often done by caricaturing the opposition as so extreme in his views as to be ridiculous—by creating a "straw man" to attack.

Question: "So now a customer who wants us to hold his hand twenty-four hours a day—write his code for him, troubleshoot his process for him, train his staff for him—wants us to give him the new software for practically nothing? And you think we should be grateful for the chance to do it?" How would you answer?

Post Hoc, Ergo Propter Hoc

Post hoc, ergo propter hoc is Latin for "it happened after, so it was caused by." This error in logic is committed when one assumes that because something happened after something else it was caused by that thing. It is often referred to as simply *post hoc*.

Question: "Last January we reorganized the sales teams, and sales increased by 15 percent for the first six months of the year. Since shuffling the players must reinvigorate the sales force, when can we reorganize again?"

How would you answer?

The Doughnut Sandwich

The doughnut sandwich has lots of names but nothing in the middle. It is known as false dilemma, false dichotomy, or excluded middle. It presents only two options, usually extremes, when more options exist. It implies that other options or compromise solutions are not possible. The bumper sticker classic is "America—love it or leave it."

Question: "If we can't dominate that market, there's no point in even being a player. Let's dump that division before it starts to be a financial drain! Then we can focus our resources on our core business. Has anybody thought about who might want to buy that division?"

How would you answer?

Short Term versus Long Term

Short term versus long term is an especially common form of the false dilemma. And it can be argued that short-term versus long-term thinking has been a major problem for many business enterprises.

Question: "How can you recommend any increase in R&D spending when Wall Street is howling about our last earnings projection?"

How would you answer?

Appeal to Ignorance

The appeal to ignorance assumes that whatever has not been proved false must be true and vice versa.

Question: "Nobody has been able to prove that the problem wasn't metal fatigue. It had to be metal fatigue! Shouldn't we narrow the investigation and focus on metal fatigue?"

How would you answer?

Ad Hominem

Ad hominem is Latin for "to the man." It is a fallacy committed when a speaker responds to an argument with a comment about the person making the opposing argument, not the merits of the argument itself. Positive or negative, the comment is usually irrelevant to the argument.

Question: "Isn't that lawyer the one who got lost on the way to our office? If she can't find her way to work, how can she be in charge of a case like this?"

How would you answer?

Hasty Generalization

The fallacy of hasty generalization happens when a generalization is induced using a sample that is too small to be conclusive. You've probably heard it called "jumping to a conclusion."

Question: "That was the third customer today who bought that book. Do you think we should order a couple hundred to get us through the month?"

How would you answer?

Unrepresentative Sample

This error occurs when the sample used, even if quite large, is not representative of the population as a whole.

Question: "Everyone I know—in my neighborhood, at the country club, even at the spa—said they were going to vote for Ashburton. How could Smith have been elected mayor?"

How would you answer?

Going Shopping

Going shopping is also known as pick and choose. Going shopping includes two closely related fallacies: observational selection and the fallacy of exclusion. Observational selection means counting the "hits" and not the "misses." Exclusion means not counting the "misses." You can observe both when you go shopping—just pick and choose the one you like best!

Question: "Wow! The California outlets are really doing well. Almost a third of them might make their sales goals, and half a dozen others are getting close. Maybe that son-in-law of mine will make it as a regional manager! Do you think he's ready to supervise Arizona and Nevada, too?"

How would you answer?

False Analogy

The false analogy compares two very different things, states or implies that they are similar, and draws a conclusion about one based on the other.

It becomes confusing when the two things may in some way be similar; recognizing the fallacy depends on seeing the differences clearly.

Question: "In both cases, the young person can cause death and mayhem to themselves and others. So isn't selling a car to a teenager like giving a loaded handgun to a toddler?"

How would you answer?

Popularity

A fallacy of popularity argues that something is true because it is believed to be true by so many people rather than because it has merit.

Question: "Don't you think the real secret to losing weight is to cut out carbohydrates? I heard that hundreds of thousands of people are switching to high-protein diets."

How would you answer?

Appeal to Authority

The appeal to authority fallacy is committed when an argument is made claiming that something is true because an authority says so, not because the argument has merit. It is a logical error because someone called upon as an authority might be wrong. Perhaps experts in the field disagree, or perhaps the authority was misinformed, misquoted, bribed, or joking. And what is the definition of an authority or expert? As the expansion of knowledge continues and fields become narrower and deeper, an expert in the exact area in question may be harder and harder to find. Perhaps the expert is actually an expert in a different field!

> Logic is not satisfied with assertion. It cares nothing for the opinions of the great—nothing for the prejudices of the many.
>
> ROBERT G. INGERSOLL

Question: "But they're the accountants! They're all CPAs! They work for a major firm! Don't you think we should let them take care of our books and focus on marketing?"

How would you answer?

Wrong-Way Street

A wrong-way street occurs when an effect is assumed to be a cause or a cause is assumed to be an effect. This often happens because of limited perspective.

Question: "But we have to keep hiring! If we slow down, the rate of production won't keep increasing. How can we keep increasing the demand and building sales if we can't continue to increase production?"

How would you answer?

Papa Don't Preach

Papa don't preach is the error in logic more formally called "prejudicial language." The use of Papa don't preach states or implies that ethical or moral goodness is associated with agreeing with the argument. It often uses emotional or value-laden terms to accomplish this.

Question: "So, the generous among us will certainly welcome this opportunity to fulfill our obligation to give back to our community by supporting the selfless work of the tireless and saintly volunteers of this noble charity. Who among you could refuse to do your part?"

How would you answer?

Red Herring

The red herring sounds like it is relevant to the question or topic being discussed but is actually irrelevant. It can throw listeners off track, confuse the issue, and make it harder to reach an agreement and a conclusion.

Question: "Before we discuss measures to encourage major urban areas to reduce their use of fresh water, don't we also need to consider how much of the world's fresh water supply is locked in both glaciers and subglacial reservoirs?"

How would you answer?

The ability to recognize the fallacy in a tough or argumentative question is the first step in being able to respond successfully. But remember, many situations are complex and emotional. What may seem reasonable and logical to you may not be to others.

Summary

The ability to recognize and respond logically to fallacious arguments (arguments that may sound convincing but are logically flawed) is an important skill for speakers. It will increase both your effectiveness and your confidence.

Many tough questions and trick questions contain logical fallacies. These questions are much easier to answer convincingly when you recognize and expose the logical flaw.

Fallacies in our own arguments are vulnerable to exposure. If the possible rewards of using a fallacious argument to persuade your listeners outweigh the risks of exposure, you can certainly choose to use it. A familiarity with common fallacies makes us less vulnerable to committing them unconsciously.

19

Something there is that doesn't love a wall . . .
And makes gaps even two can pass abreast . . .
Something there is that doesn't love a wall,
That wants it down.

ROBERT FROST

Our Small World

Overcoming Barriers to Understanding

As the world becomes smaller we find ourselves communicating with many new people and in new ways. This chapter will give you some basic guidance in overcoming three common challenges that come up in most large organizations and many small ones. These are making Web presentations, making presentations when English is a second language, and stuttering.

Web Presentations

Many of the techniques and skills that work well for a traditional in-person presentation will work well for a Web presentation. But a Web presentation does complicate matters a bit, so here are some points to consider.

What kind of Web presentation are we talking about? Let's look at some of the most common kinds. Then we can cover the challenges each presents and give some tips for managing these challenges and making the Web presentation a success.

The term *webcast* is usually used to mean a presentation via the Web to a large group of people that typically includes little or no interaction. Think *broadcast*. A *Web conference* usually includes a smaller group—as few as two people to a maximum of about twenty-five. Generally, the larger the number, as with any other kind of meeting, the smaller the proportion of time each person has to speak. A *webinar* is associated with training or teaching. It may include just a few participants or many. They may come from different organizations or from different functional areas or locations within the same organization. A webinar may include an opportunity for real-time interaction, for interaction during parts of the event or at the end, or for no interaction.

One of the obvious differences between Web presentations and in-person presentations is the Web—the technology needed to communicate over distances. Whether the Web event includes just audio or both audio and video, more technology means more details to think about. First, let's look at how the technology influences your decisions about some of the elements of your presentation.

Bandwidth Is Key

Without enough bandwidth, the participants will literally not be on the same wavelength. Each participant should receive the same content at the same time. If this can't happen, you will start with two strikes against you. Adjusting for this problem during the presentation—explaining the problem, waiting for everyone to catch up, repeating information—makes the presentation more difficult to deliver, manage, and receive. Unless you are a specialist in the technology of Web presentations, get some advice and assistance using the technology, especially the first time you use it. And make sure that technical assistance is readily and instantly available in case of a blip in the equipment or a last-minute change.

Audio Considerations

All the participants have to hear the presentation clearly. Especially when you are not using video, it is critical that all of the content can be heard. Without video or the opportunity for interaction, excellent fidelity is extremely important. It will not only help people hear the content accurately, but it is vital simply to avoid annoying, frustrating, and alienating the listeners.

Telephone land lines are still best for high-quality audio. If you are speaking through the Internet, make sure that all participants have connections fast enough to carry the audio transmission clearly, even at high-traffic periods of the day.

Wear a headset if you will be using a keyboard or physically managing other elements during the webcast. Having your hands free to handle whatever else you must do can prevent a lot of problems.

Video Considerations

As with in-person presentations, your listeners will be influenced by what they see even before you begin to speak. Following these guidelines will help you be more effective.

Keep the room environment spare. A solid-color background without unneeded objects (potted plants, pictures on the wall, a lampshade with ball fringe) will be less distracting and will also help maintain the quality of the video transmission.

Consider the lighting. Fluorescent lighting can be unflattering. Overhead lighting can make you look scary. The best lighting will be full spectrum for both brightness and warmth and will come from a variety of directions to eliminate shadows. This type of cross-lighting may require stage lighting or portable spotlights.

Dressing conservatively will keep the focus on your face. Colors that contrast with the background will make it easier to see you. Solid colors will be less distracting than patterns and will require less digital data for transmission, helping to maintain the quality of the video.

Delivery Skills

As with in-person presentations, much of the meaning will come from your tone of voice, inflections, and pauses. But when your listeners can't see you, your speech patterns and the quality of your voice become even more important. Remember to use the vocal delivery skills and the pacing and pausing skills covered in chapter 14.

If using video, avoid an extreme close-up head shot. A waist-up shot is generally best. Use gestures that are slightly subdued, or simply keep your hands at your sides. Don't shift your weight. Reducing animation keeps you from bouncing around on the screen. Keep in mind that the audience can't see everything you see. Avoid gesturing toward your visual aids. And remember to smile. It can warm up an already cool medium, and a smile can be heard as well as seen.

Facilitating the Web Presentation

Your job is to remove as many unknowns as possible from the minds of the participants. You introduce the presentation. You set the protocol. You introduce participants, including each one's role and location. You explain if, when, and how participation will take place, and you manage that interaction. If participants interact by voice, you identify each by name and location. If questions or comments are typed and displayed on-screen, especially multiple comments on the same screen, you may need to identify the source of the comment. You may choose to call on participants from various locations. This is a great way to encourage people not to just sit half-listening with their mute button pressed. If you choose this approach, let the participants know as you open the presentation that this will be part of the protocol so you don't cause delays or embarrassment by catching a participant by surprise.

Include a solid close, with a summary and an outline of the next steps to be taken by the participants.

When English Is a Second Language

Many highly skilled members of top organizations speak English as a second or third language. Their excellent technical skills and ability to write perfect e-mails and memos may not always be matched by their ability to be understood when speaking English.

An accent can be an excellent way to get and keep the attention of listeners, who may be intrigued by the different sound and rhythm. But an accent so strong that it interferes with the speaker's ability to be understood is not an asset. Differences in the sounds, intonations, and stress patterns between English and other languages contribute to the challenge of communicating clearly in a second language.

For example, English tends to stress only one word in a phrase. Stressing more than one, a common pattern in some languages, can create the impression among American listeners that the speaker is irritated or even angry. English also tends to stress the most important words, such as nouns and verbs, and reduce the emphasis on the less important ones. This creates an up and down pattern rather than one that is staccato or flat. Consider the following sentence: He *went* to the *zoo* to *study* the *snakes*. A native speaker of English would likely emphasize the words in italics.

In other languages the intonation pattern is often different, creating unintended impressions among listeners who are native speakers of English. Vietnamese, which contains single-syllable words spoken in as many as six different tones, can sound like shouting to the American ear. And Indian immigrants, although coming from a country with many different dialects, often speak English without stressing nouns or verbs and with an upward intonation at the end of sentences. To the American ear, this can be interpreted as a questioning tone. Similar to the phenomenon known as "uptalk," this can also be interpreted as lacking in confidence and authority.

What sets men at variance is but the treachery of language, for always they desire the same things.

ANTOINE DE SAINT-EXUPERY

Accent reduction classes can help speakers of English as a second language identify and practice the sounds and the stress patterns of English. Offered through corporate universities, community colleges, university extension programs, and private companies, an accent reduction class can be an excellent way to improve one's ability to be fully understood by native speakers.

Best Practices for Speakers of English as a Second Language

If English is not your native language, the first five tips below will help you present information effectively to a group. Add the next five to increase your English skills as you communicate every day.

1. Keep in mind that most people respect the fact that you are able to communicate in a second language. They want you to succeed.

2. Face your listeners and make eye contact. Use facial expressions and other nonverbal clues to increase the listeners' ability to understand. Maintain eye contact to help you judge whether or not they understand you.

3. Slow your rate of speech. This will give your listeners a chance to become accustomed to your accent and to distinguish between individual words. Invite your listeners to tell you if you speak too rapidly.

4. Pause if you need time to think. Listeners are willing to wait. The pause will give them time to consider and process the information you have already covered.

5. If appropriate (and it often is), smile frequently while you speak. It relaxes you. It relaxes your voice. It also relaxes your listeners and helps create a comfortable atmosphere where a lack of understanding can be acknowledged and overcome.

6. Immerse yourself in English. Listen to English radio stations, and engage in English conversation whenever possible.

7. Learn phonetics. You will learn how to make the sounds used in English that are not used in your native language and how to listen with greater comprehension.

8. Learn the American intonation pattern. This pattern stresses nouns and verbs, as in "*Go* to the *office* and *check* the *file*." Listen to the difference between this pattern and other patterns that may be more flat or staccato.

9. Make a list of words that are difficult to pronounce. Consciously note what makes each word difficult for you. Is it an unfamiliar consonant sound or stress on a particular syllable? Practice the words with a native speaker.

10. Record your own speech or review your voice-mail messages before you send them. Listen, monitor, and practice your pronunciation.

Best Practices for Native Speakers with Nonnatives

If English is your native language, the tips below will help you communicate effectively with nonnatives when making a presentation or participating in meetings or everyday conversations. As you use them, be sensitive to the fact that different listeners will likely have varied levels of expertise in English. Observe closely and check for understanding so that you maximize your ability to be understood without seeming to patronize your listeners.

1. Face your listeners when speaking; face the speaker when you are listening. Your facial expressions and other nonverbal clues will increase the listeners' ability to understand you. You will be better able to judge whether or not they understand you.

2. Summarize and check for understanding early and often. Whether you are making a presentation or participating in a meeting or conversation, this will help you identify barriers to good communication before they cause more problems.

3. Invite and encourage your listeners to ask for clarification if needed. Nonnative speakers may be reluctant to ask. Inviting them to do so can help put them at ease and create a more comfortable and cooperative atmosphere.

4. Slow your pace a bit. This will give your listeners a chance to identify individual words and to ask for clarification when needed.

5. Invite your listeners to tell you if you speak too rapidly. Again, nonnative speakers may be reluctant to tell you. Inviting them to do so can put

them at ease and create a more comfortable and cooperative atmosphere.

6. If you don't understand what a nonnative speaker said and asking him to repeat it doesn't help, ask to see the word in writing. Reading it can be the answer. Then say the word out loud. The nonnative speaker will be able to hear it pronounced correctly.

7. Minimize the use of slang and jargon. Many such words and phrases are puzzling and easily misunderstood.

8. Limit the use of humor, sarcasm, and word play. These are often dependent on culture and can cause serious misunderstanding, confusion, or alienation.

9. Keep your sentences short and direct. Avoid complex or rambling sentence structures. (You may want to avoid these with native speakers, also.)

10. Communicate one idea at a time. Avoid thinking out loud. Stay focused on one idea until you have finished it. Then make a clear transition to the next. Pause between ideas to allow the listeners to process information.

The rise of the global economy presents both the challenge and the opportunity to give presentations to people of other cultures. An understanding of the differences between cultures is vitally important to effective international communication. For information on making an effective presentation in cross-cultural settings, check the resource section in the back of this book. You will find both general and culture-specific resources covering a broad range of topics.

Stuttering

Many highly successful people in many walks of life have been stutterers, including Aristotle, Isaac Newton, Charles Darwin, Winston Churchill, author John Updike, former CEO of General Electric Jack Welch, and entertainers James Earl Jones, Marilyn Monroe, and Carly Simon.[1] About 5 percent of the world's population will stutter at some time in their life, most often in childhood. Most grow out of it, but about 1 percent of adults remain stutterers.[2] This means that approximately 2.8 million people in the United States—and 55 million around the world—are challenged by a stuttering disorder.[3]

Stuttering has puzzled thinkers and scientists throughout recorded history. The causes of stuttering are still not understood, although modern scientific methods are shedding new light on this mystery. The old explanations for stuttering—long thought to be caused by psychological stress or learned from family members or close acquaintances who stutter—are being supplanted by new understandings from the fields of genetics, neuroscience, radiology, and speech pathology. These new discoveries may soon help us answer many questions about stuttering. Among these are why stuttering occurs about four times as often in men as in women and why it is often, but not always, outgrown.

In late 2000, researchers announced the discovery of evidence of a genetic factor behind some cases of stuttering. And even more dramatic evidence comes from PET scans showing differences in the physiology of those who stutter. Working together, researchers at the University of California at Santa Barbara and the University of Texas have reported a difference in brain function in stutterers. This may interfere with speech production, as these differences disappear on the scan when the stutterer is speaking without stuttering. Also of interest is that the suspect brain patterns appear even when the stutterer only imagines he is stuttering. Researchers believe that this suspect brain activity is responsible for sending scrambled messages to the muscles responsible for producing the sounds of speech—the lips, tongue, vocal cords, and diaphragm.[4]

If you stutter, the chances are that you have already addressed the issue. To do so requires personal diagnosis and a program that is best tailored to the individual. However, for an excellent article full of specific tips for dealing with the challenges of stuttering, especially when interacting with a new acquaintance, read "Guerrilla Stutterer" by Eric Bourland (see the resource section in the back of the book). If you or someone you know wants more information, several organizations devoted to understanding stuttering and helping overcome the challenges it presents are also listed in the resource section at the back of this book.

If you interact with someone who stutters, the tips that follow will help overcome many of the barriers that stuttering can present.

Tips for Improving Communication with a Person Who Stutters

Communicating with someone who stutters can be an awkward or frustrating experience for everyone involved. To help keep the frustration to a minimum, use these tips to support efforts to communicate effectively.

Be patient. Wait for the speaker to finish. Do not finish his sentences. This is insulting and is especially embarrassing when the sentence is completed incorrectly. Speak at a relaxed pace but not so slowly that you sound unnatural or patronizing.

Stay connected. Use natural eye contact and facial expressions, and avoid self-conscious body language. Do not fidget. Wait through pauses. On the telephone, recognize that the nonverbal cues are missing, and be willing to wait through pauses that can seem uncomfortably long.

Do not give advice. Advice is not needed, helpful, or welcome. Avoid comments like "just relax," "slow down," or "take a deep breath." These are simplistic and demonstrate the speaker's discomfort and ignorance.

Finally, it is important to know that all of us, stutterers or not, share most of the same feelings about speaking to a group. John Alback, a stutterer and founder of a self-help group for others who stutter, wrote:

When I first learned that public speaking was the thing people feared most, I was very surprised. I thought this to be true for those of us who stutter, but not for the public at large. I had always figured that the fear of death would top this list for most people. Upon reflection, however, I came up with three advantages that death has over speaking in front of a group of people. First of all, you are only going to die once, whereas, there is no limit to the number of times you can make a fool of yourself in front of an audience. Second, death is the best way I know to avoid speaking in front of a group. And last, but not least, after you die, you do not have to walk back to your seat.[5]

Summary

The complexities of any type of human communication—the shades of meaning and subtleties that contribute to understanding—can easily become barriers to communication when language, speech, or media challenges are added to the mix. These challenges can often be met by recognizing that differences and challenges do exist. Then learning about the specifics of the challenges, planning ways to minimize and overcome them, and engaging others in cooperating in our efforts can go a long way to helping us communicate effectively.

20

Victory awaits those who have everything in order. People call this luck.

ROALD AMUNDSEN

Feeling Ready
Feels Great!

Speaker's Checklist for Perfect Planning

Planning thoroughly is a huge part of reducing anxiety and communicating effectively.

You have enough to think about at the last minute without worrying about logistical details. Your presentation probably will not go perfectly. You need to make sure that you plan thoroughly enough to eliminate the preventable problems. Then you will have the time, energy, and clarity of mind to deal with the others quickly, graciously, and with a sense of humor.

The speaker's checklist of essential information that follows will help you remember the details that need to be covered. Completing the checklist will give you the best chance of having everything you need where you need it and when you need it.

To the left of each item is a box to check when you have covered that detail. More or fewer of the items will apply depending on the nature of your presentation. You may want to photocopy this list to use whenever you need it. If you have an assistant who will handle some of the details, give the assistant the list. Then agree on who will do what. You don't need to say or hear "I thought you were going to do that!" just before your presentation.

Getting to the Venue

Gather information early about getting to the venue. Keep it where you can access it at any time while traveling.

☐ The venue's address, detailed directions, and a map.

☐ All needed travel reservations.

☐ Travel agent's phone number for help with delayed or canceled flights.

☐ Information on where to park.

☐ Information on how to enter the building. If you will arrive outside of normal business hours, get an after-hours phone number.

☐ The name and phone number of the person who will greet you.

☐ The names and phone numbers of at least two other people who could help you, for example, assistants, secretaries, building security personnel, concierge.

☐ The name and location of the room where you will present your talk.

☐ The name and phone number of the person holding any supplies you sent in advance.

☐ Confirmation of the delivery of these supplies and the location where these supplies are stored.

Hotel or Conference Center Information

Communicate early and often with the hotel or conference center staff. It is their job to give you what you need to succeed. They will appreciate your clear directions—they don't want last-minute emergencies any more than you do. The staff will be knowledgeable about the facilities. They know if a room can become too hot or cold, the best choices from their kitchen's menu, and other helpful details. Use their expertise when making arrangements. Make sure you get the following information:

- ☐ The names and phone numbers of the support staff: hotel managers, the catering manager, audiovisual support personnel, and so on.

- ☐ A list of the services provided by the staff of the facility and those that might be provided by contractors (such as audiovisual technicians). If contractors are used, make sure they will be available when you need them, such as early in the morning to set up your equipment.

- ☐ Confirmation of all pricing and payment agreements.

Seating Arrangement and Other Requirements

Send the facility the specifics (a diagram is helpful) of your requirements. Check in advance to be sure your instructions were received, but don't trust that they were followed accurately. Instructions can be too easily lost or misunderstood. Arrive early to check that the facility is set the way you need it.

- ☐ Type of seating/number of seats.

- ☐ Tables/table arrangements.

- ☐ Space required in front of room.

- ☐ Lecterns or tables needed.

- ☐ Podium (raised speaking platform) with size requirements.

- ☐ Lighting requirements.

- ☐ Audiovisual support requirements, including microphones, computer projectors, video players, easels, flip charts, whiteboards, and so on.

- ☐ Type and quantity of refreshments to be served.

- ☐ Specifics on the placement and timing of refreshment services.

Additional Detail

Here are a few extra details usually worth asking about. The staff may know about them but probably won't mention them unless you ask.

☐ Will your refreshments be served on time? Quietly? Will they be set up in a common area? If so, will they be safe from hungry "predators"?

☐ If you have bar service before your presentation, will it be closed before you begin speaking?

☐ How will your audience find you? Where and when will the staff post the information about your presentation?

☐ What types of events are scheduled in adjoining rooms? How noisy will they be? Will your noise level disturb them?

☐ Will the people in nearby rooms take their breaks at the same time as you? If so, are adequate rest room and phone facilities available? If not, can breaks be staggered?

☐ Does the room have any view-blocking pillars? This can be a concern especially in older buildings. Can tables and chairs be placed so everyone can see everything they need to?

☐ Does the room have any screen-blocking low-hanging chandeliers or other lighting challenges?

☐ Does a screen need to be moved to the side of the room? Are two screens needed?

☐ How many plants are in the room and where are they placed? You don't want to speak from a forest of potted palms.

☐ Does the room have temperature or ventilation issues? How are they dealt with?

☐ How quickly can the room be filled with and emptied of people? This is important to know when scheduling breaks.

☐ Will the hotel staff remove any empty tables or chairs from the room? You don't want to make a presentation in a room used for furniture storage.

Finally, what other details must be handled? What other information do you need to gather? What do you need to communicate to others? Make a list. Check off each item when it is done.

Summary

Planning thoroughly is a critical part of reducing anxiety. Use the above checklist to make sure that you arrive at the venue with time to spare and that the facility is appropriate for your needs and ready for you when you arrive. Thorough preparation will free you from having to deal with many problems that might otherwise occur. It will help give you the ability to deal calmly and effectively with any unforeseeable problems that might come up.

EPILOGUE

All things must change, and only that which changes remains true.

CARL JUNG

THE FRANCIS EFFECT—the reduction of anxiety and the increase in confidence that come with truly understanding the body's natural response to public speaking—starts with understanding and accepting our human nature.

Most of us will never be able to completely eliminate our natural tendency to experience some nervousness when speaking to a group. But the wisdom that comes with understanding that this anxiety is natural and normal—that we can minimize it, prepare for it, work with it, and become excellent speakers in spite of it—can make all the difference.

We can change. We can grow. To remain true to ourselves and reach our full potential, we must.

Enjoy your presentations, and enjoy the rewards they bring.

Appendix

RESOURCES

Analogies and Metaphors

Loose Cannons, Red Herrings, and Other Lost Metaphors by Robert Claiborne
New York: W. W. Norton, 2001
ISBN: 0-393-32186-X
A fun little book filled with explanations of the origins of metaphors we have used so often that most of them have become clichés. Many of the explanations are told as very short stories, making the book easy to read.

Metaphor by Zoltan Kovecses
Oxford, England: Oxford University Press, 2002
ISBN: 0-19-514511-9
An introduction to the theories about metaphor, aimed at the serious student of metaphor or linguistics.

Metaphors Dictionary by Elyse Sommer with Dorrie Weiss
Canton, MI: Visible Ink Press, 2001
ISBN: 1-57859-137-6
Covers the different types of metaphors and provides metaphors from ancient times to the present. Includes metaphors used by poets, scientists, business leaders, philosophers, and more, with hundreds from Shakespeare, indexed by both subject and author or speaker.

Metaphors We Live By by George Lakoff and Mark Johnson
Chicago: University of Chicago Press, 2003
ISBN: 0-226-46801-1
Explores the use and the power of the metaphors we use every day. A real eyeopener into the importance of metaphor in informing and persuading, it will help you recognize the use of metaphors to confuse or deceive and to appreciate how important a tool they are in speaking to a group.

Anxiety

The Anxiety and Phobia Workbook by Edmund J. Bourne
Oakland, CA: New Harbinger, 2000
ISBN: 1-57224-223-X
A good review of therapies, methods, and exercises for overcoming and managing anxiety and phobias.

Anxiety, Phobias and Panic: A Step-by-Step Program for Regaining Control of Your Life by Reneau Z. Peurifoy
New York: Warner Books, 1995
ISBN: 0-446-67053-7
Provides a thorough understanding of the roots of anxiety and how the different components interplay to interfere with comfort and productivity. Gives many good suggestions for reducing and managing anxiety and phobias.

The Breathing Book: Good Health and Vitality through Essential Breath Work by Donna Farhi
New York: Henry Holt and Company, 1996
ISBN: 0-8050-4297-0
Exercises for breathing for health and relaxation. This book is well written, the directions for the exercises are clear, and the benefits of the exercises are explained.

Freedom from Fear: Overcoming Anxiety, Phobias and Panic by Howard Liebgold, MD
New York: Citadel Press, 2004
ISBN: 0-8065-2591-6
A very readable and helpful guide to understanding anxiety. Step-by step guides for overcoming the limits caused by common phobias.

Full Catastrophe Living: Using the Wisdom of Your Body and Mind to Face Stress, Pain, and Illness by Jon Kabat-Zinn, PhD
New York: Delta, 1990
ISBN: 0-385-30312-2
Insights on the damaging effects of stress in modern life, advice and exercises to help reduce the effects of stress and stress-related illnesses.

"The Four Visual Intensity Patterns of Personal Consciousness" by Steven Paglierani
http://theemergencesite.com/Theory/Visual-Intensities-4-Events.htm
An interesting article on how the mind and body work through the four different states of consciousness: getting overwhelmed, getting wounded, reliving a wound, and healing.

The Introvert Advantage: How to Thrive in an Extrovert World by Marti Olsen Laney
New York: Workman Publishing, 2002
ISBN: 0-7611-2369-5

Learn to recognize, understand, and appreciate how and why introverts differ from extroverts. Includes information on functioning well in the workplace, in relationships, as a parent, and in social situations.

Life Is a Series of Presentations: 8 Ways to Punch Up Your People Skills at Work, at Home, Anytime, Anywhere by Tony Jeary
New York: Fireside, 2004
ISBN: 0-7432-5141-5 (also available in audio and e-book formats)
Shows how to reduce anxiety by anticipating the needs and responses of your audience, understanding and predicting the challengers ("snipers," "cheerleaders," "vacationers," and "convicts"), and encouraging audience involvement. Discusses ways to successfully influence listeners.

Living Yoga: A Comprehensive Guide for Daily Life edited by Georg Feuerstein and Stephan Bodian
New York: Jeremy P. Tarcher/Putnam, 1993
ISBN: 0-87477-729-1
A good introduction to the various types of yoga and yoga-influenced lifestyles. A variety of views on topics related to reducing and managing stress for better living. Each topic is covered by an expert on the subject.

Mastering the Art of Public Speaking: A Practical Approach to Overcoming Stage Fright, Shyness and Anxiety by Peter Desberg
New York: Barnes and Noble Books, 1999
ISBN: 0-7607-1412-6
Emphasizes the intellectual and emotional causes of anxiety. Helps the speaker analyze them and suggests helpful exercises and techniques for reducing and managing anxiety.

Overcoming Stage Fright in Everyday Life by Joyce Ashley
New York: Clarkson Potter, 1996
ISBN: 0-517-70465-X
Uses increased understanding and practical exercises to take you through a process for overcoming performance anxiety.

Relax and Renew: Restful Yoga for Stressful Times by Judith Lasater, PhD, Pt
Berkeley, CA: Rodmell Press, 1995
ISBN: 0-9627138-4-8
Focuses on restorative yoga as a means of reducing stress and stress-induced ailments. Specific programs are provided for relieving problems such as back pain, headaches, and insomnia. Special section for problems specific to women (e.g., those related to menstruation and pregnancy).

Social Phobia: From Shyness to Stage Fright by John R. Marshall
New York: Basic Books, 1994
ISBN: 0-465-07896-6
Summarizes research and current treatments for a variety of social phobias. Theorizes about the evolutionary purpose of social phobias and offers a recommended reading list.

Waking the Tiger: Healing Trauma by Peter A. Levine with Ann Frederick
Berkeley, CA: North Atlantic Books, 1997
ISBN: 1-55643-233-X
A great book for understanding the nature of trauma. Explains how to work through and move beyond the negative effects of highly stressful experiences. A valuable, insightful, and highly readable book.

Why Zebras Don't Get Ulcers: An Updated Guide to Stress, Stress-Related Diseases, and Coping by Robert M. Sapolsky
New York: W. H. Freeman, 1998
ISBN: 0-7167-3210-6
Both an excellent review and the author's interpretation of research on the causes and effects of stress. Highly readable without an extensive background in science.

Many other good books, videotapes, and audiotapes are on the market with a wide variety of mind-body approaches to reducing anxiety and increasing your ability to cope.

Body Language

Center for Nonverbal Studies
http://members.aol.com/nonverbal2/index.htm
The Center for Nonverbal Studies has the stated goal of supporting the scientific study of nonverbal information. Check out the on-line Nonverbal Dictionary for terms, definitions, explanations, interpretations, and examples of different nonverbal communication.

Conquering Deception by Jef Nance
Kansas City, MO: Irvin Benham Group, 2001
ISBN: 0-9672862-4-7
Explains how to recognize the hidden meanings of what others say by interpreting eye movements, nose gestures, and other nonverbal clues. Also covers the hidden meanings behind verbal patterns and choices.

Emotions Revealed: Recognizing Faces and Feelings to Improve Communication and Emotional Life by Paul Ekman
New York: Times Books, 2003

ISBN: 0-8050-7275-6
A review of the author's forty years studying facial expressions in humans, this book explores the evolution of facial expressions and their roots in human nature. Includes photos of faces with explanations of the subtle differences observable in facial expressions.

Facial Action Coding System
http://www.smithsonianmag.si.edu/smithsonian/issues04/jan04/readingfaces.html
http://face-and-emotion.com/dataface/misctext/iwafgr.html
http://face-and-emotion.com/dataface/facs/description.jsp
The FACS (Facial Action Coding System) is a system for recognizing and interpreting facial expressions.

Gestures: The Do's and Taboos of Body Language around the World by Roger E. Axtell
New York: John Wiley & Sons, 1997
ISBN: 0-471-18342-3
Discusses and gives examples of different gestures and their different meanings in countries around the world. This book will help you understand the nonverbal communication of those from other cultures. It will also help you to be understood without committing faux pas.

Multicultural Manners by Norine Dresser
New York: John Wiley & Sons, 1996
ISBN: 0-471-11819-2
Anthropology meets etiquette. A good guide to understanding different cultural norms and expectations. Among the topics discussed are body language, child-rearing practices, classroom behavior, clothing, colors, food, gifts, luck and supernatural forces, male-female relations, prejudice, time, and verbal expressions.

Nonverbal Communication in Human Interaction by Mark L. Knapp and Judith A. Hall
Belmont, CA: Wadsworth Publishing, 2001
ISBN: 0-15-506372-3
A textbook used in university communication and psychology classes and considered a classic work in the field of nonverbal communication. Covers research and findings on nonverbal delivery skills, reading body language (including subtle changes such as pupil dilation), smell, touch, and environmental factors. Contains an index, a comprehensive table of contents, footnotes, and suggestions for further reading at the end of every chapter.

Reading People: How to Understand People and Predict Their Behavior, Anytime—Anyplace by Jo-Ellan Dimitrius and Mark Mazzarella
New York: Ballantine, 1999
ISBN: 0-345-42587-1
A jury consultant explains how to read body language, facial expression, tone of voice, and appearance and when and how people use language to decide what people are thinking or feeling.

Color Vision Deficiency

"Color Blindness: Explaining Color Deficiency" by Stephen Holland, 2002
http://members.shaw.ca/hidden-talents/vision/color/colorblind1.html
A good article for learning the basics about color vision deficiency.

Color Vision Deficiency and Color Blindness by Mary M. Olsen and Kenneth R. Harris
Eugene, OR: Fern Ridge Press, 1988
ISBN: 0-961-53322-6
Covers the basics on color vision deficiency. Discusses the genetics behind the various types of color vision deficiency and the tests used to determine the level of blindness.

Colors for the Color Blind
http://www.toledo-bend.com/colorblind/index.html
A Web site offering a set of color charts to aid the color blind in working with computer colors on the Internet and in Web sites. It also provides software (shareware and freeware) for checking colors on your computer screen.

Vischeck
http://www.vischeck.com/vischeck/
Vischeck software, available from the Vischeck Web site, shows you what an image looks like to a color vision deficient person. Daltonize, another tool from Vischeck, corrects images for color vision deficient viewers. You can try Vischeck software on-line and run it on your own image files or on a Web page. You can also download programs to let you run it on your own computer.

Dialogue

Conversation: How Talk Can Change Our Lives by Theodore Zeldin
Mahwah, NJ: HiddenSpring, 2000
ISBN: 1-58768-000-9
This beautiful little book is filled with inspiring thoughts and ideas of what public speaking, at its best, can start.

Conversationally Speaking by Alan Garner
Los Angeles: Lowell House, 1997
ISBN: 1-56565-629-6
An easy-to-read discussion of the basics of conversation: starting conversations, listening, asking questions, resisting manipulation, managing anxiety, and more.

Dialogue: The Art of Thinking Together by William Isaacs
New York: Doubleday, 1999
ISBN: 0-385-47999-9
Brings together thinking from a variety of fields. Uses examples of how successful communication can increase understanding and cooperation and bring about positive changes.

Dialogue: Rediscover the Transforming Power of Conversation by Linda Ellinor and Glenna Gerard
New York: John Wiley & Sons, 1998
ISBN: 0-471-17466-1
A comprehensive look at the importance of the beliefs and skills that make true dialogue possible. Case studies and exercises for the readers bring the concepts to life.

First Impressions: What You Don't Know about How Others See You by Ann Demarais and Valerie White
New York: Bantam, 2004
ISBN: 0-553-80320-4
A very readable book on making a good first impression. The information and tips go well beyond first encounters. This book gives readers suggestions for identifying differences between self-perception and the interpretation by others. Each chapter covers one of the "seven fundamentals" of creating a good first impression.

Dress and Appearance

Casual Power: How to Power Up Your Nonverbal Communication and Dress Down for Success by Sherry Maysonave
Austin, TX: Bright Books, 1999
ISBN: 1-880092-48-4
Discusses the impact of body language, demeanor, and clothing on the impression you make and the response you receive from others.

Chic Simple Dress Smart for Women: Wardrobes that Win in the Workplace by Kim Johnson Gross and Jeff Stone
New York: Warner Books, 2002
ISBN: 0-446-53044-1
Focuses on dressing for the workplace. The four sections—"Get Job," "Succeed in Job," "Get Better Job," and "Goes with the Job"—take you through what to wear (when and why), how to choose it, how to buy it, and how to travel with it. Filled with practical advice, suggestions, and explanations about why it matters.

Dressing Smart for Women: 101 Mistakes You Can't Afford to Make . . . and How to Avoid Them by JoAnna Nicholson
Manassas Park, VA: Impact Publications, 2003
ISBN: 1-57023-200-8
Shows how to avoid mistakes like the wrong color, wrong style, inappropriate makeup, and buying quantity instead of quality. Color photos help illustrate the author's points.

Dressing the Man: Mastering the Art of Permanent Fashion
by Alan Flusser
New York: HarperCollins, 2002
ISBN: 0-06-019144-9
A good guide to classic dressing and a beautifully designed book. Using drawings and photos to illustrate the recommendations, it covers business, casual, and formal dressing. It explains how to coordinate patterns and colors, with special emphasis on making choices that flatter individual body types, face shapes, and coloring.

The Indispensable Guide to Classic Men's Clothing by Christopher Sulavik, Josh Karlen, and Amy Libra
New York: Tatra Press, 1999
ISBN: 0-9661847-1-8
The question-and-answer format makes this is an easy-to-read-guide to dressing. Organized by item of clothing, it shows how to identify quality and how to dress appropriately for the occasion. It includes insights and tips from many experts on men's clothing. This also is a good resource for those with a limited budget.

Men's Wardrobe (Chic Simple) by Kim Johnson Gross, Jeff Stone, Woody Hochswender, and David Bashaw
New York: Knopf, 1998
ISBN: 0-679-44576-5
A good guide to grooming and choosing and caring for your wardrobe. It is organized into five sections: "First Things," "Work Life," "Everyday Life," "Outdoor Life" (which includes the gym), and "Night Life." It addresses changing expectations and choices and gives suggestions on packing for travel and keeping your closet manageable.

The Pocket Stylist: Behind-the-Scenes Expertise from a Fashion Pro on Creating Your Own Look by Kendall Farr
New York: Gotham Books, 2004
ISBN: 1-59240-041-8
Explains how to take your true measurements and then pick clothes, shoes, fabrics, and even lingerie to make the most of them. Explains when to use—and how to find—a tailor, how to add accessories, and how to apply makeup.

Style and the Man: How and Where to Buy the Best Men's Clothes
by Alan Flusser
New York: HarperCollins, 1996
ISBN: 0-06-270155-X
Item by item—shirts, ties, casual wear, formal wear, shoes—this book shows what to look for and why. City-by-city guide shows you where to shop in the United States, Europe, and Tokyo. Includes information on packing and caring for garments when traveling.

Hostile Audiences

Controlling People: How to Recognize, Understand and Deal with People Who Try to Control You by Patricia Evans
Avon, MA: Adams Media Corporation, 2002
ISBN: 1-58062-569-X
Gives great insight into the force behind much verbally abusive behavior: the excessive need for control.

Life Is a Series of Presentations: 8 Ways to Punch Up Your People Skills at Work, at Home, Anytime, Anywhere by Tony Jeary
New York: Fireside, 2004
ISBN: 0-7432-5141-5 (also available in audio and e-book formats)
Includes information on anticipating (and preparing for) the various kinds of difficult people in an audience. Learn to identify what the author calls "snipers," "cheerleaders," "vacationers," and "convicts" (among others).

Nasty People: How to Stop Being Hurt by Them without Stooping to Their Level by Jay Carter
New York: McGraw-Hill, 2003
ISBN: 0-07-141022-8
Helps you recognize, understand, and deal with what the author calls "invalidators." Includes helpful suggestions for using verbal responses to defuse invalidation by others.

Toxic People: 10 Ways of Dealing with People Who Make Your Life Miserable by Lillian Glass
New York: St. Martin's Griffin, 1997
ISBN: 0-312-15232-9
A very readable little book that strikes a balance between understanding why and how some people create the misery they do and how to effectively deal with them. Includes a number of helpful verbal comebacks and defusing techniques that apply to presentations and other workplace encounters.

Human Nature

The Blank Slate: The Modern Denial of Human Nature by Steven Pinker
New York: Penguin, 2002
ISBN: 0-14-200334-4
An excellent summary and interpretation of the research, arguments, and rhetoric of the "nature versus nurture" debate.

Grooming, Gossip, and the Evolution of Language by Robin Dunbar
Cambridge, MA: Harvard University Press, 1997
ISBN: 0-674-36336-1

On the way to an interesting hypothesis the author reviews the research about human behavior, our similarities to and connections with other primates, and what we can learn about ourselves from them. An absolutely wonderful, highly readable, and insightful book.

The Naked Ape by Desmond Morris
New York: Laurel Books, Dell Publishing, 1999
ISBN: 0-385-33430-3
First published in 1967, this book is still fascinating reading.

Nature via Nurture: Genes, Experience, and What Makes Us Human by Matt Ridley
New York: HarperCollins, 2003
ISBN: 0-06-000678-1
Going beyond the nature versus nurture debate, this book explains and discusses the interdependence of genes and the environment. Fascinating and fun to read.

On Human Nature by Edward O. Wilson
Cambridge, MA: Harvard University Press, 1978
ISBN: 0-674-63442-X
The classic Pulitzer Prize–winning book from a great scientist and wonderful writer. A must for anyone who wants a deeper understanding of what it means to be human.

Humor

Dick Enberg's Humorous Quotes for All Occasions by Dick Enberg with Brian and Wendy Morgan
Kansas City, MO: Andrews McMeel Publishing, 2000
ISBN: 0-7407-0996-8
Good source of one-liners with general appeal, categorized by both occasion and topic, with examples and advice on how to use the material.

Do's and Taboos of Humor around the World: Stories and Tips from Business and Life
by Roger E. Axtell
New York: John Wiley & Sons, 1995
ISBN: 0-471-25403-7
The humorous aspects of many of the issues deriving from cultural differences covered in his other books, including misinterpreted gestures, signs, and cognates.

1001 Humorous Illustrations for Public Speaking: Fresh, Timely, and Compelling Illustrations for Preachers, Teachers, and Speakers by Michael Hodgin
Grand Rapids, MI: Zondervan, 1995
ISBN: 0-310-47391-8
Humorous anecdotes with illustrations by the author, categorized by topic.

The Oxford Dictionary of Humorous Quotations edited by Ned Sherrin
Oxford, England: Oxford University Press, 2003
ISBN: 0-190280045-0
Rich source of quotes from writers, entertainers, and politicians, many with characteristically British dry humor.

Podium Humor: A Raconteur's Treasury of Witty and Humorous Stories by James C. Humes
New York: HarperResource, 1993
ISBN: 0-06-273234-X
More than six hundred stories and anecdotes with excellent advice on how to use them well. Explains how to tell a story with the right amount of detail and how to use timing and humor to build suspense. Features a cross-indexed collection of anecdotes, stories, and one-liners on many topical subjects. Gives examples of "lead-in" lines and "bridge" lines to return to the topic.

2100 Laughs for All Occasions by Robert Orben
New York: Main Street Books, 1986
ISBN: 0-385-23488-0
Short anecdotes and one-liners categorized by keyword.

2400 Jokes to Brighten Your Speeches by Robert Orben
North Hollywood, CA: Wilshire Book Company, 1989
ISBN: 0-87980-425-4
Jokes, quips, and one-liners organized by category. A useful little book for incorporating a quick bit of lightness into a talk.

International Presentations

Culturegrams
http://www.culturegrams.com /products/individual.htm or 800-528-6279
Condensed reports on country-specific protocol, cultural background and issues, and nuts-and-bolts advice for getting around and getting things done. Culturegrams are four-sided hand-outs (also available as electronic downloads) designed as briefings to aid understanding of, and communication with, people of other cultures. They cover more than 125 areas of the world.

Do's and Taboos around the World: A Guide to International Behavior edited by Roger E. Axtell
New York: John Wiley & Sons, 1993
ISBN: 0-471-59528-4
Facts, tips, and instructional stories from over five hundred international business travelers. Covers etiquette and business protocol, verbal and nonverbal communication.

Do's and Taboos around the World for Women in Business by Roger E. Axtell, Tami Briggs, Margaret Corcoran, Mary Beth Lamb
New York: John Wiley & Sons, 1997
ISBN: 0-471-14364-2
Special advice for women related to culture, protocol, safety, and personal and career issues related to international business.

Do's and Taboos of Hosting International Visitors by Roger E. Axtell
New York: John Wiley & Sons, 1990
ISBN: 0-471-51570-1
Helps you anticipate the needs of your guests; how to meet, greet, host, entertain, negotiate, and do business with visitors from other countries.

Do's and Taboos of Using English around the World by Roger E. Axtell
New York: John Wiley & Sons, 1995
ISBN: 0-471-30841-2
Good advice about using English when communicating with people from other cultures. Discusses using English in non-English-speaking countries and in countries where English is spoken but with differences (e.g., England, Australia). Includes suggestions for working with interpreters.

Gestures: The Do's and Taboos of Body Language around the World by Roger E. Axtell
New York: John Wiley & Sons, 1998
ISBN: 0-471-18342-3
Discusses and gives examples of gestures and their different meanings in countries around the world. This book will help you understand the nonverbal communication of those from other cultures. It will also help you to be understood without committing faux pas.

Multicultural Manners: New Rules of Etiquette for a Changing Society by Norine Dresser
New York: John Wiley & Sons, 1996
ISBN: 0-471-11819-2
Anthropology meets etiquette. A great guide to understanding different cultural norms and expectations. Among the topics discussed are body language, child-rearing practices, classroom behavior, clothing, colors, food, gifts, luck and supernatural forces, male-female relations, prejudice, time, and verbal expressions.

Speaking Globally: Effective Presentations across International and Cultural Boundaries by Elizabeth Urech
London: Kogan Page, 2002
ISBN: 0-7494-2221-1
An easy-to-read guide to preparing and delivering presentations across cultures and around the world. A good source of general information.

For more information specific to a country or culture check with the Clearing-house for Multicultural and Bilingual Education at the David M. Kennedy Center for International Studies at Brigham Young University. You can find the clearinghouse on-line at http://departments.weber.edu/mbe/clearinghouse/K/Kennedy.htm.

Organizing Material

Brain Storm: Tap into Your Creativity to Generate Awesome Ideas and Remarkable Results by Jason R. Rich
Franklin Lakes, NJ: Career Press, 2003
ISBN: 1-56414-668-5
Covers the basic brainstorming techniques with instructions for using them as an individual or in a group. Guidelines for analyzing ideas, choosing the best ones, and implementing them successfully. It includes interviews with suggestions from well-known creative thinkers.

The Mind Map Book: How to Use Radiant Thinking to Maximize Your Brain's Untapped Potential by Tony Buzan with Barry Buzan
New York: Plume, 1996
ISBN: 0-452-27322-6
An excellent resource for developing and organizing material, it is especially valuable for those who think visually. If outlining never worked for you, you may appreciate this approach. Mind Map software is available at http://www.matchware.net/en/products/openmind/default.htm.

The Minto Pyramid Principle: Logic in Writing, Thinking, and Problem Solving by Barbara Minto
London: Minto International, 1996
ISBN: 0-960-19103-8
A good guide to organizing content, making it clear and concise, and saving time as you do so. Addresses issues in writing, thinking, problem solving, and presentation. Includes advice on designing and using visuals. Oriented toward business consulting, it uses somewhat complex examples, but with the goal of communicating as simply as possible.

Say It in Six: How to Say Exactly What You Mean in Six Minutes or Less by Ron Hoff
Kansas City, MO: Andrews McMeel, 1996
ISBN: 0-8362-1041-7
A practical, lighthearted and easy-to-read guide to help edit and structure a presentation. This is the book for you if you always run out of time or if nobody would mind if you finished sooner!

Quotations

Dick Enberg's Humorous Quotes for All Occasions by Dick Enberg with Brian and Wendy Morgan
Kansas City, MO: Andrews McMeel Publishing, 2000
ISBN: 0-7407-0996-8
Good source of one-liners with general appeal, categorized by both occasion and topic, with examples and advice on how to use the material.

The Forbes Book of Business Quotations: 14,173 Thoughts on the Business of Life edited by Ted Goodman
New York: Black Dog & Levanthal Publishers, 1997
ISBN: 1-884822-62-2
Another excellent source, especially for business speakers. Over fourteen thousand quotations in more than three hundred categories, and indexed by author.

Great Quotes from Great Leaders by Peggy Anderson
Franklin Lakes, NJ: Career Press, 1997
ISBN 1-56414-286-8
A good selection of quotes from twentieth-century business, political, military, religious, and sports leaders, categorized by speaker.

The Harper Book of Quotations edited by Robert I. Fitzhenry
New York: HarperResource, 1993
ISBN: 0-06-273213-7
Another collection of quotes on a wide variety of topics, categorized and indexed by author. This one is small enough to be easily portable.

The International Thesaurus of Quotations compiled by Eugene Ehrlich and Marshall De Bruhl
New York: HarperResource, 1996
ISBN: 0-06-273373-7
An excellent source for quotations. Sixteen thousand quotations indexed by authors and sources, keywords, and more than one thousand subject categories.

The Oxford Book of Aphorisms chosen by John Gross
Oxford, England: Oxford University Press, 2003
ISBN: 0-19-282015-X
A good source for quotes with a philosophical tone.

The Oxford Dictionary of Humorous Quotations edited by Ned Sherrin
Oxford, England: Oxford University Press, 2003
ISBN: 0-190280045-0

Rich source of quotes from writers, entertainers, and politicians, many with characteristically British dry humor.

The Oxford Dictionary of Modern Quotations edited by Tony Augarde
Oxford, England: Oxford University Press, 1991
ISBN: 0-19-283086-4
The book to use if you want to trace down a quote, provide the source of a quote, or choose a quote with the assurance that you can provide the correct source. Quotations are indexed by keywords and are traced to the original or authoritative source. Includes about five thousand "widely known and used" quotes.

Speaker's Lifetime Library: The Wordsmith's Collection of Pithy Quotations, Witty Aphorisms, Captivating Anecdotes, Apt Comparisons, Historical Allusions and Insightful Observations for All Occasions by Leonard Spinrad and Thelma Spinrad
New York: Prentice Hall, 1997
ISBN: 0-7352-0020-3
A comprehensive reference book organized into four sections: "The Speaker's Reference Guide" is a collection of more than 150 sets of definitions, quotations, aphorisms, anecdotes, and facts; "Apt Comparisons" lists metaphors, symbols, and opposites for almost one thousand common words; "The Day and Date Book" details great events for each day of the year; "The Special Occasions Book" includes speech ideas for over fifty different occasions.

3,500 Good Quotes for Speakers by Gerald F. Lieberman
New York: Broadway Books, 1987
ISBN: 0-385-17769-0
A handy book with a good mix of wise and funny quotes arranged by topic.

The Viking Book of Aphorisms selected by W. H. Auden and Louis Kronenberger
New York: Viking, 1981
ISBN: 0-88029-056-0
Quotes from writers, categorized by topic and indexed by keywords. An excellent source of quotes for the sophisticated audience.

Searching the Web is an easy way to find quotes. Many Web sites specialize in quotes by topic, by author, and so on.

Sales Presentations

Heavy Hitter Selling: How Successful High-Technology Salespeople Use Language and Intuition to Persuade Customers to Buy by Steve W. Martin
Rancho Santa Margarita, CA: Sand Hill Publishing, 2002
ISBN: 0-9721822-0-9
The advice in this book will help throughout the sales cycle.

New Sales Speak by Terri L. Sjodin
New York: John Wiley & Sons, 2001
ISBN: 0-471-39570-6
Discusses nine common mistakes made when delivering sales presentations. Includes advice on how to avoid them and suggestions for more effective alternatives.

Presenting to Win: The Art of Telling Your Story by Jerry Weissman
New York: Financial Times/Prentice Hall, 2003
ISBN: 0-13-046413-9
A good step-by-step guide to preparing a sales presentation, oriented toward the high-tech environment.

Scientific and Technical Presentations

The Craft of Scientific Presentations: Critical Steps to Succeed and Critical Errors to Avoid by Michael Alley
New York: Springer-Verlag, 2002
ISBN: 0-3879-5555-0
An excellent guide for scientific and technical speakers. Includes examples from scientists who became great speakers, good advice on how to avoid common errors. Helpful for speakers in any field who must communicate specialized information to a general audience.

Effective Communication Skills for Scientific and Technical Professionals by Harry E. Chambers
New York: Perseus, 2000
ISBN: 0-7382-0287-8
Full of excellent advice for technical specialists who must communicate in a business environment. Helps the technical expert better understand the needs and preferred communication style of the less technical person. Information from many different topic areas will help you improve your technical presentations.

The Essence of Technical Communication for Engineers: Writing, Presentation, and Meeting Skills by Herbert L. Hirsch
New York: IEEE Press, 2000
ISBN: 0-7803-4738-2
Covers planning and managing a variety of communication challenges in technical environments. Good advice on tailoring technical information for a more general audience.

Even a Geek Can Speak: Low-Tech Presentation Skills for High-Tech People by Joey Asher
Atlanta, GA: Longstreet Press, 2001
ISBN: 1-56352-628-X
A lighthearted look at presentation skills. Good general advice.

Presenting to Win: The Art of Telling Your Story by Jerry Weissman
New York: Financial Times/Prentice Hall, 2003
ISBN 0-13-046413-9
A good step-by-step guide to preparing a sales presentation, oriented toward the high-tech environment.

Speakers Organizations

Toastmasters International
Toastmasters clubs typically consist of twenty to thirty members who meet once a week to learn the skills needed to deliver speeches and conduct meetings. The organization has many products and services available for continued learning, practice, and support. Find Toastmasters on-line at www.toastmasters.org or contact Toastmasters International, PO Box 9052, Mission Viejo, CA 92690, Phone: 949-858-8255.

National Speakers Association
The National Speakers Association is an organization for professional speakers. It provides professional development assistance and serves as a clearinghouse for those looking to hire a professional speaker. You can find the National Speakers Association on-line at http://www.nsaspeaker.org or call 480-968-2552.

Stories

FINDING STORIES

Forbes Greatest Business Stories of All Time by Daniel Gross and the editors of *Forbes Magazine*
New York: John Wiley & Sons, 1997
ISBN: 0-471-19653-3
The stories of twenty great American business leaders. Especially useful is the index—find a principle you want to discuss, then turn to the story to tell.

Forbes Great Success Stories: Twelve Tales of Victory Wrested from Defeat by Alan Farnham
New York: John Wiley & Sons, 2000
ISBN: 0-471-38359-7
Inspiring stories of business leaders who overcame business and personal obstacles. Some very well-known as well as less-famous folks.

In the Words of Great Business Leaders by Julie M. Fenster
New York: John Wiley & Sons, 1999
ISBN: 0-471-34855-4
Short stories, anecdotes, and quotations about and from famous American business leaders of the twentieth century. Good source of classic short stories with powerful business lessons.

Great Presidential Wit . . . I Wish I Was in the Book: A Collection of Humorous Anecdotes and Quotations edited by Robert (Bob) Dole
New York: Scribner, 2001
ISBN: 0-7432-0392-5
A good source for short stories about and quotes from U.S. presidents. Many of the stories have a lesson with broad applications for business and life.

The Wit and Wisdom of . . . by James C. Humes
Winston Churchill, New York: HarperCollins, 1994, ISBN: 0-06-092577-9
Benjamin Franklin, New York: Gramercy Books, 2001, ISBN: 0-517-16345-4
Abraham Lincoln, New York: Gramercy Books, 1999, ISBN: 0-517-20719-2
In each of these three books, a former presidential speechwriter shares anecdotes about (and one-liners by) one of the greatest leaders and speakers in modern history.

USING STORIES

Using Stories and Humor: Grab Your Audience by Joanna Slan
Boston: Allyn & Bacon, 1997
ISBN: 02-05-26893-5
A guide to finding, developing, and telling stories. The section on humor gives suggestions for using humor effectively and appropriately. The emphasis is on developing your own fresh and pertinent material.

Never Be Boring Again: Make Your Business Presentations Capture Attention, Inspire Action, and Produce Results by Doug Stevenson
Colorado Springs, CO: Cornelia Press, 2003
ISBN: 0-9713440-9-4
Instructions on how to choose, craft, and tell stories, all in the context of presentations. Practical and useful information about how to use stories in sales and technical presentations.

The Springboard: How Storytelling Ignites Action in Knowledge-Era Organizations by Stephen Denning
Woburn, MA: Butterworth-Heinemann, 2001
ISBN: 0-7506-7355-9
Shows how storytelling can be a powerful tool to communicate values, vision, strategy, and goals. An excellent source for learning to use stories strategically and tactically in even very large organizations.

The Story Factor: Inspiration, Influence and Persuasion through the Art of Storytelling by Annette Simmons
Cambridge, MA: Perseus Publishing, 2001
ISBN: 0-7382-0369-6
An excellent book on both the why and how of using stories.

Managing by Storying Around: A New Method of Leadership by David M. Armstrong
New York: Doubleday, 1992
ISBN: 0-9648027-1-6
A business owner/manager gives advice and examples of how to use stories to train, motivate, and inspire employees.

The Storyteller's Guide: Storytellers Share Advice for the Classroom, Boardroom, Showroom, Podium, Pulpit and Center Stage by Bill Mooney and David Holt
Little Rock, AR: August House Publishers, 1996
ISBN: 0-87483-482-1
Written by and for professional storytellers, this book has lots of good advice for successfully, ethically, and legally incorporating stories into your communications. Includes advice on how to adapt stories from printed text and how to create your own stories.

Stuttering

Several organizations are devoted to understanding stuttering and helping overcome the challenges it presents. Among these are

> National Stuttering Association
> http://www.nsastutter.org
> The American Institute for Stuttering
> http://www.stutteringtreatment.org
>
> The Stuttering Foundation of America
> http://www.stutteringhelp.org

Guerrilla Stutterer by Eric Bourland
http://ebwebwork.com/stutter/
This article, written by a stutterer, gives excellent practical advice and encouragement for stutterers. It includes many tips for dealing with the challenges of stuttering, especially when interacting with a new acquaintance.

Sweating

International Hyperhidrosis Society
An organization devoted to understanding excessive sweating and sharing information about treatment options. Find it at http://www.sweathelp.org.

"Hyperhidrosis: Current Understanding, Current Therapy" by Markus Naumann, MD; Jonathan R. T. Davidson, MD; and Dee Anna Glaser, MD
A summary of recent medical research into the causes of and treatments for excessive sweating. Find it on-line at http://www.medscape.com/viewprogram/1540_pnt.

Videoconferencing

Smart Videoconferencing: New Habits for Virtual Meetings by Janelle Barlow, Peta Peter and Lewis Barlow
San Francisco: Berrett-Koehler Publishers, 2002
ISBN: 1-57675-192-9
A good guide on how to prepare for and successfully participate in videoconferences. Helpful tips on everything from when to use a videoconference to how to dress.

Videoconferencing: The Whole Picture by James R. Wilcox
Gilroy, CA: Telecom Books, 2000
ISBN: 1-57820-054-7
Covers all aspects of videoconferencing: business considerations for videoconferencing, including hardware and software; selecting and accessing videoconferencing networks; developing a videoconferencing request for proposal. Includes case studies.

"Virtual Collaboration: Pitfalls and Best Practices" by Andrew Black
http://www.interactionassociates.com/html/article_downloads_page.html
This article has great suggestions for helping to overcome the barriers created when communicating and collaborating over distances with electronic media.

Visual Aids

DESIGNING VISUAL AIDS

Beyond Words: A Guide to Drawing Out Ideas by Milly Sonneman
Berkeley, CA: Ten Speed Press, 1997
ISBN: 0-89815-911-3
A useful guide to drawing shapes, symbols, and graphics. If you work with flip charts, whiteboards, or chalkboards, this can help you add clarity and pizzazz to visuals you create on the spot. This is also a good guide for understanding how to use simple graphics and make good color choices when designing visual aids.

Looking Good in Presentations by Molly Joss
Scottsdale, AZ: Paraglyph, 1999
ISBN: 1-932111-56-5
A graphic designer gives comprehensive advice on choosing the appropriate types of visual aids, designing them, and using them effectively. If you will be using a variety of types of visual aids, this is a great book to get.

How to Do Everything with Microsoft Office PowerPoint 2003 by Ellen Finkelstein
Emeryville, CA: McGraw-Hill Osborne Media, 2003
ISBN: 0-07-222972-1
An easy-to-read and comprehensive guide.

PowerPoint 2003 Bible by Faithe Wempen
New York: John Wiley & Sons, 2003
ISBN: 0-7645-3972-8
A comprehensive guide to using PowerPoint.

PowerPoint 2003 for Dummies by Doug Lowe
Hoboken, NJ: John Wiley & Sons, 2003
ISBN: 0-764539-08-6
A lighthearted and easy-to-read guide.

Teach Yourself Visually PowerPoint 2002 by Kelleigh Johnson and Ruth Maran
New York: Hungry Minds, 2002
ISBN: 0-7645-3660-5
A good choice for the visual learner.

In addition, check out the four-page laminated QuickStudy guides on the basics of using PowerPoint available at http://www.barcharts.com. They contain good basic information and are easy to access. They are great for bringing on an airplane when you don't want to juggle a book.

CREATING AND USING IMAGES

These classics are written by Edward Tufte and published by Graphics Press in Cheshire, Connecticut. They are beautiful books with many examples from the very simple to the complex. The text is comprehensive and clear.

Envisioning Information
1990
ISBN: 0-9613921-1-8

Visual and Statistical Thinking: Displays of Evidence for Decision Making
1997
ISBN: 0-9613921-2-6

The Visual Display of Quantitative Information
2001
ISBN: 0-9613921-4-2

Visual Explanations: Images and Quantities, Evidence and Narrative
2001
ISBN: 0-9613921-2-6

Say It with Charts: The Executive's Guide to Visual Communication by Gene Zelazny
New York: McGraw-Hill, 2001
ISBN: 0-07-136997-X
Discusses when to use different types of charts—bar, column, dot, line, and pie—as well as how to use lettering size, colors, and other elements effectively. Also covers using imported images, animation, sound, video, and links to pertinent Web sites.

Style Guide for Business and Technical Communication by Franklin Covey Company
Salt Lake City, UT: Franklin Covey, 1985–1997
ISBN: 0-9652481-1-9
An excellent source of information on when and how to use a variety of visual elements. Sections on charts, graphs, tables, illustrations, photos, and maps. If you use different visual elements when you create visual aids, this is a great place to start. It will satisfy the needs of most business presenters. (It's also a comprehensive style guide.)
Create a Graph
http://nces.ed.gov/nceskids/graphing/
Follow this link to a Web site that explains the fundamentals of graphs and gives you an easy way to create your own version of a basic graph. The site is designed for children, which makes it easy to use.

How to Lie with Charts by Gerald Everett Jones
Lincoln, NE: iUniverse, 2000
ISBN: 1-58348-767-0
Learn to use different design elements to create charts and graphs that help you make the point you want to make. You will find before-and-after versions using different kinds of charts, graphs, and software products.

How to Lie with Statistics by Darrell Huff
New York: W. W. Norton and Company, 1993
ISBN: 0-393-31072-8
Shows how to use the statistics you have to make the point you want and includes examples of how to design charts and graphs that help accomplish this. Also gives you something even more valuable: the ability to recognize when these techniques are being used on you!

FINDING IMAGES

Many other sites offer stock photos and clip art. Do an Internet search using the keywords "clip art" or "stock photos."

Design Gallery Live
http://dgl.microsoft.com
Design Gallery Live from Microsoft offers both photos and clip art by category.

iStockPhoto
http://www.istockphoto.com/
This is one of many Web sites offering stock photos by category.

You might also try Google: select "images," type in your subject, and choose (unless your subject is obscure) from the photos, illustrations, and other images that pop up. Be careful not to use copyrighted material inappropriately.

Voice

Change Your Voice, Change Your Life: A Quick, Simple Plan for Finding and Using Your Natural Dynamic Voice by Morton Cooper
North Hollywood, CA: Wilshire Book Company, 1996
ISBN: 0-87980-441-6
Solid coverage of the components of an effective voice, with examples of prominent public figures. Covers issues such as breathing, pacing, nasality, and accents with exercises for identifying and improving vocal quality.

Voice Power: Using Your Voice to Captivate, Persuade, and Command Attention by Renee Grant-Williams
New York: American Management Association, 2002
ISBN: 0-8144-7105-6
Good information on the fundamentals for developing a strong and pleasant voice. Covers breathing, enunciation of sounds, variety in tone and volume, and appropriate use of the voice in professional settings.

Web Presentations

Looking Good in Presentations by Molly Joss
Scottsdale, AZ: The Coriolis Group, 1999
ISBN: 1-932111-56-5
A graphic designer gives useful advice on Web presentations as part of a comprehensive look at visuals in presentations.

NOTES

Chapter 1: You Are Not Alone

1. J. C. McCroskey, "The Communication Apprehension Perspective," in *Avoiding Communication: Shyness, Reticence, and Communication Apprehension,* ed. J. A. Daly and J. C. McCroskey (Beverly Hills, CA: Sage Publications, 1984).
2. Chuck Martin, "How Well Do You Hear the Message?" Darwin, April 2004, http://www.darwinmag.com/read/040104/hear.html/ (accessed June 25, 2004).

Chapter 2: The Downward Spiral

1. Reneau Z. Peurifoy, *Anxiety, Phobias, and Panic* (New York: Warner Books, 1995), 1–2.
2. James Trefil, *Are We Unique?* (New York: John Wiley & Sons, 1997), 21–22.

Chapter 3: Wolves and Other Phobias

1. Antonio Damasio, *The Feeling of What Happens* (San Diego, CA: Harcourt, 1999), 228.
2. George H. Fried and George J. Hademenos, *Theories and Problems of Biology* (New York: McGraw Hill, 1999), 66, 206, 438.
3. Damasio, *The Feeling of What Happens,* 54.
4. Antonio Damasio, *Descartes' Error* (New York: G. P. Putnam's Sons, 1994).
5. Steven Pinker, *The Blank Slate* (New York: Penguin, 2002).
6. Ann Gibbons, "Which of Our Genes Make Us Human?" *Science* 281 (September 4, 1998): 1432–1434.
7. Derek E. Wildman, Lawrence I. Grossman, and Morris Goodman, "Human and Chimpanzee Functional DNA Shows They Are More Similar to Each Other Than Either Is to Other Apes," conference paper, http://www.uchicago.edu/aff/mwc-amacad/ biocomplexity/conference_papers/goodman.pdf (accessed June 1, 2004).
8. Edward O. Wilson, *Sociobiology: The Abridged Edition* (Cambridge, MA: Harvard University Press, Belknap Press, 1980), 265–270.
9. Carl Zimmer, "Searching for Your Inner Chimp," *Natural History,* December 2002–January 2003.

10. Wilson, *Sociobiology,* 90–117.
11. Martin E. P. Seligman, "Phobias and Preparedness," *Behavior Therapy* 2 (1971): 307–320.
12. R. J. McNally, "Preparedness and Phobias: A Review," *Psychological Bulletin* 101 (1987): 283–303.
13. Edward O. Wilson, *On Human Nature* (Cambridge, MA: Harvard University Press, 1978), 68.
14. David Wallechinsky, *Book of Lists,* (Philadelphia, PA: Lippincott Williams and Wilkins: 1995); John W. Newstrom and Edward E. Scannell, *The Big Book of Business Games: Icebreakers, Creativity Exercises and Meeting Energizers* (New York: McGraw-Hill, 1995).
15. Desmond Morris, *The Naked Ape* (New York: Dell Publishing, 1984), 26.
16. Robin Dunbar, *Grooming, Gossip, and the Evolution of Language* (Cambridge, MA: Harvard University Press, 1997), 17–18.
17. Noel T. Boaz and Russell L. Ciochon, "The Scavenging of 'Peking Man,' *Natural History,* March 2001, 46–51.
18. Ibid.
19. C. K. Brain, *The Hunters or the Hunted? An Introduction to African Cave Taphonomy* (Chicago: University of Chicago Press, 1981); Alex MacCormick, *The Mammoth Book of Maneaters* (New York: Carrol and Graf Publishers, 2003).
20. Bruce Chatwin, *The Songlines* (New York: Penguin Books, 1987), 232–256.
21. Ibid., 232, 233.
22. Ibid.
23. "Cognitive-Behavioral Therapy," Dr. Joseph F. Smith Medical Library, http://www .chclibrary.org/micromed/00043200.html (accessed June 10, 2004).
24. John Shea, *Starlight* (New York: Crossroad Publishing Company, 1996), 47–51.
25. Omer Englebert, *St. Francis of Assisi* (Ann Arbor, MI: Servant Books, 1979), 136–138.

Chapter 4: Recognize Your Wolf

1. L. G. Ost and K. Hugdahl, "Acquisition of Phobias and Anxiety Response Patterns in Clinical Patients," *Behaviour Research and Therapy* 19 (1981): 439–447.
2. Joseph LeDoux, *The Emotional Brain,* (New York: Touchstone, 1996), 237.
3. Matt Ridley, *Nature via Nurture* (New York: HarperCollins, 2003), 192–195.
4. Ibid.
5. Ridley, *Nature via Nurture,* 195.
6. R. A. Kleinknecht, "The Origins and Remission of Fear in a Group of Tarantula Enthusiasts." *Behaviour Research and Therapy* 20 (1982): 437–443.
7. Susan Mineka, "The Frightful Complexity of the Origin of Fears," in *Theoretical Foundations of Behavior Therapy,* ed. F. R. Brush and J. B. Overmier (New York: Plenum, 1985), 81–111; S. Mineka, M. Cook, and S. Miller, "Fear Conditioned with Escapable and Inescapable Shock: The Effects of a Feedback Stimulus," *Journal of Experimental Psychology: Animal Behavior Processes* 10 (1984): 307–323.
8. R .J. McNally, "Psychological Approaches to Panic Disorder: A Review," *Psychological Bulletin* 108 (1990): 403–419.

9. Eddie Harmon-Jones and Judson Mills, *Cognitive Dissonance: Progress on a Pivotal Theory in Social Psychology* (Washington, DC: APA Books, 1999).

10. Rick Brenner, "The Fundamental Attribution Error," *Point Lookout* 4, no. 18 (May 5, 2004), http://www.chacocanyon.com/pointlookout/040505.shtml (accessed July 27, 2004).

Chapter 5: Doing What Comes Unnaturally

1. John Bowlby, *A Secure Base* (New York: Basic Books, 1988), 7–8.

2. Ann Gibbons, "Solving the Brain's Energy Crisis," *Science* 280 (1998): 1345–1347.

3. This behavior, in an extreme form and accompanied by exceptional abilities in areas not involving social interaction, may be a sign of Asperger's Syndrome. To learn more, see Tony Attwood, *Asperger's Syndrome: A Guide for Parents and Professionals,* (London: Jessica Kingsley Publishers, 1998).

4. Herbert H. Clark and S. A. Brennan, "Grounding in Communication" in *Perspectives on Socially Shared Cognition,* ed. Lauren B. Resnick, John M. Levine, and Stephanie D. Teasley (Washington, DC: APA Books, 1991).

5. Martin Clayton, Rebecca Sager, and Udo Will, "In Time with the Music: The Concept of Entrainment and Its Significance for Musicology," final draft before publication, http://perso.wanadoo.fr/esem/ECP_WEB/Articles/Vol. 1/IYWTM.htm (accessed June 19, 2004).

6. Edward T. Hall, *Beyond Culture* (New York: Anchor Books, 1981), 71–84.

7. Clayton, Sager, and Will, "In Time with the Music."

8. Hall, *Beyond Culture,* 72–73.

9. Peter Senge, *The Fifth Discipline* (New York: Currency Doubleday, 1994), 248.

Chapter 6: Getting to Know Your Wolf

1. Fried and Hademenos, *Theories and Problems of Biology,* 312.

2. Ibid., 207, 289, 290.

3. Ibid., 230.

4. Elaine Morgan, *The Scars of Evolution* (Oxford, England: Oxford University Press, 1994), 85–87.

5. John D. MacArthur, "The Human Brain: How Your Brain Responds to Stress," Franklin Institute Online, http://www.fi.edu/brain/stress.htm (accessed August 15, 2004).

6. Ibid.

Chapter 7: Feeding Your Wolf

1. Edmund J. Bourne, *The Anxiety and Phobia Workbook* (New York: MJF Books/Harbinger Publications, 1995), 225.

2. Ibid.

3. "Drinking the Night Away," *Night Writer Magazine,* http://www.nightworkers.com/drink.html (accessed June 20, 2004).

4. Peggy Papathakis, "Five Signs Your Diet Needs Help," http://www.ucdmc.ucdavis.edu/pulse/scripts/99_00/fyi_nutrition_help.pdf (accessed June 15, 2004).

5. Walter J. Edwards, "Low Blood Sugar," Health Gallery, http://www.getwel.com/lo_bls.htm (accessed June 15, 2004).

6. Paul S. Saenz, OD, "What Exercise Really Does for You," http://www.proteamphysicians.com/article/index.asp?showarticle=yes&articleId=187&articletype=13 (accessed June 16, 2004).

7. Ann Underwood and Claudia Kalb, "Stress-Busters: What Works," *Newsweek,* June 14, 1999, 61.

8. Ibid., 60, 61.

9. For more insights into the soothing power of walking see Chatwin, *The Songlines,* 229, 230.

10. "Beta Blocker," in *The Columbia Encyclopedia,* 6th ed. (New York: Columbia University Press, 2003).

11. "Beta Blockers," Dr. Joseph F. Smith Medical Library, http://www.chclibrary.org/micromed/00039720.html (accessed December 21, 2004).

12. MacArthur, "The Human Brain."

13. Namarata Bose and Elizabeth Tsang, "The Stress Conundrum: How Much Is Too Much? Issues, *Berkeley Medical Journal* (Fall 2002).

14. Ibid.

Chapter 9: Getting It Together

1. Philip Theibert, *Business Writing for Busy People* (Franklin Lakes, NJ: Career Press, 1996), 20, 21.

2. John Suler, PhD, "Brainstorming," http://www.rider.edu/~suler/brainstorm.html (accessed February 7, 2005).

Chapter 10: Words That Work

1. "The Power of Words," Hoops U, http://hoopsu.homestead.com/motivpowerofwords.html (accessed December 6, 2004).

2. "Secretary Rumsfeld Press Conference at NATO Headquarters, Brussels, Belgium," United States Department of Defense, http://www.defenselink.mil/transcripts/2002/t06062002_t0606sd.html (accessed December 6, 2004).

Chapter 11: Rising above the Noise

1. Thomas H. Davenport and John C. Beck, *The Attention Economy* (Cambridge, MA: Harvard Business School Press, 2001).

2. Saul J. Berman, "Ten Strategies for Survival in the Attention Economy," http://www-8.ibm.com/services/pdf/ten_strategies.pdf (accessed February 8, 2005).

3. Bill Jensen, *Simplicity* (Cambridge, MA: Perseus Publishing, 2001).

4. J. L. McGaugh, "Significance and Remembrance: the Role of Neuromodulatory Systems," *Psychological Science* I (1990): 15–25.

5. "Words That Resonate," The Healing Spectrum, http://www.thehealingspectrum.com/quotes.html (accessed December 3, 2004).

6. Carl Sagan, *The Dragons of Eden* (New York: Ballantine Books, 1977), 17.

7. P. J. O'Rourke, "Zion's Vital Signs," *Atlantic Monthly,* November 2001.

8. Kenneth M. Morris, *User's Guide to the Information Age* (New York: Lightbulb Press, 1999), 12.

9. Ibid., 19.

10. Steve W. Martin, *Heavy Hitter Selling* (Rancho Santa Margarita, CA: Sand Hill Publishing, 2002), 56.

11. Annette Simmons, *The Story Factor* (Cambridge, MA: Perseus Publishing, 2001), 5.

12. Ibid., 4.

13. Kieran Egan, "Memory, Imagination and Learning: Connected by the Story," http://www.educ.sfu.ca/kegan/MemoryIm.html (accessed February 10, 2005).

14. David M. Armstrong, *Managing by Storying Around* (New York: Doubleday Currency, 1992).

15. Jim Kerstetter, "Information Is Power," *Business Week,* June 24, 2002.

16. Julie Fenster, *In the Words of Great Business Leaders* (New York: John Wiley & Sons, 2000), 137, 138.

17. Jerry Rice, "Next Stop: Atlantis," *Inland Valley (CA) Daily Bulletin,* Entertainment, 6, May 29, 2004.

18. Michael Kinsley, "Please Don't Quote Me," *Time,* May 13, 1991, 82.

19. "Psychiatrist's Joke 'World's Funniest,'" BBC News Front Page, October 4, 2002, http://news .bbc.co.uk/2/hi/uk_news/england/2297365.stm (accessed July 2, 2004).

20. "Official! World's Funniest Joke," CNN.com/Science and Space, October 7, 2002, http://www.cnn.com/2002/TECH/science/10/03/joke.funniest/ (accessed July 2, 2004).

21. Ted Cohen, *Jokes: Philosophical Thoughts on Joking Matters* (Chicago: University of Chicago Press, 1999).

22. Ibid.

23. "Hunt for the World's Funniest Joke Is Over," iol news, Front Page, October 3, 2002, http://www.iol.co.za/index.php?click_id=79&art_id=qw1033641001893B216&set_id=1 (accessed July 2, 2004).

Chapter 12: Can You Picture It?

1. G. Anglin, R. Towers, and H. Levie, "Visual Message Design and Learning: The Role of Static and Dynamic Illustrations," in *Handbook of Research on Educational Communications and Technology,* ed. D. H. Jonassen (New York: Simon and Schuster Macmillan, 1996).

2. Edward O. Wilson, *Biophilia* (Cambridge, MA: Harvard University Press, 1984).

3. Terrace L. Waggoner, OD, "What Is Colorblindness and the Different Types?" Colorblind HomePage, http://colorvisiontesting.com/ (accessed December 6, 2004).

4. Anglin, Towers, and Levie, "Visual Message Design and Learning."
5. Edward R. Tufte, "PowerPoint Is Evil," *Wired,* September 2003.

Chapter 14: Your Body Speaks

1. David B.Givens. "Proxemics," http://members.aol.com/doder1/proxemi1.htm (accessed July 10, 2004).
2. A groundbreaking and frequently referenced work in this area is A. Mehrabian, *Silent Messages: Implicit Communication of Emotions and Attitudes.* (Belmont, CA: Wadsworth, 1981), currently distributed by Albert Mehrabian, am@kaaj.com. For an interesting article summarizing the way A. Mehrabian's findings have been misinterpreted and misused, and for recommendations for and implications of accurate interpretation, see Herb Oestreich, "Let's Dump the 55%, 38%, 7% Rule," Transitions 7, no. 2 (1999): 11–14, http://www.cob .sjsu.edu/oestreich_h/Communic percent20Article.doc (accessed Aug. 18, 2004).
3. For a close look at the effect these "disfluencies" have on listeners, see Susan E. Brennan and Michael F. Schober, "How Listeners Compensate for Disfluencies in Spontaneous Speech," *Journal of Memory and Language* 44 (2001), 274–296, http://www.psychology .sunysb.edu./brennan-/papers/brenscho.pdf (accessed July 20, 2004)
4. LeDoux, *The Emotional Brain,* 117–118.
5. Philip Ball, "Loud Voices Music to Our Ears," *Nature News Service,* 2001, http://www.nature.com/nsu/010524/010524-2.html (accessed May 21, 2001).
6. Simmons, *The Story Factor,* 87.
7. Robert M. Krauss, Yihsiu Chen, and Rebecca F. Gottesman, "Lexical Gestures and Lexical Access: A Process Model," http:// www.columbia.edu/~rmk7/PDF/GSP.pdf (accessed June 15, 2004).

Chapter 15: Tools of the Trade

1. Charles Gladwin, "Time Capsule," http:// www.dotpharmacy.co.uk/upmela.html (accessed July 1, 2004).
2. Paul E. Miller, DVM, "Vision in Animals," http://www.vin.com/VINDBPub/SearchPB/ Proceedings/PR05000/PR00515.htm (accessed December 28, 2004); F. J. Ollivier, D. A. Samuelson, D. E. Brooks, P.A. Lewis, M.E. Kallberg, and A.M. Komaromy, "Comparative Morphology of the Tapetum Lucidum (among Selected Species)," http://www.ncbi .nlm.nih.gov/entrez/query.fcgi?cmd=Retrieve&db=PubMed&list_uids=14738502&dopt= Abstract (accessed December 28, 2004).

Chapter 16: Can We Talk?

1. John Bowlby, *A Secure Base* (New York: Basic Books, 1988), 7–8.
2. Robin Dunbar, *Grooming, Gossip, and the Evolution of Language* (Cambridge, MA: Harvard University Press, 1997), 121.
3. Ronald P. Marks, "Improving On-line Sales Education," *Learning Developer's Journal* (October 1, 2002), http://www.elearningguild.com/pdf/2/100102des-1.pdf (accessed June 25, 2004).

4. Gerald D. Fischback, *Mind and Brain: A Scientific American Special Report,* 1994, 8.
5. Tedd Tripp, *Shepherding a Child's Heart* (Wapwallopen, PA: Shepherd Press; 2003).

Chapter 17: Meeting of the Minds

1. Fischback, *Mind and Brain,* 8.
2. Harry E. Chambers, *Effective Communication Skills for Scientific and Technical Professionals* (New York: Perseus Publishing, 2001), 125.
3. Del Jones, "Execution Does More Than Get Things Done: Honeywell Chief Talks about Making Great Ideas Work," *USA Today,* p. B.04. June 10, 2002.

Chapter 19: Our Small World

1. Laura Doty, "Famous People Who Stutter," http://www.d.umn.edu/~cspiller/stutteringpage/famous.htm (accessed August 15, 2004).
2. Kenneth O. St. Louis, PhD, "Providing Help for People Who Stutter: A World View," 2004, http://www.mnsu.edu/comdis/isad7/papers/stlouis7/stlouis.pdf (accessed January 15, 2005).
3. Eric Bourland, "Guerrilla Stutterer," 1994, 2004, http://ebwebwork.com/stutter/.
4. Rachel K Sobel, "Anatomy of a Stutterer," *U.S. News and World Report,* April 2, 2001, 44–51.
5. John Alback, ed. *To Say What Is Ours: The Best Ten Years of* Letting Go (San Francisco: National Stuttering Project, 1990), 13.

GLOSSARY

active voice A grammatical structure in which the subject of the verb performs the action, for example, "The speaker walked across the stage." This focuses attention on the subject. *See also* passive voice.

ad hominem Latin for "to the man." An error in logic that occurs when a speaker responds to an argument with a comment about the person making the opposing argument, not the merits of the argument itself. Positive or negative, the comment is usually irrelevant to the argument.

adrenal glands Two small endocrine glands, one located above each kidney, consisting of the cortex, which secretes several steroid hormones, and the medulla, which secretes adrenaline.

adrenal medulla The inner portion of the adrenal glands that manufactures, stores, and releases adrenaline.

adrenaline A hormone produced by the body and released into the bloodstream in response to physical danger or mental stress. It starts many bodily responses that help the body cope with emergencies. Among other things, it stimulates heart action to increase the body's oxygen supply and increases blood sugar levels to provide extra energy.

aldosterone A hormone secreted by the adrenal glands that helps regulate blood pressure and blood saline levels.

analogy A comparison made to show some similarity between two things. Analogies can be used to infer that if things agree in some respects they probably agree in others.

analyze To separate into essential parts and examine or interpret each part.

anxiety Concern, restlessness, and agitation about some thing or event. Anxiety is the result of a future vague, uncertain, or ill-defined threat.

appeal to authority An error in logic made by arguing that something is true because an authority says so, not because the argument has merit.

appeal to fear An error in logic made by using a threat of harm to advance one's position. The appeal to fear is also known as the argument from adverse consequences or swinging the big stick.

appeal to ignorance An error in logic made by assuming that something that has not been proved false must be true and vice versa.

argument from adverse consequences An error in logic made by using a threat of harm to advance the speaker's position. The argument from adverse consequences is also known as the appeal to fear or swinging the big stick.

autonomic nervous system The part of the nervous system concerned with the control of activities that do not require thought, such as breathing. It regulates the function of glands (especially the salivary, gastric, and sweat glands), the adrenal medulla, smooth muscle tissue, and the heart. The autonomic nervous system may act on these tissues to reduce or slow activity or to initiate their function.

begging the question Also known as assuming the answer or circular reasoning, this error in logic is made when an argument uses the proposition to prove itself. It may sound as if the speaker is giving a reason for something when he or she is simply restating it using different words.

beta blockers A class of drugs used to treat high blood pressure and heart disease by lowering blood pressure and slowing the heart. Beta blockers can be used to reduce the symptoms of anxiety, especially if they are physical symptoms. Beta blockers decrease the force and rate of heart contractions.

body language Facial expressions, gestures, postures, movement, and proximity to others by which one communicates nonverbally.

c cubed A shorter name for an argument known more formally as the fallacy of confusion of correlation and causation. This error in logic is made when an argument assumes that because two events happened together—in time, in place, or to the same person or group—one must have caused the other. It is also known as the fallacy of false cause.

Cartesian Of or pertaining to the French philosopher Rene Descartes or his philosophy.

cliché A phrase that was originally effective and vivid but has become trite or banal through overuse.

cognitive dissonance A state of discomfort resulting from behavior that is at odds with an established attitude. To reduce or eliminate the dissonance, a change is needed to achieve consistency between the behavior and the attitude. *See also* theory of cognitive consistency.

compare To examine two or more things in order to identify similarities and differences.

conclude To end or close including a summary, result, inference, or decision.

content concerns Anxiety-provoking concerns related to selecting and preparing content: the topic, the information covered, the support material used, who the audience will be, what they want and need.

contrast To set in opposition in order to show differences. Also, the visual effect of the juxtaposition of different colors, shades, or tones.

coping self-statements Positive and true statements made to oneself and used to help one feel more confident and relaxed.

cortisol A hormone produced principally in response to physical or psychological stress and secreted by the adrenal glands.

criticize To make judgments about merits and faults. Criticism often accompanies analysis.

define To state the meaning of, to explain the essential qualities or nature of, to determine the precise limits of.

describe To convey an image or impression with words that reveals the appearance or nature of; to give an account of; to list parts, qualities, and characteristics of.

dialogue A conversation or interaction between two or more people intent on gaining insight or learning from one another.

diaphragmatic breathing A method of breathing more slowly and deeply than we tend to do when anxious. It helps us use the diaphragm correctly to expend less effort and energy to breathe. It can reduce many of the physical symptoms of anxiety.

discuss To examine by argument, consider and debate the pros and cons of an issue, explain conflicts; discussion often includes analysis, criticism, and comparison.

doughnut sandwich An error in logic made by using an argument that presents only two options, usually extremes, when more options exist. It implies that other options or compromise solutions are not possible. The doughnut sandwich is also called excluded middle, false dilemma, and false dichotomy.

downward spiral A debilitating increase in anxiety resulting from the interplay of content and performance concerns.

entrainment The synchronization of vibrations and behaviors that results in one body influencing and being influenced by another.

enumerate To list several things: ideas, aspects, events, qualities, reasons, and so on; to mention separately.

evaluate To appraise carefully, to determine the value or amount of.

excluded middle An error in logic made when one presents only two options, usually extremes, when more options exist. It implies that other options or compromise solutions are not possible. Also called the doughnut sandwich, false dilemma, and false dichotomy.

explain To make clear and understandable, to make clear the cause or reason, to assign a meaning or interpret.

expound To give a methodical, detailed, scholarly explanation.

extemporaneous Given (as an unmemorized speech or presentation) from notes or an outline.

fallacy An argument that sounds convincing but is essentially flawed. Fallacies are errors in logic usually born from an attempt to persuade through nonlogical means. They can also be caused by careless thinking.

fallacy of popularity An error in logic that occurs when it is argued that something is true because it is believed to be true by so many people rather than because it has merit.

false analogy An error in logic made by using an argument that compares two very different things, states or implies that they are similar, and draws a conclusion about one based on the other. It becomes confusing when the two things may in some way be similar; recognizing the flaw in the argument depends on seeing the differences clearly.

false dichotomy An error in logic made by using an argument that presents only two options, usually extremes, when more options exist. It implies that other options or compromise solutions are not possible. Also called the doughnut sandwich, excluded middle, and false dilemma.

false dilemma An error in logic made by using an argument that presents only two options, usually extremes, when more options exist. It implies that other options or compromise solutions are not possible. Also called the doughnut sandwich, excluded middle, and false dichotomy.

fear An emotion of alarm and agitation caused by the anticipation, expectation, or realization of some specific pain or danger. Fear is usually accompanied by a desire to fight or flee.

fight-or-flight response The reaction and collective changes that occur in the body when faced by a sudden, unexpected threat or source of stress. The physical changes of the fight-or-flight response include a sharpening of the senses to help us detect and avoid physical dangers. They also give us increased physical strength and speed to fight or flee if the danger can't be avoided.

fundamental attribution error The tendency to attribute behavior, especially that of others, to fundamental character traits rather than to the situation and context.

germane Vital to understanding. An element is germane if it cannot be removed without reducing comprehension.

grounding The processes by which we let our dialogue partners know how we have understood their messages—what we think they mean—and by which we seek evidence from them that our messages have been understood the way we meant them.

hasty generalization An error in logic made by generalizing using a sample that is too small to be conclusive. Also known as jumping to a conclusion.

homeostasis The physiological process by which the internal systems of the body (e.g., blood pressure, body temperature) are maintained within a narrow range of equilibrium despite changes in the external environment.

homeostatic Possessing a tendency to stability in the normal body states (internal conditions) of the organism; relating to homeostasis.

illustrate To explain by giving examples or making comparisons.

impromptu Given (as a speech or presentation) without preparation and at a moment's notice.

inclusive language Language that avoids false assumptions about people regardless of their gender, marital status, ethnicity, disability, and age.

innate Inborn, native, natural. Not acquired by learning or conditioning.

interpret To explain, construe, or understand in a certain way; to give the meaning of something by paraphrase.

lexical gesture A gesture that helps the speaker remember a word or words.

loaded question A question that includes an assumption as an attempt to damage the position of the other party. This sidetracks the argument and can antagonize others by making them feel manipulated or bullied.

metaphor A figure of speech that identifies one object or idea with another in one or more ways, for example, "The tiger's eyes were burning coals." Metaphors are used to suggest a similarity. *See also* simile.

monologue A speech or utterance by one person, usually at least several sentences long. Monologues often discourage others from participating in a conversation.

non sequitur Latin for "it doesn't follow." A non sequitur is an error in logic made when the conclusion of an argument fails to follow from its premise or premises.

nonverbal delivery skills Prosody and paralanguage used as part of the delivery of information in a presentation or speech.

nonvocal paralanguage Body language. Variations in posture, gestures, facial expressions, and eye contact patterns are all nonvocal paralanguage. Examples include slumping, waving, smiling, and batting the eyes.

outline To give a general account or report including only the main points or features.

Papa don't preach The error in logic made by using value-laden language. The use of Papa don't preach states or implies that ethical or moral goodness is associated with agreeing with the argument. It often uses emotional or value-laden terms to accomplish this.

paralanguage Communication apart from the verbal communication of a message. Paralanguage changes or supplements the meaning of language. Gestures and tone of voice are examples of paralanguage.

passive voice A grammatical structure in which the subject of the verb receives the action, for example, "The winning point was made by the guard." Passive voice should be used when the action itself is more important than the person, persons, or thing that is acting. *See also* active voice.

performance concerns Anxiety-provoking concerns related to personal performance, that is, how the speaker delivers the content.

phobia A persistent and seemingly irrational fear of a specific object, activity, or situation that results in a strong fear of and a desire to avoid it.

positive language Word choices and grammatical structures that communicate optimism and an expectation of the positive.

post hoc, ergo propter hoc An error in logic made by one assuming that because something happened after something else it was caused by that thing. Latin for "it happened after, so it was caused by," it is often referred to as simply post hoc.

prepared learning The theory that the potential for some learning is innate and triggered by a direct experience or observation. The theory of prepared learning holds that without the specific experience or observation, the learning will not take place. For example, a fear of snakes will be triggered by seeing another person recoil in fear of a snake.

prosody The qualities of voice and vocal delivery that change the meaning of the verbal communication used. Volume, inflection, tone, rhythm, and pacing are examples of prosody. Humor and sarcasm are largely dependent on prosody.

prove To establish the truth or genuineness of by evidence or argument.

proxemics The study of the ways in which individuals use physical space within their cultures. This includes their use of space in interactions with others and in the planning and use of interior space (architectural layouts) and exterior space (town, city, and transportation system layouts). Proxemics includes the study of how this use of physical space influences the thinking and behavior of individuals, groups, and cultures.

psychographics The study of the attitudes, values, belief systems, and ideologies of an individual, group, or culture.

rate To estimate quality or value, assign to a classification, or assign comparative worth.

red herring A error in logic made when something is said that sounds like it is relevant to the question or topic being discussed but is actually irrelevant. It can throw listeners off track, confuse the issue, and make it harder to reach an agreement and a conclusion.

redundancy The use of more words than necessary; that part of a message that can be eliminated without loss of essential information.

rhetorical question A question asked to encourage thought rather than elicit an answer. Rhetorical questions are often used to express an opinion or to emphasize a point.

salient object A thing having a quality that thrusts itself into attention; the center of attention or focus.

simile A figure of speech that expresses a resemblance between two things usually using the words like, as, or than, for example, "The tiger's eyes shone like burning coals." *See also* metaphor.

simple externalization The conscious and deliberate use of your senses to focus on something around you. Simple externalization can be used to redirect your attention from thoughts that provoke anxiety to thoughts that help you relax.

slippery slope An error in logic made by arguing that if a first step is taken, a disastrous and inevitable set of consequences will follow. These consequences are presented as the reason for not taking the first step. The slippery slope assumes an inability to make exceptions, set limits, or make decisions on a case-by-case basis.

straw man A error in logic committed when a speaker attacks an argument different from and weaker than the opposition's best argument. This is often done by caricaturing the opposition as so extreme in his views as to be ridiculous.

summarize To briefly and concisely state or restate main points.

swinging the big stick A argument in which the threat of harm is used to advance the speaker's position. Swinging the big stick is more formally known as the argument from adverse consequences or the appeal to fear.

sympathetic-adreno-medullary axis (SAM) The fight-or-flight response. The first of two phases of the response of the sympathetic nervous system to perceived danger.

sympathetic nervous system That part of the autonomic nervous system that controls the fight-or-flight response.

theory of cognitive consistency This theory predicts that when a person behaves differently than his or her attitude would predict that person will change his or her attitude to achieve consistency and reduce discomfort. *See also* cognitive dissonance.

trace To follow the course, development, or history of; to show the order of events or progress of a subject or event.

transition A verbal device used to move from one section of a presentation to the next.

unrepresentative sample An error in logic that occurs when the sample used, even if quite large, is not representative of the population as a whole.

vocal paralanguage Utterances that can be heard but can't be found in the dictionary. Laughter, crying, sighing, grunting, snorting, and giggling are all examples of vocal paralanguage.

wrong-way street An error in logic that occurs when cause and effect are confused, that is, when an effect is assumed to be a cause or the cause is assumed to be an effect. This often happens because of limited perspective.

BIBLIOGRAPHY

Adler, Jerry. "Stress: How It Attacks Your Body." *Newsweek,* June 14, 1999.

Ariniello, Leah. "Stuttering." Brain Briefings, http://web.sfn.org/content/Publications/BrainBriefings/stuttering.html (accessed July 25, 2004).

Armstrong, David M. *Managing by Storying Around: A New Method of Leadership.* New York: Doubleday Currency, 1992.

Ashley, Joyce. *Overcoming Stage Fright in Everyday Life.* New York: Three Rivers Press, 1996.

Attwood, Tony. *Asperger's Syndrome: A Guide for Parents and Professionals.* London: Jessica Kingsley Publishers, 1998.

Axtell, Roger E. *Gestures: The Do's and Taboos of Body Language around the World.* New York: John Wiley & Sons, 1991, 1998.

Ball, Philip. "Loud Voices Music to Our Ears." Nature News Service, Macmillan Magazines, 2001, http://www.nature.com/nsu/010524/010524-2.html (accessed May 21, 2001).

Begley, Sharon. "Culture Club." *Newsweek,* March 26, 2001.

Begley, Sharon. "Living Hand to Mouth: New Research Shows That Gestures Often Help Speakers Access Words from Their Memory Banks." *Newsweek,* November 2, 1998.

Best, Joel. *Damned Lies and Statistics: Untangling Numbers from the Media, Politicians, and Activists.* Berkeley, CA: University of California Press, 2001.

Blake, Gary, and Robert W. Bly. *The Elements of Business Writing: The Essential Guide to Writing Clear, Concise Letters, Memos, Reports, Proposals, and Other Business Documents.* New York: Macmillan General Reference, 1991.

Boaz, Noel T., and Russell L. Ciochon. "Headstrong Hominids." *Natural History,* February 2004.

Boaz, Noel T., and Russell L. Ciochon. "The Scavenging of Peking Man." *Natural History,* March 2001.

Bose, Namarata, and Elizabeth Tsang. "The Stress Conundrum: How Much Is Too Much?" *Berkeley Medical Journal,* Fall 2002.

Bossidy, Larry, and Ram Charan. *Execution: The Discipline of Getting Things Done.* New York: Crown Business, 2002.

Bourne, Edmund J. *The Anxiety and Phobia Workbook.* New York: MJF Books/Harbinger Publications, 1995.

Bowlby, John. *A Secure Base: Parent-Child Attachment and Healthy Human Development.* New York: Basic Books, 1988.

Bowlby, John. *Attachment.* New York: Basic Books, 1969.

Brain, C. K. *The Hunters or the Hunted? An Introduction to African Cave Taphonomy.* Chicago: University of Chicago Press, 1981.

Brink, Susan. "Sleepless Society." *U.S. News and World Report,* October 16, 2000.

Brown, Nina. "Edward T. Hall: Proxemic Theory, 1966." http://www.csiss.org/classics/content/13 (accessed June 22, 2004).

Brussat, Frederic, and Mary Ann Brussat. *Spiritual Literacy: Reading the Sacred in Everyday Life.* New York: Scribner, 1996.

Buzan, Tony, with Barry Buzan. *The Mind Map Book: How to Use Radiant Thinking to Maximize Your Brain's Untapped Potential.* New York: Plume, 1996.

Byatt, A. S. "Narrate or Die." *New York Times Magazine,* April 18, 1999.

Carducci, Bernardo. "Confidence! With a Special Report on Shyness." *Psychology Today,* January/ February 2000.

Carducci, Bernardo. *Shyness: A Bold New Approach.* New York: HarperCollins, 1999.

Cartmill, Matt. "The Gift of Gab." *Discover,* November 1998.

Chambers, Harry E. *Effective Communication Skills for Scientific and Technical Professionals.* New York: Perseus Publishing, 2001.

Chatwin, Bruce. *The Songlines.* New York: Penguin Books, 1987.

Clark, Herbert H., and S. A. Brennan. "Grounding in Communication." In *Perspectives on Socially Shared Cognition,* edited by Lauren B. Resnick, John M. Levine, and Stephanie D. Teasley. Washington, DC: APA Books, 1991.

Clayton, Martin, Rebecca Sager, and Udo Will. "In Time with the Music: The Concept of Entrainment and Its Significance for Musicology," final draft before publication, http://perso.wanadoo .fr/esem/ECP_WEB/Articles/Vol. 1/IYWTM.htm (accessed July 15, 2004).

"Cognitive-Behavioral Therapy." Dr. Joseph F. Smith Medical Library, http://www.chclibrary.org/ micromed/00043200.html (accessed August 14, 2004).

Cohen, Ted. *Jokes: Philosophical Thoughts on Joking Matters.* Chicago: University of Chicago Press, 1999.

Cooper, Morton. *Change Your Voice, Change Your Life: A Quick, Simple Plan for Finding and Using Your Natural Dynamic Voice.* North Hollywood, CA: Wilshire Book Company, 1996.

Cousineau, Phil. *Once and Future Myths: The Power of Ancient Stories in Modern Times.* Berkeley, CA: Conari Press, 2001.

Cowley, Geoffrey. "The Language Explosion." Special Edition, *Newsweek,* Spring/Summer 1997.

Cowley, Geoffrey, with Anne Underwood and Claudia Kalb. "Stress-Busters: What Works." *Newsweek,* June 14, 1999.

Damasio, Antonio. *Descartes' Error: Emotion, Reason and the Human Brain.* New York: G. P. Putnam's Sons, 1994.

Damasio, Antonio. *The Feeling of What Happens: Body and Emotion in the Making of Consciousness.* San Diego, CA: Harcourt, 1999.

Daniels, Cora. "Stress: The Last Taboo." *Fortune,* October 28, 2002.

Davenport, Thomas H., and John C.Beck. *The Attention Economy: Understanding the New Currency of Business.* Cambridge, MA: Harvard Business School Press, 2001.

Dell, Michael, with Catherine Fredman. *Direct from Dell: Strategies That Revolutionized an Industry.* New York: HarperBusiness, 1999.

Diamond, Jared. T*he Third Chimpanzee: The Evolution and Future of the Human Animal.* New York: HarperCollins, 1992.

Di Monte Santa Maria, *Ugolino. The Little Flowers of St. Francis of Assisi.* Edited by and adapted from a translation by W. Heywood. New York: Random House Spiritual Classics, 1998.

Dole, Robert, ed. *Great Presidential Wit . . . I Wish I Was in the Book: A Collection of Humorous Anecdotes and Quotations.* New York: Scribner, 2001.

"Drinking the Night Away." *Night Writer Magazine,* 2000. http://www.nightworkers.com/drink.html (accessed June 20, 2004).

Dunbar, Robin. *Grooming, Gossip, and the Evolution of Language.* Cambridge, MA: Harvard University Press, 1997.

Edwards, Walter J. "Low Blood Sugar." Health Gallery. http://www.getwel.com/lo_bls.htm (accessed June 15, 2004).

Eichenbaum, Howard. "The Topography of Memory." *Nature,* December 9, 1999.

Ellinor, Linda, and Glenna Gerard. *Dialogue: Rediscover the Transforming Power of Conversation.* New York: John Wiley & Sons, 1998.

Englebert, Omer. *St. Francis of Assisi: A Biography.* Ann Arbor, MI: Servant Books, 1979.

Fallows, James. "Inside the Leviathan: A Short and Stimulating Brush with Microsoft's Corporate Culture." *Atlantic Monthly,* February 2000.

Farhi, Donna. T*he Breathing Book: Good Health and Vitality through Essential Breath Work.* New York: Owl Books, 1996.

Fenster, Julie. *In the Words of Great Business Leaders.* New York: John Wiley & Sons, 2000.

Feuerstein, G., and S. Bodian, eds., with the staff of *Yoga Journal. Living Yoga: A Comprehensive Guide for Daily Life.* New York: Jeremy P. Tarcher, 1993.

Feynman, Richard. *The Pleasure of Finding Things Out.* Cambridge, MA: Perseus Publishing, 1999.

Fischback, Gerald D. *Mind and Brain: A Scientific American Special Report,* 1994.

Fisher, Helen. *Anatomy of Love: A Natural History of Mating, Marriage and Why We Stray.* New York: Fawcett Columbine, 1992.

Fox, Jeffrey J. *How to Become CEO.* New York: Hyperion, 1998.

Franklin Covey Company. *Style Guide for Business and Technical Communication.* Salt Lake City, UT: Franklin Covey, 1998.

Fried, George H., and George J. Hademenos. *Theories and Problems of Biology.* New York: McGraw Hill, 1999.

Gallagher, Leigh. "Sweat Equity." *Forbes,* September 15, 2003.

Garner, Alan. *Conversationally Speaking.* Los Angeles: Lowell House, 1997.

Gerstner, Louis V. *Who Says Elephants Can't Dance? Inside IBM's Historic Turnaround.* New York: HarperCollins, 2002.

Gibbs, Nancy. "If We Have It, Do We Use It?" *Time,* September 1999.

Givens, David B. "Proxemics," http://members.aol.com/doder1/proxemi1.htm (accessed July 10, 2004).

Gladwell, Malcolm. *The Tipping Point: How Little Things Can Make a Big Difference.* Boston: Back Bay Books, 2000, 2002.

Gladwin, Charles. "Time Capsule," http://www.dotpharmacy.co.uk/upmela.html.

Goffman, Erving. *Interaction Ritual: Essays on Face-to-Face Behavior.* New York: Pantheon Books, 1982.

Goldberg, Bernard. *Bias: A CBS Insider Exposes How the Media Distort the News.* Washington, DC: Regnery Publishing, 2002.

Gore, Rick. "New Find: The First Pioneer?" *National Geographic,* August 2002.

Gorman, Christine. "The Science of Anxiety." *Time,* June 10, 2002.

Gould, Stephen Jay. *I Have Landed: The End of a Beginning in Natural History.* New York: Three Rivers Press, 2002.

Grant-Williams, Renee. *Voice Power: Using Your Voice to Captivate, Persuade, and Command Attention.* New York: American Management Association, 2002.

Green, Julien. *God's Fool: The Life and Times of St. Francis of Assisi.* San Francisco: HarperSanFrancisco, 1985.

Grove, Andrew. *Only the Paranoid Survive: How to Exploit the Crisis Points That Challenge Every Company.* New York: Doubleday Currency, 1999.

Hall, Edward T. *Beyond Culture.* New York: Anchor Books, 1981.

Harby, K., K. Kucharski, S. Tuck, and J. Vasquez. "Beta Blockers and Performance Anxiety in Musicians," published with permission of Karla Harby, http://www.ethanwiner.com/BetaBlox.html (accessed July 1, 2004).

Harmon-Jones, Eddie, and Judson Mills. *Cognitive Dissonance: Progress on a Pivotal Theory in Social Psychology.* Washington, DC: APA Books, 1999.

Hayden, Thomas. "A Theory Evolves: The New Reality of Evolution." *U.S. News and World Report,* July 29, 2002.

Hayden, Thomas. "Anatomy of a Punch Line." *U.S. News and World Report,* March 5, 2001.

Herold, Ann. "On the Corporate Stage, Delivery Is Everything." *Los Angeles Times Magazine,* July 27, 2003.

Hillyard, Stephen, P. Malinowski, John Moores, and T. Gruber. "UCSD Researchers Demonstrate Enhanced Ability to Divide Visual Attention." ScienceDaily, http://www.sciencedaily.com/releases/2003/07/030723085509.html (accessed August 12, 2004).

Hoff, Ron. *Say It in Six: How to Say Exactly What You Mean in Six Minutes or Less.* Kansas City, MO: Andrews and McMeel, 1996.

Huff, Darrell. *How to Lie with Statistics.* New York: W. W. Norton & Company, 1993.

"Hunt for the World's Funniest Joke Is Over." iol news, Front Page, October 3, 2002, http://www.iol.co.za/index.php?click_id=79&art_id=qw1033641001893B216&set_id=1 (accessed July 2, 2004.)

Isaacs, William. *Dialogue: The Art of Thinking Together.* New York: Currency Doubleday, 1999.

Jensen, Bill. *Simplicity: The New Competitive Advantage in a World of More, Better, Faster.* Cambridge, MA: Perseus Publishing, 2001.

Jones, Chuck. *Make Your Voice Heard: An Actor's Guide to Increased Dramatic Range through Vocal Training.* New York: Watson-Guptill Publications, 1996.

Jones, Del. "Execution Does More Than Get Things Done: Honeywell Chief Talks about Making Great Ideas Work." *USA Today,* June 10, 2002.

Keleman, Stanley. *Myth & the Body: A Colloquy with Joseph Campbell.* Berkeley, CA: Center Press, 1999.

Kelly, Kevin. *New Rules for the New Economy: Radical Strategies for a Connected World.* New York: Penguin Books, 1998.

Kenny, Peter. *A Handbook of Public Speaking for Scientists and Engineers.* Bristol, England: Adam Hilger, 1983.

Kinsley, Michael. "Please Don't Quote Me." *Time,* May 13, 1991.

Kluger, Jeffrey. "Phobias." *Time,* April 2, 2001.

Koch, Richard. *The 80/20 Principle: The Secret to Success by Achieving More with Less.* New York: Currency Doubleday, 1998.

Koch, Richard. *The Natural Laws of Business: How to Harness the Power of Evolution, Physics, and Economics to Achieve Business Success.* New York: Currency Doubleday, 2001.

Krauss, Robert M., Yihsiu Chen, and Rebecca F. Gottesman. "Lexical Gestures and Lexical Access: A Process Model," http:// www.columbia.edu/~rmk7/PDF/GSP.pdf (accessed June 15, 2004).

Langreth, Robert. "Betting on the Brain." *Forbes,* January 7, 2002.

Larkin, T .J., and Sandar Larkin, *Communicating Change: Winning Employee Support for New Business Goals.* New York: McGraw Hill, 1994.

LeDoux, Joseph. *The Emotional Brain: The Mysterious Underpinnings of Emotional Life.* New York: Simon and Schuster Touchstone, 1996.

Lemonick, Michael D. "The First Butcher." *Time,* May 3, 1999.

Lemonick, Michael D. "Smart Genes? How Memory Works." *Time,* September 13, 1999.

Lemonick, Michael D., and Andrea Dorfman. "Up from the Apes: How Man Evolved." *Time,* August 23, 1999.

Levine, Peter A., with Ann Frederick. *Waking the Tiger: Healing Trauma.* Berkeley, CA: North Atlantic Books, 1997.

Maas, James B. *Power Sleep: The Revolutionary Program That Prepares Your Mind for Peak Performance.* New York: HarperPerennial, 1999.

MacCormick, Alex. *The Mammoth Book of Maneaters.* New York: Carrol and Graf Publishers, 2003.

Marks, Ronald P. "Improving On-line Sales Education: Learning Styles and Streaming Media." *The Learning Developer's Journal,* October 1, 2002.

Martin, Chuck. "How Well Do You Hear the Message?" On the Mind, *Darwin,* April 2004, http://www.darwinmag.com/read/040104/hear.html (accessed June 25, 2004).

Martin, Steve W. *Heavy Hitter Selling: How Successful High-Technology Salespeople Use Language and Intuition to Persuade Customers to Buy.* Rancho Santa Margarita, CA: Sand Hill Publishing, 2002.

Masson, Jeffrey Moussaieff. *The Pig Who Sang to the Moon: The Emotional World of Farm Animals.* New York: Ballantine Books, 2003.

Masson, Jeffrey Moussaieff, and Susan McCarthy. *When Elephants Weep: The Emotional Lives of Animals.* New York: Delta/Bantam Doubleday Dell, 1995.

Maxwell, John C., and Jim Dornan. *Becoming a Person of Influence: How to Positively Influence the Lives of Others.* Nashville, TN: Thomas Nelson, 1997.

May, Rollo. *The Cry for Myth.* New York: W. W. Norton & Company, 1991.

McCaskey, Michael B. "The Hidden Messages Managers Send." *Harvard Business Review,* November–December 1979.

McDonald, John J. "UCSD Neuroscientists Find That Attention to Sound Influences Ability to See," http://www.sciencedaily.com/releases/2000/10/001020092509.htm (accessed August 12, 2004).

McKay, Matthew, Martha Davis, and Patrick Fanning. *Messages: The Communication Skills Book.* Oakland, CA: New Harbinger Publications, 1995.

McNally, R. J. "Preparedness and Phobias: A Review." *Psychological Bulletin* 101 (1987).

McNally, R. J. "Psychological Approaches to Panic Disorder: A Review." *Psychological Bulletin* 108 (1990).

Mehrabian, Albert. "Communication without Words." *Psychology Today,* September 1968.

Mehrabian, Albert. *Silent Messages: Implicit Communication of Emotions and Attitudes.* Belmont, CA: Wadsworth, 1981.

Miller, Paul E., and Christopher J. Murphy. "Vision in Dogs." *Journal of the Veterinary Medical Association* 207, no. 12 (December 15, 1995).

Mineka, S. "The Frightful Complexity of the Origin of Fears." In *Theoretical Foundations of Behavior Therapy,* edited by F.R. Brush and J. B. Overmier. New York: Plenum, 1985.

Mineka, S., M. Cook, and S. Miller. "Fear Conditioned with Escapable and Inescapable Shock: The Effects of a Feedback Stimulus." *Journal of Experimental Psychology: Animal Behavior Processes* 10 (1984).

Mohan, A. G. *Yoga for Body, Breath and Mind: A Guide to Personal Reintegration.* Boston: Shambhala Publications, 1993.

Mooney, Bill, and David Holt. *The Storyteller's Guide: Storytellers Share Advice for the Classroom, Boardroom, Showroom, Podium, Pulpit and Center Stage.* Little Rock, AR: August House Publishers, 1996.

Morgan, Elaine. *The Scars of Evolution: What Our Bodies Tell Us about Human Origins.* Cambridge, England: Oxford University Press, 1994.

Morris, Desmond. *The Human Zoo.* New York: Kodansha America, 1996.

Morris, Desmond. *Intimate Behaviour.* New York: Kodansha America, 1997.

Morris, Desmond. *The Naked Ape.* New York: Dell Publishing, 1984.

Morris, Kenneth M. *User's Guide to the Information Age.* New York: Lightbulb Press, 1999.

Murray, Barbara. "Forgetful? It Could Just Be Stress." *U.S. News and World Report,* June 21, 1999.

Nicholson, Nigel. "Evolved to Chat: The New Word on Gossip." *Psychology Today,* June 2001.

Norton, Amy. "Fear of Math May Temporarily Cloud Memory." Reuters Health Headlines, May 14, 2001.

"Official! World's Funniest Joke." CNN.com/Science and Space, October 7, 2002, http://www.cnn.com/2002/TECH/science/10/03/joke.funniest/ (accessed July 2, 2004).

Olsen, Mary M., and Kenneth R. Harris. *Color Vision Deficiency and Color Blindness.* Eugene, OR: Fern Ridge Press, 1988.

O'Rourke, P. J. "Zion's Vital Signs." *Atlantic Monthly,* November 2001.

Paley, William S. *As It Happened: A Memoir.* New York: Doubleday, 1979.

Papathakis, Peggy. "Five Signs Your Diet Needs Help," http:// www. ucdmc.ucdavis.edu/pulse/ scripts/99_00/fyi_nutri-tion_help.pdf (accessed June 15, 2004).

Pei, Mario, and Frank Gaynor. *Dictionary of Linguistics.* New York: Philosophical Library, 1954.

Peurifoy, Reneau Z. *Anxiety, Phobias and Panic: A Step-by-Step Program for Regaining Control of Your Life.* New York: Warner Books, 1995.

Pfeffer, Jeffrey. *The Human Equation: Building Profits by Putting People First.* Cambridge, MA: Harvard Business School Press, 1998.

Pinker, Steven. "Against Nature." *Discover,* October 1997.

———. *The Blank Slate: The Modern Denial of Human Nature.* New York: Penguin, 2002.

———. *The Language Instinct: How the Mind Creates Language.* New York: HarperPerennial, 1994.

Plumwood, Val. "Being Prey." *Utne Reader,* August 23, 2000.

Port, Robert, Keiichi Tajima, and Fred Cummins. "Self-Entrainment in Animal Behavior and Human Speech." Indiana University Linguistics, Computer Science, Cognitive Science, April 25, 1996.

Preston, Richard. "The Genome Warrior." *New Yorker,* June 12, 2000.

"Psychiatrist's Joke 'World's Funniest.'" BBC News Front Page, October 4, 2002, http://atnews .bbc.co.uk/2/hi/uk_news/england/2297365.stm (accessed July 2, 2004).

Quammen, David. *Monster of God: The Man-Eating Predator in the Jungles of History and the Mind.* New York: W. W. Norton and Company, 2003.

Rainey, Robert. "The Phobia List Class Categories," http://www.phobialist.com/class.html (accessed August 10, 2004).

Ridley, Matt. *Genome: The Autobiography of a Species in 23 Chapters.* New York: HarperCollins, 1999.

Ridley, Matt. *Nature Via Nurture: Genes, Experience, and What Makes Us Human.* New York: HarperCollins, 2003.

Ridley, Matt. *The Origins of Virtue: Human Instincts and the Evolution of Cooperation.* New York: Penguin Books, 1996.

Saenz, Paul S., OD. "What Exercise Really Does for You," http://www.proteamphysicians.com/ article/index.asp?showarticle=yes&articleId=187&articletype=13 (accessed June 16, 2004).

Sagan, Carl. *The Demon Haunted World: Science as a Candle in the Dark.* New York: Ballantine Books, 1997.

Sagan, Carl. *The Dragons of Eden: Speculations on the Evolution of Human Intelligence.* New York: Ballantine Books, 1977.

Sagan, Carl, and Ann Druyan. *Shadows of Forgotten Ancestors.* New York: Ballantine Books, 1992.

Sapolsky, Robert M. *Why Zebras Don't Get Ulcers: An Updated Guide to Stress, Stress-Related Diseases, and Coping.* New York: W.H. Freeman and Company, 1998.

Schacter, Daniel L. *Searching for Memory: The Brain, the Mind and the Past.* New York: Basic Books, 1996.

Schrof, Joannie M. "Why Everyone Gets Stage Fright." *U.S. News and World Report,* June 21, 1999.

Seligman, Martin E. P. "Phobias and Preparedness." *Behavior Therapy* 2 (1971) 307–320.

Senge, Peter. *The Fifth Discipline: The Art and Practice of the Learning Organization.* New York: Currency Doubleday, 1994.

Serpell, James. *In the Company of Animals: A Study of Human-Animal Relationships.* Cambridge, England: Cambridge University Press, 1996.

Shea, John. *Starlight: Beholding the Christmas Miracle All Year Long.* New York: Crossroad Publishing Company, 1996.

Shepard, Paul. *The Others: How Animals Made Us Human.* Washington, DC: Shearwater Books, 1997.

Shepard, Paul. *The Tender Carnivore and the Sacred Game.* Athens: University of Georgia Press, 1998.

Simmons, Annette. *The Story Factor: Inspiration, Influence and Persuasion through the Art of Storytelling.* Cambridge, MA: Perseus Publishing, 2001.

Sinclair, Sandra. *How Animals See: Other Visions of Our World.* Kent, England: Croom Helm, 1985.

Sobel, Rachel K. "Anatomy of a Stutterer." *U.S. News and World Report,* April 2, 2001, 44–51.

Sonneman, Milly R. *Beyond Words: A Guide to Drawing Out Ideas.* Berkeley, CA: Ten Speed Press, 1997.

Stewart, Thomas A. "The Cunning Plots of Leadership." *Fortune,* September 7, 1998.

Strathern, Andrew J. *Body Thoughts.* Ann Arbor: University of Michigan Press, 1996.

Strunk, William Jr., and E. B. White. *The Elements of Style.* Needham Heights, MA: Allyn & Bacon, 2000.

Sutton, Robert R. "Weird Rules of Creativity." *Harvard Business Review,* September 2001.

Tattersall, Ian. "The Laetoli Diorama." *Scientific American,* September 1998.

Tattersall, Ian. "Once We Were Not Alone." *Scientific American,* January 2000.

The Columbia Encyclopedia, 6th ed., New York: Columbia University Press, 2003.

Theibert, Philip. *Business Writing for Busy People.* Franklin Lakes, NJ: Career Press, 1996.

Trefil, James. *Are We Unique? A Scientist Explores the Unparalleled Intelligence of the Human Mind.* New York: John Wiley & Sons, 1997.

Tripp, Tedd. *Shepherding a Child's Heart.* Wapwallopen, PA: Shepherd Press, 2003.

Tufte, Edward R. *Envisioning Information.* Cheshire, CT: Graphics Press, 2001.

Tufte, Edward R. "PowerPoint Is Evil." *Wired,* September 2003.

Tufte, Edward R. *The Visual Display of Quantitative Information.* Cheshire, CT: Graphics Press, 2001.

Tufte, Edward R. *Visual Explanations: Images and Quantities, Evidence and Narrative.* Cheshire, CT: Graphics Press, 1997.

Underwood, Ann, and Claudia Kalb. "Stress-Busters: What Works." *Newsweek,* June 14, 1999.

Von Kreisler, Kristien. *Beauty in the Beasts: True Stories of Animals Who Chose to Do Good.* New York: Jeremy P. Tarcher/Putnam, 2001.

Wildman, Derek E., Lawrence I. Grossman, and Morris Goodman. "Human and Chimpanzee Functional DNA Shows They Are More Similar to Each Other Than Either Is to Other Apes," http://www.uchicago.edu/aff/mwc-amacad/ biocomplexity/conference_papers/goodman .pdf (accessed June 1, 2004).

Wilson, Edward O. *Biophilia.* Cambridge, MA: Harvard University Press, 1984.

Wilson, Edward O. *Consilience: The Unity of Knowledge.* New York: Alfred A. Knopf, 1998.

Wilson, Edward O. *On Human Nature.* Cambridge, MA: Harvard University Press, 1978.

Wilson, Edward O. *Sociobiology: The Abridged Edition.* Cambridge, MA: Harvard University Press, Belknap Press, 1980.

Wilson, Edward O., ed. *The Best American Science and Nature Writing 2001.* New York: Houghton Mifflin Company, 2001.

Wrangham, Richard, and Dale Peterson. *Demonic Males: Apes and the Origins of Human Violence.* New York: Mariner Books, 1996.

Zeldin, Theodore. *Conversation: How Talk Can Change Our Lives.* Mahwah, NJ: Hidden Spring, 2000.

Zeldin, Theodore. *An Intimate History of Humanity.* New York: HarperPerennial, 1996.

Zimbardo, Philip. *Shyness: What It Is, What to Do about It.* Cambridge, MA: Perseus Publishing, 1990.

Zimmer, Carl. "Searching for Your Inner Chimp." *Natural History,* December 2002–January 2003.

ABOUT THE AUTHOR

M. F. FENSHOLT is a cofounder and principal of GenuSpeak, a business presentations training and consulting firm. She has over twenty years of training, consulting, and management experience. She works with executives and sales, marketing, and technical professionals to help them improve their ability to communicate important messages in a trustworthy and memorable way. Her clients include many Fortune 500 companies.

Educated at the University of California at Los Angeles and the University of Kansas, she graduated Phi Beta Kappa with a bachelor's degree and master's degree in communication studies and has completed additional postgraduate work in the areas of adult learning methods and training in business enterprises. She lives with her family in Claremont, California.

INDEX

QUICK ORDER FORM

FAX ORDERS: Complete this form and fax it to 1-866-TFE-7388 (1-866-833-7388).

E-MAIL ORDERS: Send the following information to franciseffect@oakmont.com.

MAIL ORDERS: Complete this form and mail it to Oakmont Press, 2890 Inland Empire Boulevard, Suite 102, Ontario, CA 91764, USA.

Please send _____ copies of *The Francis Effect: The Real Reason You Hate Public Speaking and How to Get Over It* ($19.95 each). $_____

SHIPPING AND HANDLING:
- United States standard: Add $2.50 for first book and $2.00 for each additional book. (Allow 1-3 weeks for delivery.)
- United States priority: Add $5.00 for first book and $3.00 for each additional book. (Allow 1 week for delivery.)

SALES TAX: Add 7.75% for products shipped to California addresses. $_____

TOTAL: $_____

PAYMENT: ❏ Check   ❏ Credit Card
                    ❏ VISA   ❏ MasterCard   ❏ AMEX   ❏ Discover

Card number: _____

Name on card: _____ Exp. date _____

Please send FREE information on
❏ Speeches   ❏ In-house Workshops   ❏ Public Workshops   ❏ Consulting

SEND TO (please print or type):

Name: _____

Address: _____

City: _____ State: _____ Zip:_____

Telephone: _____ Fax: _____

E-mail address: _____